# THE
# 32

Edited by Paul McVeigh

# THE

# 32

An Anthology of Irish
Working-Class Voices

unbound

First published in 2021

Unbound
Level 1, Devonshire House, One Mayfair Place, London W1J 8AJ

www.unbound.com

Text Design by PDQ Digital Media Solutions Ltd

A CIP record for this book is available from the British Library

ISBN 978-1-80018-024-6 (paperback)
ISBN 978-1-80018-025-3 (ebook)

Printed and bound in Great Britain by Clays Ltd, Elcograf S.p.A.

1 3 5 7 9 8 6 4 2

*The 32* was made possible by generous funding from the
Arts Council of Northern Ireland.

Thanks to Janine Kane and The Last Drop bar and restaurant, Belfast.

THE
LAST
DROP
BEER & WINE
LOUNGE
BAR
LOST IN THE LAST

This book also received grant support from the Government of Ireland's Reconciliation Fund, operated by the Department of Foreign Affairs, which aims to promote reconciliation between communities and traditions in Northern Ireland, between North and South and between Ireland and Britain. The views expressed in the book do not necessarily reflect those of the Irish Government.

# Contents

# Introduction

*Paul McVeigh*

If one of the defining characteristics of the wealthier members of our society is the desire to pass on their riches and privileges to their progeny to maintain the status quo, I find that for the working class who've achieved success in the arts, many become passionate, if not warrior-like, about passing on their wealth in precious knowledge to those of their feather who are following behind, to bring about change; the cartography for navigating the obstacles on the way to joining them. I've also described it as 'leaving a trail of breadcrumbs' and Kerry Hudson recently in the *Guardian* as 'send[ing] the elevator down'. As a working-class artist, it can often feel that on your journey you watch others flying past because they have a car while you are on foot, watch others waved through at gatekeepers' checkpoints while you are stopped and found to be carrying the wrong papers. Successful working-class artists often travel between worlds and are likely to pull over and offer you a lift.

Kit de Waal is a prime example. Having won a substantial three-book deal on the back of her debut, *My Name is Leon*, Kit de Waal used some of the money to set up an annual scholarship at a London university for a student from a marginalised background. She also came up with the idea, and raised the funding for, *Common People: An Anthology of Working-Class Writers*. The book contained thirty-two pieces of memoir about working-class life, sixteen established and sixteen new writers, including an essay by Dave O'Brien on the impact that class background has on your chances of breaking into the publishing industry as a whole. The statistics are shocking in the UK and you can check out that essay, or, online, find surveys conducted by a number of organisations, such as the Society of Authors, some including data on Northern Ireland. Though some research has been done in Ireland recently, the statistics are largely unknown, but you can read an essay that raises the subject at the end of this book from Dr Michael Pierse.

How did *The 32* come about? The short version is: *Common People* was a huge success, and while touring festivals in Ireland with the book, Kit de Waal was asked on many occasions, 'Will there be an Irish version?' – and *voilà*! It was by no means a simple transplant, however. Some questions I've been asked might be best answered here briefly. The name change: the phrase 'common people' didn't have the same connotations in Ireland as it did across the water, so we needed a new title. As there were thirty-two contributors and the book would be all-island, I thought *The 32* would work and changed 'writers' to 'voices', as there were a couple of contributions that wouldn't be from writers.

Those commissioned were chosen due to a number of factors. Most, I, or in some cases Kit, had worked with in the past; we knew their background and interests, and that they could be persuaded to come on board to lend their talent and literary weight to the topic and the project. I tried to find a spread around the island and a variety of forms and genres. The expression 'you have to see it to be it' was on my mind. As a working-class boy from Belfast, I never thought I could be a writer. This may sound strange to some, but if I'd known a working-class boy from the north became the books editor of the *Irish Times,* I think it would have impacted what I thought might be open to me. For those concerned with detail, one of the commissioned writers pulled out at the last moment so, rather than replace them with a named writer, I chose to commission a new writer whose work I admire.

We have a Baileys Women's Prize winner, an IMPAC Award winner, a Booker Prize winner, two *Sunday Times* Short Story Award winners, a newspaper editor, playwrights, poets, a radio presenter and a senator among those commissioned. We are delighted with the outcome and we hope you are too.

Last word of explanation: I had asked Lyra McKee to participate before her tragic death. Lyra and her partner were my guests at the Belfast Book Festival launch of *Common People* and I was helping her prepare for the upcoming publication of her work in progress, *The Lost Boys*. I'm moved to have an extract from that book included here, thanks to her partner, family and Faber & Faber.

A major difference between producing *Common People* and *The 32* was that there are more people in London than in the whole island of Ireland. Using the same crowdfunding publisher, the same commitment to paying all thirty-two contributors a fee, but without the administrative and financial backing from Britain's regional writer-development agencies, *The 32* cost more to produce than *Common People*. Effectively, I was asking an island a tenth of the population of Britain to crowdfund a larger amount than its counterpart. With this in mind, *The 32* was made possible by a substantial contribution from the Arts Council of Northern Ireland, with particular support from Chief Executive Roisín McDonough.

With the book funded, the commissioned writers could go ahead and write, and the call-out for the sixteen new writers could be launched. Again, without the applicants being filtered regionally through support agencies, the process was tougher than with *Common People*, as all entries had to be read and chosen by me and Rachael Kerr from Unbound. And here may I add that Rachael Kerr is the silent editor of this anthology, working on all the pieces more closely than myself. Much praise is deserved for her hard work and fundamental contribution to this publication.

Of course, there were other issues: those who questioned the need for such a book, challenged the choices I made in commissioning, and no doubt there will be more to come. I've already had multiple online run-ins demanding I define what I mean by 'working class'. I was asked repeatedly how would I make applicants prove their class? How am I qualified to edit this? And, with disbelief, how I can claim to be a writer and working class when that's just not possible. For an island where some say class doesn't exist, there sure has been a lot of concern about policing this book.

One thing I've noticed along the road is that working-class writers often come out of the artistic closet later in life. A mixture of lack of confidence, pressure to get a proper job to contribute to the family, or giving up the dream on the long road to publication because bills needed paying. Becoming a writer is often only possible later because financial independence has been achieved elsewhere first. Or, if you've stuck at it, more or less as in my own case, you risked sacrificing the spoils of financial independence. I can now claim that being a writer is my sole source of income, and that means I review, interview, take commissions, chair events, programme festivals and teach. Oh, and write. Writer as self-employed entrepreneur – few of us are lucky enough to 'just' write. Still, sounds pretty good, huh? What's he complaining about? He's middle class now.

A recent Authors' Licensing and Collecting Society (ALCS) report found that 'the top 10 per cent of writers still earn about 70 per cent of total earnings in the profession' (where have we heard this kind of thing before?), so how many authors do you think are lifted out of their class by a book deal, or even two? As Nicola Solomon of the Society of Authors told me, outside of the rare big deals, to mid-list novelists 'the top five publishers may offer £1,000 to £3,000, but often nothing [advances are paid for a *tiny* proportion of published fiction]; smaller publishers rarely pay advances and, if they do, rarely more than £1,000'. I was published by a wonderful independent publisher who paid below that. An amount that wouldn't cover your rent for a month, never mind your living costs, and, to some, you've become middle class, apparently.

All the issues around being working class in the arts mentioned in this introduction have been part of my story. I gave up writing essentially to become a teacher because, as I got older, it became harder to justify writing while having huge bills to pay, living in London. The best writing advice really is 'keep your overheads low'. As you get older, try dating in your late thirties or early forties while sleeping on sofas at your mates' and telling some sweet one that you're, you know, writing that novel, so you're skint and that one pint has to last the whole night. After giving up writing for a few years, hitting forty, I decided to give it one more shot. In order to do it, I elected to sleep on two cushions on a friend's floor for six months. Then a further six months in another friend's cloakroom under the coats. But I did it. Wrote the book, got the deal. The novel didn't come out until I was in my mid-forties. I was over fifty before I bought my first car and had the first home I didn't have to share – a home that I could finally call mine.

When I read that now, it seems made-up. There is a shame attached to living through and even admitting the above: your own don't like you talking out of school, and from others, a sense that if it didn't come easy then the victory is somehow sullied; if it was that hard maybe it wasn't for you in the first place. I wear the shame not as a cry for sympathy but to lessen its power; I've found shame is a garment whose colour fades with use. Having less and being seen as lesser often go hand in hand. Ironically, my mortgage is a third of what my rent was. It really proves James Baldwin's point: 'Anyone who has ever struggled with poverty knows how extremely expensive it is to be poor.' I can think of a number of people who are the most talented I've ever met in their field, be it acting, dancing or writing, who gave up because they couldn't afford to be an artist. Think of those talents unused, those seminal works of art lost. Of course, we can't have it all, we have to make choices, but working-class artists often have to settle for less and have fewer choices available to them.

Although there are a lot of similarities in the working-class story, and I'm sure you'll recognise a lot of the experiences related in this book, one of the purposes of *The 32* is to show that there are many stories and all are worthy of telling – the working class suffer from what Chimamanda Ngozi Adichie calls the 'danger of a single story'. Even the notion of an Irish working class is up for debate, and the differences between the inner-city working-class life and its rural cousin can be compared. We are lucky to have a myriad of experience explored here.

We want *The 32* to be a success, not only to showcase the talent and experience of working-class lives, but for the new writers to have a chance to be published and get a leg up in their literary career. We are building a professional-development programme with the help of leading publishers and the Irish Writers Centre. The new writers included in *Common People* have read at literary festivals, been published in newspapers and magazines, been on the radio, made a video; five have found agents and one has a book deal, with another on the way. Let's hope we have a similar result for *The 32*. Here's to some new, Irish working-class heroes!

# Two-Word Terms

*Rick O'Shea*

I grew up surrounded by two-word terms,
Ones I never thought about,
Tiny sentences, like fences, fraught with meaning,
I was just a kid.

'Social housing' is a term of shifting meaning,
Particularly if you didn't come from it,
I've heard:
Freeloading, feckless, wasters, a drain on your important taxes,
Full of people,
People like me.

I was born in the seventies,
In a block of flats in Drimnagh, bordered by a paint factory, a
    community centre, the canal,
Everyone knew everyone,

Full of coal sheds, coddle, oul' wans who spent summers toasting
    in the sun,
Full of families who plugged away.

My grandparents were a scaffolder and a cleaner,
A car-park attendant and a housewife,
They lived on opposite balconies,
That's how my parents met.

My mum grew up in a tenement,
An actual tenement,
Crumbling Georgian Dublin falling down around her ears,
Seventeen to a floor,
Outdoor toilet in the yard,
One of the last to be demolished,
To make way for the brand new 1960s,
Moved from The Liberties to a maisonette in Drimnagh,
Two miles or so,
May as well have been the Moon, she told me once.

My brother and I grew up in a 1930s council house in Crumlin,
Mortgaged from the Corporation by my mum and dad,
Back when that was still a thing.
Now I live in a 1950s council house,
Long since in private hands, a different space,
My home costing exactly fifty times what my father paid for his,
No longer 'social housing',
The act of purchase magically transforming it
And all of us, into a better sort of person.
Ask anyone.

Drimnagh and Crumlin,
They were nine tenths of my world as I grew up,
I was born in one, grew up in the other,
Spent all of my childhood shuttling back and forth,
Today I live just across the canal,
Drawn back like a homing pigeon.

But 'Crumlin-Drimnagh', that's a different sort of place,
It's a journalistic hand grenade,
Shorthand for dealing, shooting, feuding, tit for tat,
Headlines have long proclaimed it Gangland,
A theme park nobody asked for full of attractions no one rides,
Car chase rollercoasters,
Target practice ranges,
A ghost train where everybody shoots up in the dark,
I've never been there.

We played rounders,
Threw snowballs, played hide and seek, cycled round the block,
I remember endless football on the green,
Always the little fat kid in the goal,
Mostly though I stayed indoors, reading Famous Fives and comic
    books,
Playing endless primitive computer games,
I watched every hour of telly ever made.

I come from South-Central, Dublin South-Central,
At election time,
Funny, right?

South-Central in the movies it was not.

It still isn't.

Although people I know living there these days are the most
    disreputable sort,

Broadcasters, producers, writers, musicians, podcasters...


'Working class' is who I am,

Growing up that meant gets their hands dirty,

Greases wheels, sits at tills, drives trains, stacks bricks, fills shelves,
    builds, makes, delivers,

That's not me though, is it?

I talk for a living,

Is that really work at all?

Still, I am, still I always will be,

Working class.

I have never called myself anything else, regardless of the
    contradictions,

The older I get, the more it means,

I'm still not sure why that is.


Before I was born my mum sewed for a living,

For a furrier,

An end product that was never meant for her,

My dad is listed as a plumber's mate on my birth certificate

But that's only part of what he did.

Sort of builder,

Occasional scaffolder,

Minibus driver,

On the dole for a lot of the eighties, but weren't they all?

I remember my mum driving him to work,
Us dozing in the back seat every morning,
Down to the East Wall docks,
To build a new electricity plant,
Just before the city woke, before the City woke,
Before The Point, before the IFSC, before the East Link Bridge,
Through collapsing phantom acres of abandoned identity,
Rusting, warehoused, atrophied,
Echoes of dockers and ferries and Big Jim Larkin,
Things I discovered in my twenties, when I read *Strumpet City*.

A few years ago, I walked my parents through the grounds of
    Trinity College,
My mum said, 'I've never been in here,'
As if it was something only a certain kind of person could do,
In her mind it was.
She was born a mile from there,
Lived her whole life no more than three miles away,
It may as well have been the Moon.

# Working Class
# Is Authenticity

## *Erin Lindsay*

'Are you working class?' A bit of a stark question to answer about yourself. There is no catch-all definition, no definitive description – when the dictionary describes the working class as those who are employed for wages, in this day and age it isn't that simple.

As with all my fellow millennial/Gen Z-ers who struggle with identity in their twenties, questions of self-definition are a big source of overthinking for me. I think about whether I am 'working class' a lot – or rather, I suppose a more accurate question is, 'Am I working class *enough*?'

The question of class is one largely unspoken in Irish society. We steal glimpses around street corners and overhear it in conversations. It ripples under the surface of all our discourse, unmentioned but unavoidable, an awkward, uncomfortable presence for those of every background.

Only now, in 2021, has the question begun to bubble to the surface – beginning its journey into common conversation on the ever-gracious and context-filled platforms of social media. Users argue their case about the definition of 'working class' – what it means, what it entails, and how deserving each of us are of the title.

Where did you grow up? How did you make ends meet? What do your parents do? Who had it harder? Who is *more* working class? The contention of proving who had a more hardening childhood, who had to deal with more adversity, who has more anecdotes of their personal struggle to overcome the barriers of class, is always there.

This battle, as overdramatised and futile as social media forms it, is the reason that the question of whether I can say that I am working class is ever-present in the back of my mind. It's not there because I can't answer these questions – it's the opposite. I know the answer to how hardening my childhood was. It wasn't.

I grew up in Tallaght. I was born and bred and lived there until my mid-twenties. I had both parents growing up. My dad worked in the same company for almost my entire life, while Mam provided the idyllic home life that stay-at-home mothers tend to give.

My mam and dad are two of the most intelligent and interesting people I know. This is down to their endless enthusiasm for learning, even when it is not in a classroom – neither of them finished school, but it is from them that I learned that education does not result in common sense, and money does not result in class. Growing up, my house was full of conversations and debates about history, philosophy, politics, life, ethics, love – they taught me everything I know.

Drugs were never an issue. Drink never presented more than hangovers or embarrassing tales to bring up the next day. Violence did not enter my world. Poverty was not there either.

I spent my teenage weekends alternating between the Metro and the Plaza, two of Tallaght's finest nightlife establishments, sharing a €50 wristband with a friend so we could split the free drinks for the night (you can already tell that offer isn't still around).

When I left school, I went to college in town, spending my weekends with the same friends I'd had since playschool. Throughout jobs and degrees, we all maintained the same sense of community that has coloured my idea of Tallaght and what it means to me since childhood. I loved living there – I think myself very lucky to have had the life I did growing up.

It's not exactly the callous surroundings that the rest of the country imagines when they think of Tallaght. I did not have this fabled 'working-class' struggle growing up – because what does that even mean?

Class has never struck up a barrier to my successes in life. I never felt as if I didn't deserve a seat at the table, and when I had one, I never felt like my opinion wasn't valid. I've never felt held back by it.

Tales of leaving school at fifteen to work, of eighties dole queues, of emigration, as told to me by my parents, the truth of their own youth, were fables, warnings, but not my reality. While not living in luxury, we wanted for nothing, and I felt as far removed from the TV depictions of where I lived as I did from the affluent seaside towns elsewhere in Dublin that were a setting for second and third homes whose occupants enjoyed holidays to the Caribbean.

Because class never provided a barrier, there is a certain level of strange apprehension in describing myself as such – almost guilt.

Can I authentically call myself working class, when class has never been an obstacle? As a journalist and writer, can I authentically tell the stories of other working-class people, when my background, although geographically close, may be contextually much further away?

But if there is a level of guilt associated with calling myself working class, God knows the guilt of not doing so is worse.

Every day I question if I'm remaining true enough to my background, if I'm being authentic enough. I try not to use a phone voice. My accent becomes more pronounced when I'm around people who aren't from Tallaght, not less. I talk frequently and at length about where I'm from, my school, my friends. I question if I represent working-class issues enough in my work, if I talk about them enough in debates and conversations, when I'm surrounded by people who have no concept of what being working class really means. I'm constantly trying to find a balance that feels authentic.

I feel that pressure because class only becomes an issue when other people make it so. I only feel different when others project that image of otherness onto me.

The first time I truly became aware of what class means, I was fourteen years old. Introducing myself as being from Tallaght, I was met with a look of disdain, a voice that was hesitant – from another fourteen-year-old. That was the first time that the idea of 'us and them' came into my head. This person saw me as other, beneath, and not from their own experiences, but from what they'd been told by older, should-know-betters.

I started to realise that the stereotypes of what working class looks like would be projected onto me – without my consent, without my input – and it would be my job to reckon with them.

Maybe this is what they mean by 'working class', I thought: my work, as a woman who happens to be from a working-class community, to dispel rumours and prejudices and preconceptions would never be over.

Similar incidences followed and have continued well into adulthood. Anger rose and fell (and still rises). As I moved through college and out into the world, I encountered countless people who thought they understood the working-class experience better than anyone and had no embarrassment in telling me such. My attention turned to politics, to cultural issues, to stories of poverty, of injustices, and I wondered if these stories would ever permeate the attitudes around me that reared their heads in often the most subtle of ways.

I am the same as the rest of the room – until someone does a crass impression of a homeless person with an accent that sounds a lot like mine. Until someone starts in on why they wouldn't raise their kids in 'certain areas', where Tallaght is almost certainly near the top of the list. Until I celebrate an accomplishment but know that others are questioning how deserving I am. Until I state where I'm from and am met with a sympathetic smile, as if to lament my answer.

Until I hear the passive-aggressive comments, made through sweetly sneering mouths – 'I had no idea people were so well educated there!' 'I had no idea you had those facilities.' I had no idea that people from Tallaght are like everyone else.

I believe that this struggle about remaining true to one's background is one that I am not alone in. The nature of being working class is struggling with authenticity.

Every day working-class people are faced with those who think they understand their experience better than they do – depictions, impersonations that all ring hollow to those who have actually lived it. Whether it's in film, music, or conversations overheard on the street, the idea of being working class is contorted and presented back to us without our presence in its creation.

Constantly having to correct others' presumptions about working-class existence, formed because of what they've seen and heard from other non-working-class people, is exhausting. Smiling through gritted teeth, correcting misconceptions, letting certain jokes go so as not to be seen as no craic. It's tiresome, and it grates, and it doesn't take long to stop being funny.

I don't want to have to internally debate whether to call myself working class. I want the world's idea of what the working class looks like to match what I picture – diversity, community; that includes interests, jobs, life stories of every shape and detail. There is no one box of what the working class looks like – it is not me, nor is it the person in the next estate. Working class is community, support, humour, love. Working class is authenticity.

# The Likes of You

*Roddy Doyle*

Years ago – it might be twenty years ago – I was at a gathering of family and friends. It wasn't my family and I wasn't really a friend, so my memory of the occasion – where I was, and why – is vague. It might have been after a christening and it might have been a hotel function room, or a room over a pub. The walls were green – I remember that – and there was a group of people to my left, including the daughter of the man who came and stood in front of me.

He told me who he was. Had I heard of him?

No, I hadn't.

That was his daughter over there, he told me. He was retired now but he had, for a time, been the manager of one of the banks in – he named a place on the Northside of Dublin, about a mile from Kilbarrack, where I grew up, where my parents still lived at the time when the episode I'm remembering occurred.

He waited for me to say something.

I'd grown up near there, I told him.

He knew.

I went to primary school there, I told him.

He knew that too.

I'm going to tell you something, he said. Something funny.

Go on.

Years ago, he started, a man from Kilbarrack came into his bank.

He stopped, and looked at me again; he wanted to see amusement on my face.

I smiled.

The man was dressed like he owned the place, he said.

I knew: he was talking about my father.

The man was wearing an elegant tweed jacket, he told me. And a hat – not a cap. A fedora, no less. Like the lord of the manor. He even had a walking stick. Like a shareholder in the bank itself – the outright owner. Saying hello to all around him.

He stepped back, and looked at me again – examined me.

But do you know why he was there? he asked. Do you know why he was in my bank?

No, I didn't.

I'll tell you, he said.

He was there to pay the last instalment of his Corporation house loan.

Do you know who that man was? he asked me.

My father, I said.

Isn't it gas? he said.

He laughed.

The lord of the manor and all he was doing was paying off his Corporation loan.

I smiled.

I wish I'd hit him. I wish I'd drawn back a fist – something I hadn't done since I was twelve or thirteen – and put it into his face. Hard. He was inviting me to laugh at my father, and at other working-class men who had notions. I wish now – *now* – twenty years after the event, years after that man died, more than six years since my father died – I wish I'd smashed his fuckin' face.

But I smiled.

I don't remember how I got away. I probably went looking for my children.

I don't think the man was being malicious when he told me that story. But he had thought that I'd find it amusing, and that I'd get it, that – somehow – I was no longer my father's son. In the couple of years between the release of *The Commitments*, a film based on a book I'd written and the script of which I'd co-written, and winning the Booker Prize – 1991 to 1993 – I'd stopped being Roddy Doyle and had become 'Roddy Doyle'. I'd been a schoolteacher who taught in a community school on the Northside and who'd self-published a book, and had metamorphosed into an internationally known author whose name appeared in the *Guardian* and the *New York Times*. I'd crossed over a line; I'd become a useful accessory.

I sat at a dinner table one Saturday evening, a year or so after *The Commitments* had been released.

What do you do? the woman sitting to my left, a well-known interior designer from London, asked me.

I'm a teacher, I told her.

The evening's hostess almost climbed over the table to correct my error.

He wrote *The Commitments*! she shouted.

She did: she shouted. The message was clear: I was there because I'd been involved in the making of a successful film and she didn't give a continental fuck if, in fact, teaching is much more interesting.

That man – the bank manager – had thought that I was one of his tribe now, someone who could laugh affectionately – and viciously – at the foibles of the working classes, and at my own father.

Isn't it gas? he'd said.

The cunt.

My father, Rory Doyle, was a customer of that particular bank because, when he'd gone to a different bank looking for a mortgage – this was in 1950 – he'd been told by a different bank manager that his bank didn't give mortgages 'to the likes of you'. It was 1950, not 1850; my father was a printer – a compositor. He'd served a seven-year apprenticeship and the man on the other side of the desk probably got a C in maths in the Leaving Cert. But he'd gone to the right school and my father had had to leave one of the wrong schools when he was fifteen so he could become the skilled craftsman whose labour had produced the newspaper – the *Independent* – that the bank manager probably had hidden in the top drawer of his desk.

As I'd told the other bank manager, I'd gone to primary school, the national school, very near his bank. I started there in 1963, by which time my father was a teacher of print and design in Bolton Street College of Technology – now part of TUD, Technological University Dublin. I was invited back to the school – Scoil Íde – a few years ago. It was lovely, walking into the building more than fifty years after I'd left it; nothing bad came at me. I'd loved it there, and in the boys' school next door, Scoil Assaim. The walls, the tiles, the angle of the light at that hour of the morning – the building was immediately familiar, and I felt welcome and happy. The principal, Clare Ring, had put the old registration book on her desk, open on the page for 1963. My name was there, in Irish – Rúairí O'Dúbhaill – and my date of birth. My father's name was there too, also in Irish, also Rúairí O'Dúbhaill. Three things struck me: there was no sign of my mother's name – there were no mothers on the page; I'd always hated having to say that my name was Rúairí O'Dúbhaill – it was never my name; my father's occupation was 'vocational teacher'. Today, it would be 'lecturer'. But back then, when he was thirty-nine, a much younger man than I am now, the adjective – 'vocational' – put him back in his box. More notions smothered.

But my father refused to notice.

The last time I went anywhere with him – just the two of us – it was to the National Print Museum in Beggar's Bush, about six months before he died. I watched him carefully that day as he gazed at the printing and compositing machines. That was what he did: he *gazed*. And the retired printers who volunteer at the museum, who demonstrate the machinery, gazed at him as they came to realise that the old man explaining how the Monotype caster worked to the man in his late middle years – me – was their old teacher from Bolton Street, Rory Doyle.

He was both of those things when I was a child, a printer and a teacher, with a foot in each camp, working class and middle class. Both but neither – and both, and more. He refused to be defined, even as the banks and the state tried to define – and to confine – him.

I remember, a few days after Trump was elected, I was listening to a discussion on RTÉ radio about the voting patterns, and one of the panellists referred to 'educated voters', by which she meant women and men with college degrees. I think I stared at the radio. By that definition, many of my closest friends and members of my family were uneducated. No one in the studio queried this; no one said, 'Hang on – are you serious?' Had no one there a sense of how hurtful that categorisation was? I remember being upset, and angry. But I knew how my father – an utterly uneducated man by that definition, without even an Inter Cert (a state exam which students had to sit at the end of their third year of secondary school), one of the most intelligent people I've known – would have reacted.

Gobshites.

That was how he dealt with the put-downs, the 'likes of you' moments. They hurt. I know that, because he told me, when we were both men, and friends, and he no longer had to teach me how to live. I never mentioned the bank manager episode to him. I could have altered it. I could have changed a few words and swapped ridicule for admiration. Or I could have told him exactly what had happened. And I know what he'd have said.

The gobshite.

But I know too: he'd have been hurt.

I still wish I'd hit that man that day. Because, I think – and I know I'm not being fair to myself when I think it: I betrayed my father when I walked away. I know, I didn't. I don't have to explain away my guilt. My father would have been appalled if I *had* hit the man. I felt so hurt as I listened, so powerless, useless, so trapped in the occasion – whatever it was – so trapped by my success, whatever that was. If I could relive the moment, I wouldn't hit him. I'd tell him he was a gobshite, then I'd walk. It wouldn't help, but I'd be honouring my father.

# Finding Words

*Theresa Ryder*

My dad died on his hands and knees. There is no grand statement after that fact. Just a modest man leaving as quietly as he lived, his hand still clutching the paving trowel. At the age of twenty-eight and a novice to grief, I was left speechless. I had no words to offer at his funeral, not for ceremony or small talk. But I listened. And it was amid the epithets of praise and expressions of condolence that I discovered another part to my dad's story: that he had been unable to read or write. The revelation came with an, 'Ah, that explains...' But, of course, things are never that simple. This discovery made me consider the ways in which my dad communicated and the impact he had on my life choices.

In 1964, when I was a year old, my migrant parents moved into our council house in north-west London. The big, noisy Irish family became part of the street landscape. But Dad never really left Ireland. For the next twenty-six years he had the same neighbours and he always addressed them by formal title and surname. Dad established us as different in other ways. Neighbours' gardens flourished in floral display; ours was dedicated to plots and rows of potatoes, cabbage, onion and carrot. A persistent mint grew at the front door; an aggressive gooseberry bush stole the path under the street windows. By the back door, a paint-layered kitchen chair was reserved for Mum to take the sun and watch Dad shuffle the clay with hoe and spade.

Indoor life was at times chaotic. My struggle for space and control of the two-channel television was often abandoned to four brothers. Three bedrooms were split between kids, parents and a long-term resident uncle, my dad's younger brother. But outside was idyllic, sent off to play unfettered around the common land of woods and ponds. On Sundays Dad would take us on long rambles through those woods, pointing out animal burrows, edible berries, and trees for climbing. I would take leg-stretch jumps to land in the safety of his long footsteps, afraid of quicksand beneath the leafy woodland floor.

On those Sunday excursions he wore his best blazer, a navy double-breast with a shamrock crest. The real sprig flounced, fresh from Ireland, from his lapel on his birthday, St Patrick's Day. Everything he said harked back to his homeland, or 'beyond', as he called it. His actions reflected the etiquette of his upbringing, including bringing home bar stragglers from his Sunday-morning pint to sit them down for a home-cooked dinner. We'd squeeze in another seat. Plate up another serving. Make small talk with another grizzled man presenting with slurred accent and age-shined suit.

For the long summer holidays Dad would bring us back to Ireland, always our mum's home-place in County Meath. As we settled in for lazy weeks on farm and bog, he pitched hay and turf, sweating with the farm men. While there he referred to London as 'behind', a telling word that expressed his censure for his chosen home.

Words were not a concern in our house. There were no books, no daily papers, no ethos of helping with homework or encouraging education. Our parents, like many of the time, didn't get involved in school matters. I missed the bus and stayed home so often that when I did attend school my name wasn't on the register. I eventually quit for good at fifteen. No one seemed to mind my lengthy absences. On those days I would go with Mum to her cleaning jobs. Our council house was in a predominantly wealthy area and Mum's work gave me access to the finest homes. I would happily shine brass or silverware and vacuum to pick up coins purposely dropped under a couch to ensure a thorough job. I delighted in polishing the pianos, relishing the sounds from my prodding fingers on the tuned keys. And all the houses had bookshelves. In the clutches of desire I lovingly dusted and organised the books, opening the shabbier volumes to smell the pages. That intoxicating odour of age and permanence that for me intimated the foreverness of a story, an essence that lived on with the reader long after the physical book was closed. I snatched an hour or two around those shelves, leaving with the treasure of characters and their half-told tales.

Dad loved stories. I would sit with him through Saturday-afternoon matinees of Danny Kaye films or his beloved westerns. Mum spent Saturday seeking out jumble sales in a bike-ride radius. She would return with garments to cut for buttons and zips, old jumpers unravelled for the wool. And she often brought me back an equally cast-off book. Over time, I grew a shabby collection that I stacked on the bedroom floor for want of a shelf. One great favourite, *Five Little Peppers and How They Grew*, she bought for me when I was ten and confined with tonsillitis. I read it again and again. I coloured in the drawings of characters and scenes depicted at the opening of each chapter. Love was planted on every page, evident in crude crayon and tattered spine. It has followed me to all my adult bookcases and sits proudly on the shelf behind me as I write, forty-six years later. I have even made it a focus of my novel in progress, giving me the opportunity to take down the delicate hardback, the spine long gone but the covers still attached by a web of binding thread, and indulge again.

Dad was a willing ear for my enthusiastic retelling of reading matter. Mum was just too busy. An early critic, I announced favourite lines such as, 'Katy's name was Katy Carr. She lived in the town of Burnet.'* That succinct introduction that urged me to find out *What Katy Did*. I can put a hand now to my bookshelves and return to *The Secret Garden* of Mary and Dickon. Smell *The Smoke in Albert's Garden*. And I'll hear the click on Dad's 'baccy' box lid as he lent me full attention. Armed with a pot of tea and a lick-sealed roll-up, Dad was a good listener. I later found this to be the case with others unable to communicate with the written word: listening is a vital survival tool.

I had no perception of Dad's struggle to live in a literate world. I saw none of the signs. All I saw was the kindly man, fond of a Guinness, a beautiful singer. He sang ballads such as 'The Banks of the Foyle', 'The Green Fields of France' and 'Spancil Hill'. Laments to a place left behind. He learned by ear and delivered in a soothing

* Susan Coolidge, *What Katy Did*, Little, Brown, New York, 1925.

croon. An old radio and tape deck played his favourites. The radio, that ally of those who rely on the spoken word, brought him the news, for which we all had to 'whisht' on the hour, every hour. He wouldn't use the phone, a heavy black rotary dial. He would offer up the earpiece to one of us if he needed to make a call and mutter about the numbers being too small. On the days he was out of work and Mum had gone to hers, he would shy away from writing a permission or absence slip for a teacher, which was all the excuse I needed to stay home again. Only after his death did I realise that Mum had to work, as, on the frequent days when he had no labouring job, Dad wouldn't sign on the dole. Because he couldn't make his mark on paper. He had no identifying logo of his own, knew no written word to give him singular distinction.

But he was not wordless. In his soft Mayo tone he layered his speech with a mountain vernacular not found in any Irish dictionary. He used words that did not trip lightly from my London tongue. Our ears were tuned to the dialect of our city youth, but his words resided somewhere deeper in us, words we knew only phonetically but never questioned their meaning. And he used his voice, not for debate or argument but to tell us snippets of his life. He told us stories flavoured with poetic imagination. Raised on a mountain close to Croagh Patrick or 'the Reek', as he knew it, he told of how he would listen for the 'penny whistle' of the ships docking in the harbour. A penny earned offloading cargo. How he would skip up one side of the Reek and down the other four or five times a day on hearing that whistle. Those ships, in my mind as tall as that tale, are long gone. So too the neighbour who died and was seen sitting on a rock smoking his pipe as my dad returned from that same man's funeral. The apparition raised his hat and acknowledged Dad by name before fading into the moonlight. There was the Disney-worthy tale of a neighbour who lived in a house tucked away on a mountain ledge with no accessible road. Animals of all description, farm dogs, mountain goats, cats, birds and hares found their way to the door. As a boy Dad had been sent with a pot of blue paint to this neighbour's house with instruction to paint until the pot was emptied. Dad set off through gorse bushes to reach his neighbour and was met by an assortment of animals forming a protective barrier. Dad explained his quest to the four-legged force, and they let him pass.

When we were adults, we took him back to his mountain. His old home a ruined monument to memories. He picked at a gap in the stone wall beside what had been a fireplace and told us that was where, as a boy, he used to hide his Woodbines. He wept then, but recovered to guide us over rocks to a pathless plateau where an old man still lived in a house painted blue, inside and out. Chimney smoke curled from the two blue-framed windows, the blue ledges piled with books and an old radio. Crows lined the roof. Three dogs rose to meet us, a rabbit dashed for cover and assorted cats flicked their tails on our approach. Dad assured the animals we came in peace and they let us pass.

But the saddest story was of the death of Dad's mother when he was twelve. His father, left with five children and a living to earn on the land, soon married again. This time to a widow with five children of her own. The three eldest, my dad, his only sister and one brother, were put out of the house to fend for themselves. We don't know where they went or how they lived until the story skips on ten years to London in 1950, where the three arrived to earn a living. A living unachievable on the rough-hewn Mayo land, or from the ships, long since diverted to other ports. Born to rock and gorse, and sparing mountain air, Dad was content to find his way by digging into the London soil. I thought I had a lifetime to discover the missing sections of that story.

A year after Dad died I achieved his ambition and left London for good, relocating to Ireland, where I have lived now for over thirty years. I raised my own family and later in life I took up the slack on my education, graduating with a Master of Arts and a teaching degree from Maynooth University. Along the way I volunteered as a literacy tutor. My admiration for those courageous adults who step up to learn to read and write knows no bounds. Through them I learned the truth in the concept of multiple intelligences. I have been privileged to work with people who enabled themselves to help their kids with homework, or complete college courses of their own. Some starting from a position of being so afraid of the written word they would hide when the morning post hit the mat. Almost all having to constantly fight against a deep-rooted sense of failure, overwhelmed by a shadow of shame. I wish Dad could have had the opportunity to share their joy of achievement.

But it is obvious that Dad was not without influence. I wish now as a writer that I had his ability to summon a memory and air it with fresh enthusiasm for a familiar audience. To have that passion spill into my fiction. My first submitted short story won an award and it was because he was there; his character seeped into the sentences. And he taught me to listen, that most undervalued skill. He gave me an early platform to express myself and I learned not to be afraid of my voice. And in the pursuit of a story I still gladly leap into his footsteps. It was Dad who, with lyric and lilt, paved my way to find words.

# The Gaatch

*Kevin Barry*

My father's family kept an uncle in the attic. This was in the house on Brown's Lane, which was off Lord Edward Street, about 500 yards from Colbert Station in Limerick city. The McCourt family of *Angela's Ashes* fame lived a couple of lanes away. In my father's house there were five children, the two parents, and the uncle in the attic. I don't know what this uncle's name was, or whose side he was on, or whether he was an invalid or just a bit odd in himself, but I know that he was kept in the attic.

This must have been around the late 1920s or early 1930s. My father left school at about ten years old, as did most of the kids who lived in the inner city at that time. He became a messenger boy around town before eventually getting work with CIÉ down at Colbert Station – a lot of the family ended up working there, mostly as wagon-makers.

Of the family lore that survives, much of it concerns my grandmother, Mary Kate, who died long before I was born. She was an unconventional woman for the time in that she went to the pub alone – the lounge bar of the Railway Hotel – and also she went to the bookmaker's. This was considered close to scandalous at the time.

The Railway Hotel is on Parnell Street, opposite Colbert Station, the same street where my mother's family lived. They had moved in from west Limerick in the 1930s, and my grandfather and grandmother on that side always seemed to me like country people. After living in a flat on Parnell Street for a while, they got a council house in Ballinacurra Weston, a house that stayed in the family until my aunt, the last of the family in Limerick, died in 2005.

When I was born, in 1969, we lived in a council house on Hyde Road, about a half-mile down from Colbert Station, and about the same again from the site of Brown's Lane, which by then had been knocked down. Working-class families tend to move around in fairly tight circles. In 1972 we bought a house – I think for about £1,500 – in a new estate of semi-ds called Ballinacurra Gardens, about a mile from my mother's parents' house in Weston. A lot of the families who moved into the raw new estate were also coming from council houses. Most houses had about five or six kids knocking around in them and the estate was teeming, especially on the summer evenings – it's very quiet now. The estate was close to the Catholic Institute tennis club, long established to service the very respectable neighbourhoods of Rosbrien and Greenfields nearby. We didn't join the tennis club.

I went to school at CBS Sexton Street, a couple of hundred yards from Colbert Station. Thinking about my schoolmates, I'd say about three quarters of us were from working-class backgrounds and the rest were lads from the county who tended to be the good hurlers. I'd wanted to go to Crescent College Comprehensive for secondary, not least because it had girls in it. I sat the entrance exam, which consisted of multiple-choice questions, and I came out of it pretty certain that I'd scored 100 per cent. I didn't get offered a place in Crescent Comp – you generally had to have a brother or sister who'd gone there before you, and it was the case with Crescent Comp that the brothers and sisters were mostly from the better areas, from the middle-class estates, and from the old, established roads. The casual way schools in Ireland are segregated very strictly along class lines still astonishes me.

About a month before I sat my Leaving Cert in 1987, one of our teachers came in one morning and gave us a talk about our destinies. We were the top-streamed class in the school, considered to be the smarter kids, the good workers. But still and all, he said, Ye're likely to end up in bum office jobs around the town. I remember the phrase exactly – 'bum office jobs'. He spoke for quite some time, and he painted a grim enough future. If we didn't watch ourselves, he said, we'd be working in dreary little insurance offices, and we'd be answering to bosses who had gone to the Crescent Comp. They would be no smarter than us, he said, but they'd have gone directly to university, while we'd have been doing bookkeeping courses in the tech. He explained that it was systemic. His message, quite passionately delivered, was that we should struggle with all of our resources not to be placed in the boxes that were waiting for us. He suggested that the limits of our futures were very often set by the limits our families foresaw for us. He had been watching all this play out for years, he said, and it made him angry. We were all a bit rattled by this talk. We hadn't seen it coming.

A couple of years later, I began working my first job as a junior reporter on a local newspaper. On Thursday mornings I attended the sittings of Limerick District Court. I did the courts for a couple of years, and I can't remember ever hearing a working-class defendant's word taken over the word of a guard. You could predict with high accuracy the forthcoming judgements from the look of the defendant taking to the witness stand. If he or she had a working-class kind of *gaatch* to them – as we'd say in Limerick, meaning that they carried themselves in a certain way, dressed in a certain way, spoke in a certain way – they would very likely be found guilty. We'd often discuss it in the reporters' box. Some lad in a tracksuit would be sauntering up to give his account of the night in question, with a face on him, and we'd nudge each other, and slyly wink. Not a chance, we'd say, not a chance.

With regards to the gaatch...

Very often, when I'm writing fiction, I think first of all not about how characters sound or about what they're saying, I think about how they physically hold themselves. If you can see in your mind's eye the level of physical affront one of your creations is offering to the world, it can work as a powerful insight to their personality, to their soul. Stance is character. As often as not, I'm writing about characters from working-class backgrounds, and very often I'm writing about men from such a background, and the physical stance is always defensive. It's a kind of shoulder-forward stance, a feet-planted, rooted hold of the body, with a single shoulder jutting, a very tense and knotted pose, and there are hundreds of years of history and stress contained within it. There is politics and there is religion and there is a very particular colonial history contained within this stance, too, but most of all, most importantly, it is made out of class.

From my late teens through to my early thirties, I freelanced as a journalist, working first for local newspapers and then for music and lifestyle magazines and then for the national papers in Ireland and then for the national papers in Ireland and in the UK. The higher you ascended on the freelance ladder, the fewer working-class people you were dealing with – at the very top-end publications, you weren't dealing with any at all. This wasn't surprising, of course – we are none of us innocents, and we know how the world works. What was surprising was the fact that people in the media industry from middle-class backgrounds, and from higher, genuinely didn't seem to see this at all. They seemed entirely unaware that they viewed the world through a very particular prism, that they were coming from a very particular set of circumstances and expectations. It wasn't that they lacked empathy or suss or ability – they were just blind to it, and it was reflected so plainly in their publications, in their slants, in their reads of things.

This morning, as I write this at the raging height of the coronavirus pandemic, the number-one most-read story on the *Irish Times* website concerns property: 'Is Now The Time To Buy?'

In the arts, when I came to enter that zone as a practitioner rather than as a reporter, I found that there was a particular expectation about the type of material writers from working-class backgrounds should produce. There is, for example, what I came to think of as the 'bag of cans' school of working-class literature. If you were writing about young men from working-class housing estates, a bag of cans would at some point, like the primed gun in a Raymond Chandler novel, have to put in an appearance. The language should be kind of stripped-down and tough-as-nails and street-ready. This expectation is unspoken but is absolutely commonplace.

Now, as a writer of fiction in various forms, I operate in the interlinked realms of publishing, film and theatre. Film is an industry with very little regular cash flow in it, and those who survive are the ones who can hang around long enough without money coming in on a steady basis – for this reason, an almost comically large proportion of the Irish film industry comes from the well-heeled pastures of south Dublin. In Irish theatre there is so little money going around by this stage that you would again need independent means to keep going at a fully professional level – I suspect that working-class participation in Irish theatre is by now falling rather than increasing. In publishing there has been a bit of an effort at the lower echelons, but at the senior editorial and directorial levels there is still hardly anyone from working-class backgrounds; in the UK, there is still hardly anyone not from Oxbridge.

As a result, the stories that are told in film and books and theatre come through very particular prisms, and working-class material is very often considered almost as anthropological report, as news from elsewhere.

Chippy? I can see certain eyebrows ascend as this piece is read, and the word coming to the lips as if freshly minted – Chippy; he's chippy enough, all the same.

Expectations around class persist in this way – they persist in clichéd formulations.

I have just now googled 'Brown's Lane, Limerick' and found a reference from a census of 1907 in which it is listed as part of the holdings in the city owned by the Earl of Limerick. We were serfs, essentially.

I have seen a single photograph of the house my father grew up in on the lane. It looks tiny, and my grandmother Mary Kate fills the doorway, with a kind of brazen or dismissive look on her face, as if she is in no way impressed by the fact of a camera or by the fact that this moment will be held.

Not that I noticed it at the time, but Limerick when I was growing up there, in the 1970s and 1980s, was a very working-class town. It was the only place in Ireland with working-class rugby clubs, and remains so. When Clontarf or Terenure would come down from Dublin to play Young Munster or Shannon, the dissonance between the accents of the supporters was very pronounced and ripely comical. Of course, there was always some old money about the city, too; there were always the 'respectable' roads where the older trees grew. There were fine houses on the Ennis Road and on O'Connell Avenue, and the area of Castletroy was then considered very posh. I had friends from Castletroy, and the rest of us used to wind them up relentlessly and make fun of their accents. There was a particular taxi-cab base on Shannon Street, and when somebody came in late on a raucous Saturday night and asked for a cab to Castletroy, the dispatcher lady used to exaggerate the word 'poshly' when she got on the mike to alert the taxi drivers – 'Have we anyone for *Castletroy*, lads?' – and how we all laughed.

I now live in splendid isolation in the Sligo countryside. We have rooms full of books and lots of nice bottles of wine. It's a former barracks of the Royal Irish Constabulary, no less, and we have no neighbours for half a mile in any direction. I work in the arts. To all intents and purposes, I would be considered to be a member of the middle classes. But as I sidle up to the window now to look out on the garden – it's a night of big wind and the sally trees are dancing madly – I find my own reflection looking back at me in the half-light of a Maytime dusk and one thing is absolutely certain: I have a big serf head on me still.

It takes half a lifetime to see out beyond the immediate shadows of yourself and of your own biography. It takes for ever and a day to recognise the systems and the streams that are in place to divert you from your true will and ambitions. It takes a steady nerve, and a steady voice, to begin to question them, and to unpick them.

# The In-Between

## *Trudie Gorman*

In 1989 my parents move with my brother from their fifteenth-floor flat in Ballymun to a newly built council estate in Dublin West. My mam leaves her seamstress job at a factory in East Wall because there is no transport in this new place. There are no shops. There is nothing but a constellation of concrete homes and fields for miles and miles. This is an in-between place, a not-quite-here-or-there place. The people who live here exist and don't all at once. This not-quite-existence, this outsideness, settles into the bones and blooms whole gardens of not-enoughness. Shortly after the estate is built, heroin arrives, and our community is splintered with addiction and fear. My mam becomes sick. My parents go on social welfare and must make decisions like choosing between coal and food. My brother is only a few months old and has hair so white blond it's like snow. I have not arrived yet; I'm not even an idea, but here in this suburban wilderness my history begins.

*

Four years later I'm born three months too soon, and the doctors say I won't live through the night. Granny says she's never seen anything like me. My entire body fits into my dad's hand, machines breathe for me and my organs are still becoming. I spend those first months in an incubator with no human touch. I learn how to rock myself to sleep. I learn how to survive in a liminal space between life and death. I'm an in-between girl. And I'll carry the memory of this somewhere deep inside my body for years to come. After two months my parents take me home to the house on the hill in the in-between place and I become part of the architecture of living on the edge of society.

In the millennium I am seven years old. I'm not like the other children on the road. I'm too afraid to imagine a future most of the time, and I don't speak outside the house. I don't smile. I never let my mam hug me. I carry a sad animal in my chest that I don't have a name for, but I'm pretty sure it's dying. A teacher in school asks my mam if my jaw muscles are broken and that's why I don't smile. She doesn't understand. The schoolyard is a battlefield. The other children have parents who are addicts and parents who are poor and they hurt each other out of all this pain. They call me things I can't unhear years later, only because I am unspeaking and unsmiling. I don't fully know why I don't speak, only that it's how I survive the slow violence of the everyday. The teacher suggests raising money to send me to Lourdes. I wonder what it would be like for so many people to be praying just for my smile.

There are good days too. Like the days I build forts in the fields with my brother, playing in burnt-out cars and eating Black Jack bars by the frogs' pond. Most weekends my mam takes us both on outings around the city, to museums and libraries and parks. Or we cycle out the back roads and along the canal with our dad. We don't spend many weekends in the estate because our mam wants us to know the world is bigger than pockets of fear. In the summer a local Traveller man goes around our estate and charges £1 to take the children up and down the hill on a horse and cart. I fall in love with the feeling of sitting in the back and watching the horse run.

Some nights we move the couch closer to the TV to watch a film and my mam cuts a packet of King Crisps in half for me and my brother. Other nights we sit around the kitchen table and she makes us cinnamon toast on white bread, and the fragrance of sugar and butter and cinnamon melts us. This is our favourite supper. Mam reads us the Harry Potter series until book five, then the books get too big and her voice goes hoarse. After this she gets me the book-on-tape version from the library and I lie on my back on the sitting-room floor to listen to it after school.

In 2003 I love things like *Buffy the Vampire Slayer* and my pet mouse. On a mild spring morning, I'm sitting on my front wall with another girl from the road. I know she doesn't like me and is only waiting until someone else comes out to play. But I'm used to this feeling and I hold my lonely in my mouth, let it hang in the silence between us. The girl's parents are alcoholics and years later her brother will leave the country to escape a prison sentence. I wonder where she held her lonely. On that morning the silence is split open with a scream. The woman from number 9 comes running up the road.

'He's dead! He's dead on the kitchen floor!'

Her shrieks fill the morning with sudden tremors, and people begin to come out of their houses. My mam comes outside to the garden and tells me to stay where I am before she walks down to number 9. Later that day I learn the man died of a heroin overdose. The violence of it pouring out onto the street, the private and public blurring in our in-between world. People round here don't have the luxury of quiet reactions to the way life sparks out. In the following days the family go house to house, collecting for his funeral. Collections like this are common here and I don't yet know there are people in other places, with other lives, who can afford to put the ones they love in the ground.

In 2005 I go to secondary school. My parents send my brother and me to school outside the area. I'm grateful for this because I've been silent for too long, shuddering away from a world I've been so afraid of. I start to speak outside the house. My words leave me in avalanches. They are prayers for a new beginning. At school I make friends, and I speak fast and excited just like them. I tell stories. I begin to write furiously and always. I'm high on the power of my own voice. Around the same time, my mam starts to say a mantra she'll repeat throughout the rest of our school lives: that education is our passport to freedom. She means freedom from the in-between place. The not-quite-hereness of our lives. And I want that, the freedom. I begin to follow words like they are my passport, my imagination finally opening to its own survival. I decide I want to become a writer.

I come apart from the in-between place, separate from it. The children on my road grow into teenagers and start taking drugs and joyriding and mitching off school. Meanwhile, I'm in a different world where teachers encourage me and I begin to believe in a future. Things continue to happen in the in-between place, aggressive and stormy things. Heroin begins to give way to cocaine. The movement of migrants to the area sparks an onslaught of racist attacks. But I am separate from these things; I don't fully let them into my body until I'm lying in bed at night. I am the in-between girl. I straddle a life between my middle-class school and my council-estate home. I meet new people. They have cars and go on family holidays and wear designer school bags. I learn words like 'skanger' and 'scumbag' and 'knacker'. When I'm getting dressed to go out with friends, I show my mam my outfit before I leave the house.

'I don't look like a skanger?' I ask her. 'I don't look common, do I?'

She says no, that I look lovely. Common is bad.

Language is powerful. I try to become the opposite of these bad words. When people ask me where I'm from, I start to say the name of the village nearby. I don't try to change my accent, but somehow it becomes less working class. I never wear tracksuit bottoms or hoop earrings. But I don't belong in the un-common world either. I come home every evening to my council estate and the dead thing in my chest never quite leaves.

In 2011, I go to college to study English literature and sociology. My brother and I are two of only a few young people in the estate to finish secondary school. At college I learn about social class and inequality. I learn a language for my own life and it gives me a power I never had before. My life, my whole life, didn't have to be this way.

It's only the system we live in that is hurting us. It's only generations of working-class people beaten into the ground and worlds made smaller because of poverty. Choices limited and expectations snuffed out. We were never taught that the sky was our limit; we were taught the sky didn't even belong to us, so why bother?

But college is alienating too. I don't belong there, not really. In sociology we look at case studies of working-class communities and the voyeurism of it all makes me feel sick. I go to lectures to learn about the injustice of my own life and get the bus home to my estate where we're all still living it. I am still an in-between girl living in an in-between place.

I get disillusioned with college and go in search of other voices who aren't middle class or white or men. I discover bell hooks and her raging belief in subjective knowledge, in the power of our own story. She says we have power in coming from the outside, from the in-between places of the world. I discover Audre Lorde and her insistence that poetry has never been a luxury but a necessity in the face of oppression, Paulo Freire and his conviction in education and freedom. Their words light a fire in me, and I begin to write from my body, from my very centre. I go to open mics and poetry slams and I listen and observe. Then one not-so-special day, I get up on stage and I tell my story.

This is not the whole story. There are so many other things: first kisses and bike rides and how the colour of the sky at night looks over a housing estate in Dublin West. There's how I learned to be hugged. There's six years at university, emigrating to Spain and London and back again. There's the one and only family holiday we took to Wexford, sponsored by the Vincent de Paul. We rented a horse-drawn caravan, and Stamper the horse pulled us around the Hook Peninsula for a week. In the photographs my hair trails down my back in plaits and my brother is wilful, smiling. There's the first time I got paid to perform poetry. The last time I ever left my parents' house in the in-between place.

I am twenty-seven and I no longer live in the in-between place but the memory of it lives in me. Poverty does that, sticks around inside of you. I don't always see a future because sometimes all my possibilities get snuffed out with bills and how I'll pay the rent this month and my past weighing heavy on my chest. But I know now that all those years of silence was my whole being crying out for things to be different. For little girls to not live in-between lives in hurt places. I was scared, and so I chose silence until I couldn't any more, until the sound of my own will to survive was deafening. And then I spoke. I am a woman. I am a working-class woman. I speak on stages now. I speak loud.

# Once You Solve the Mystery, the Story Ends

*Lisa McInerney*

My cousins and I called ourselves 'The Dectives'. It was meant to be 'The Detectives', but we couldn't spell. Nor did we detect much. We looked for clues – footprints, sweet wrappers, snapped twigs – and debated what these clues might mean, heads full of Enid Blyton whodunnits with their casts of plucky, plummy Brits. There were real mysteries in the council estate, but they were of the domestic and sleazy bent, and we were too young to care about what adults got up to in each other's bedrooms or what was lifted from whose garden shed. In fact, we had no interest at all in the bigger picture. We just wanted to look for clues; we wanted orphaned components and no conclusion at all. As part of this clue-hunting compulsion, we would organise expeditions to nearby fields.

There were eight of my cousins in the one family, though the youngest were too small to come with us. In summer the

Corkonian cousins arrived to add to our numbers. Sometimes a friend or neighbour kid was allowed to come along as well. And there was me. I was an anomaly, a child for whom cousins were about the closest thing, the only family that felt like definitive family.

It was summer, and the Corkonians had arrived. We were staying at the eight cousins' three-bed terraced house and were going to explore an abandoned tract over a gulley that ran along the bottom of the estate. This modest plan tugged at the heartstrings of the dad of the eight cousins – my aunt's husband – and he decided to give us a real chance to explore. Rather than laugh at us marching a mighty one hundred metres into waste ground, he would instead lead us cross-country from my cousins' estate to Coole Park, about three and a half kilometres away.

I don't have a dad. I have instead two mothers: one biological, who is legally my sister, and the other adoptive, who is biologically my grandmother. This is because when I arrived into the world – in the 1980s, not so long ago – children born outside marriage were still legally deemed 'illegitimate'. No one was certain what this archaic-sounding term meant in practice, which meant it could mean anything. My grandparents had lived through a fair dose of hateful Catholic nonsense; they remembered, for example, when overseas adoption of Irish children was prohibited unless those children were illegitimate. They did not trust the state with me. My mother was twenty and, according to my aunts' anecdotes, had no maternal instinct. It was decided that the best thing for both of us would be to promote me to my grandparents' ninth child from my biological position as second grandchild: to adopt me into the legitimate family. Instead of a young wan who slept through my crying and some feckless, faceless young fella, my parents would be a tradesman and housewife in their fifties, who had loads of experience in this sort of thing.

The eight cousins' dad was much younger than my grandfather; he had loads of experience, too, but also a little more energy. He was open-minded in a way that was pleasing to kids and befuddling to adults. He didn't like his children using the word 'hate' because he thought 'hate' was too powerful a word. He was interested in alternative remedies. Sometimes he talked about auras and naturally we all pretended we could see them. (He had a bad habit of playing favourites, though we didn't understand that at the time, so one or two of us he believed as being able to see auras, and the others, he crossly said, were only liars.)

So imagine this man, now: around thirty years of age, striding across fields towards the woods, a whoop of small children with short legs in his wake. It felt like it took hours to reach Coole Park, though of course it must not have. When we had scrambled over enough stone walls to reach the reserve, we trudged as exhausted pilgrims to the walled garden at the middle and collapsed dramatically on the grass. Some sixty seconds later we were grand again, and my cousins ran off to climb trees.

'Will you come, Dad?' they asked, but their father said it would be wise to rest; we had to walk home yet. This sounded right to me. Being a reader, I knew that expeditions were gruelling and reserves of energy important; possibly we would need some sustenance soon, though the eight cousins' father hadn't packed sandwiches and there wasn't a Blytonesque babbling brook anywhere in the vicinity. Besides, I wanted very much to please him. I didn't have a dad. I lived in my own head most of the time. The world was as

I made it. So as my cousins ran off, I sat quietly with their father, pretending he was mine.

Recently, my aunt – the eight cousins' mother – recalled that as a child, I had asked her husband if I could call him my father. I remember the expedition to Coole Park but I don't remember this. My aunt seemed to find it amusing, then and now. Her anecdote didn't include his answer. I imagine it was, *No, I have enough of my own children, and besides, I don't like that you use actual people as toys, and your aura, which by the way I can definitely see, is a most menacing colour.*

I was informed early that my older 'sister' was actually my birth mother. I was informed so early, in fact, that it seemed totally normal. In a sense, it was. Plenty of people in Ireland have discovered that their 'sisters' gave birth to them. Plenty of people outside Ireland, too; I share this quirk with Jack Nicholson, Nobel Prizewinner Sir Paul Nurse, and the somewhat less distinguished Ted Bundy. There was no mention of my biological father, but, y'know, being a reader and all, I knew that if I had a 'real' mother, I had to have had a 'real' father, too. In childish curiosity, I asked about him, and eventually I got an awkward answer. His name. That he'd been a drinker. That I had his eyes.

I didn't miss him, this fella with the name and the eyes. I had my grandfather and uncles, and four uncles by marriage, one of them, of course, the eight cousins' dad, so there were plenty of father figures around if I wanted them, and most of the time I didn't. When I did want a stand-in dad, it was for some narrative rather than practical reason.

Narratively, fathers had duties. In the stories I read, they were wise figures, occasionally stern, and whose praise meant everything. They drove cars.

I'd have very much liked a car. My grandfather suffered from arthritis, and couldn't grip the steering wheel. He knew how to drive, but his driving days had ended before I'd come along. As had his working days, pretty much. A carpenter, he once did a nixer at my primary school; I ran over excitedly when I saw him in the yard, perhaps hoping that I might show him off, and he ignored me because he was talking to another adult, and children should be seen and not heard. This is why it pissed him off when I had nightmares and came into my grandparents' room in the middle of the night. When this happened, my grandmother would keep me on the outside of the bed, and she would go into the middle. Once I tried to snuggle in between her and my grandfather instead, and my grandfather unceremoniously dumped me out onto the floor, rolled over and went back to sleep.

None of the fathers in my books did such things, though they were busy men who were scientists and captains of frigates and bank managers. I looked for their qualities in other people's fathers, not having found them in my grandfather and not having a clue what qualities my biological father had, apart from his eyes and his love of the gatt. Hence the brief elevation of the eight cousins' father to my own. All he had to do was sit quietly, catching his breath; he could be the cornerstone of a world in which I had a father who was wise and kind and had a car.

My grandfather was a magnificent raconteur, great in the company of adults, but he was cantankerous with children and fond of threatening me and my cousins with 'the hurl'. He never actually hit us with the hurl, but he was very insistent that he might. *Spare the rod, spoil the child* was still in vogue, at least in my family in the 1980s, though really, wasn't it very Dev, very Archbishop McQuaid?

Catholic Ireland was itself a cantankerous beast and Archbishop McQuaid was the holy father of Catholic Ireland. The list of things he was opposed to on the grounds of the nation's moral health included tampons, Protestants, communism, the Gardaí daring to investigate allegations of clerical sexual abuse, and Noël Browne's plan to reduce child mortality, which McQuaid seemed to think was secretly a plan to socialise medicine, so I suppose you could say communism again. His was the Ireland social campaigners had battled so hard to modernise in the decade or so before my birth, though the war wasn't yet won: the legal status of 'illegitimacy' existed until 1987, and until 1990 lone parents who wanted welfare from the state had to be widowed, or otherwise prove desertion.

There was a bit more to this moralising than families like mine offending the Lord. The issue – still prevalent in religious conservatism, here and abroad – wasn't that the family unit must be protected; it was that the traditional family unit was a respectable family unit, meaning a family unit of a particular social class. The likes of us bred like rabbits anyway. Important not to further encourage us. Children born outside of the respectable family unit could starve or be reared in industrial schools or sold to America, so long as the behaviour that had led to their being born was punished, and so long as the burgeoning middle class of Ireland was warned off partaking in this kind of freewheeling. Anyway sure, how could you save something that hadn't sinned? Or how, in fact, could you frighten the respectable with stories about damnation if there were no wretches around to exemplify it?

My grandfather was a product of Catholic Ireland, but he knew it, and he was a clever man for an ostensibly uneducated man. It was his decision to adopt me; I was blood. He'd have clattered anyone who looked down on me. He didn't seem altogether fond of me, but I don't think my existence bothered him. He didn't seem altogether fond of anyone.

I don't know if I'm correct either on my grandfather or on Catholic Ireland. These are just the conclusions drawn when the clues are put together. Unpleasant, aren't they?

My biological mother went on to marry a strong, silent type and they had a daughter of their own. I was told recently that the man who might be my stepfather made enquiries as to whether it was possible to adopt me when he married my biological mother. It wasn't: a child cannot be adopted twice. He never mentioned this to me, or gave me any clues as to his ever feeling this way, so I don't even know if it's true. I'd rather not know. It's much easier to be quietly grateful, to imagine an understanding or bond, to fabricate knowing looks. Anyway, despite it being about me, it feels rude to ask.

A few years ago, during an event about working-class writing, I was asked whether it was difficult writing dialogue for working-class characters, considering how working-class people didn't say much, particularly working-class men. I still think about this question a lot. My life has been soundtracked by anecdotes, jokes, admonishments, complaints, rebel songs, welts of wooden spoons, and gossip, so much gossip. Not just from the women, either. My clan is full of blethering men.

But when I think hard about it, the men around me, the fathers who stood in for a father in my make-believe world, riffed constantly on absolutely nothing. They could talk endlessly about politics, history, sport, this gobshite or that gobshite, and remain unknowable. They were only intense or sincere when they sang. They wouldn't even tell doctors what was wrong with them.

The place was full of riddles and its inhabitants dropped clues in perpetuity. Useless things. Cantankerous words, historical actions, favouritism. Footprints, sweet wrappers, snapped twigs. It was imperative that no one ever solved the mystery.

Before Twitter and Facebook and even Bebo, there was Friends Reunited, a social-media site that aimed to connect old schoolmates. Even though it was pitched at people in their thirties and forties who'd fallen out of touch with old confidants and crushes, and I, hardly out the school gates, still knew everyone I cared to know from school, I set up an account. And one day, Friends Reunited sent me an email that read: 'Your father has sent you a message.'

I had his name and it was flickering at me from my computer screen. He had noticed my surname and home town, and wanted to ask, on the off-chance, whether I knew a certain woman from the area. My sister. Or mother. Herself. Whoever.

I hurried over to her house to tell her what had happened and ask if she thought I should reply.

She said, tersely, 'I hope he's not coming here!'

I was put out. It was as though she believed he was only contacting me so he could make contact with her. That I was only a conduit for more inappropriate carry-on from him.

I went back home and replied to the message. 'I'm her daughter,' I said. 'And I think I know who you are.'

He replied with, 'I don't know what to say.'

My biological father and I exchanged photographs and anecdotes. He told me he'd gone on to have three more kids of his own, all boys. I was his only daughter. My child was his only grandchild. But we never used those terms; we never said the words 'father' or 'daughter' or 'grandchild', or talked about our connection, which, though biological and therefore true as anything could be, felt tenuous and vague. We talked about politics instead. He was a bit of a socialist, very fond of Cuba and such. We didn't discuss meeting.

Between my email exchanges with him and clipped conversations with my two mothers, I figured out some details. When my mother became pregnant, my father, her boyfriend-or-whatever-he-was, was not welcomed. He came to see me once as a baby. I don't know how it went. I don't know how hard, if at all, he was partying at the time. Was it that he had no interest in supporting my mother? Did he come for a gawp at his baby and take to his heels again afterwards? Did he break my mother's heart? Or was it just too shameful to have a scut or dandy hanging about the family home, after he'd impregnated one of the daughters? 'He was no good,' my grandmother told me, and I saw the damage he did when I looked in the mirror.

How strange to have parents who don't want to admit your relationship. It's one of those things it doesn't pay to think about that much. Here were the two people without whom there wouldn't have been a me. Whatever fucked-up or inappropriate or damaging or blissfully ignorant relationship they had, if they hadn't had it, I wouldn't be here. Neither of them wanted to talk about it. Both were happy to keep the most visible reminder of it at a safe emotional distance. Both semi-strangers; there, and then not there.

My father got in touch, but the only thing I got out of it was confirmation that yes, I did have his eyes.

Years later, my biological father went from being left wing to supporting UKIP; it's funny how the two ends of the political spectrum can loop around to bite each other's arses. I didn't confront him, because I couldn't be bothered. I unfollowed him on Twitter and haven't heard from him since.

It's a good job that I never cared much for endings, because that's not a very satisfying ending. It's a fine thing that my interest lies in gathering clues, arranging them in ways where they might catch the light rather than shed light. All I want are prompts around which I can build my own narratives. UKIP arseholery doesn't fit at all. I don't want a real father if he's going to be messy. Why should I? How can it be my duty to compromise now, when it was never his duty to come see me or drive cars or provide wisdom or any of that?

The everyday functions of fatherhood fascinate me, even still. My interest in what fathers are or what they're meant to do or how they feel about their children and their role comes through in a lot of my fiction. The narratives I pin on other people started with me not knowing who I am and, more importantly, not wanting to know, either. Is it that all writers are 'dectives', hunting for clues without the drive to solve the mystery? Common to us all is the belief that it's the expedition that's important.

# Spricks

*Maurice Neill*

The race at the head of the Green Dam is full of spricks, said Aunt Annie. My little book of British fishes contained detailed references to, and drawings of, all manner of sporting creatures that could not be found in Ireland – such as barbel, tench, chub, grayling and dace. It mentioned in passing some that could be found in abundance such as salmon, trout, perch, eels and pike – but there was no mention of spricks. 'Wee spricklybacks,' added Annie, in a failed effort to end my puzzlement. Despite the communications problem, we set off with my first fishing rod, a jam jar full of garden worms and a plastic seaside bucket for a keep net. The hunt was on for the mysterious spricklyback that lived in the fabled race. I had not been well. This trip outside was a treat because I was finally on the mend. It was hard to tell who was more excited, Annie or me, her nine-year-old nephew in my short trousers and a woolly pom-pom hat.

When William Clark & Sons built a linen business in the little valley of Upperlands, it was because it had a good source of running water. The Knockoneill River tumbles swiftly down from the boggy Sperrin Mountains and across County Derry along a stony course. It passes through the historic mill village on its way to join with the 'fruitful fishy Bann' described by Elizabethan poet Edmund Spenser. The Bann is the only river to flow out of Lough Neagh and drains most of Northern Ireland before it enters the sea among the sand dunes at Castlerock. The Clarks built a series of strong dams to ensure a steady supply of water all year round, water that could turn the mill wheels and drive the hammers of the beetling engines where my grandfather worked. It was also required to soak the flax, for the plant must be allowed to rot in water before the valuable fibres can be made workable.

The race – a Scots term for a man-made channel of running water – fed these artificial reservoirs. The race could be opened and closed when required using a series of sluice gates. The Knockoneill River was named after Ulster's last great Gaelic chieftain, but Upperlands folk were largely people from the Scottish Lowlands. The first Ulster settlement, in the time of James I, was funded by London businessmen in a failed effort to pacify the king's most troublesome province. Fishing rights were still owned by their descendants, The Honourable The Irish Society. The Scots brought their industry and their rich tongue with them. Their speech was not the lyrical Gaelic of the Scottish and Irish Highlands but that of another famous poet – Robert Burns. The sick were said to be 'failed'. To be cold was to be 'starved' of heat. Twilight was 'dayligaun'. To shout was to 'gulder' or 'gowl'. To be underhand was to be 'sleekit'. Children were 'weans' and young girls 'wee cutties' or 'blades'. If I ate too many sweets, I was a 'gorb' – like the greedy fledgling in the nest. If I misbehaved, I was threatened with a 'skelp on the bahookie', which would make me 'gurn' and run and hide in the 'glory hole' beneath the stairs.

Hand in hand, Annie and I set off down the road and past the towering cathedral of brickwork that was the factory wall behind which, on weekdays, Annie and her sister Jean toiled at making fine linen that would become expensive Italian suits in the gentlemen's outfitters of London, Paris and New York. In its time, Clark's linens provided troopers' tents during the American Civil War and the fuselages of aircraft during the Great War. But the glory days of linen were long gone. It had been eclipsed as the everyday fabric by softer man-made fibres and cheap cotton from overseas. The Clarks built themselves a series of fine and comfortable houses before the profits dried up. All of my father's family worked in the factory and grew up in a company cottage by the river. As children they kept the lids of cocoa tins, said Annie. 'We nailed them over the knot-holes in the floor to keep the rats out.' They had no sanitation and had to bathe in a tin tub before the open fire. It was the 1950s, when a Labour government invested in the building of decent public housing, before the family became the proud owners of a flushing toilet.

We crunched along a cinder path that once accompanied the factory branch of the Derry Central Railway line and arrived at the head sluice for the Green Dam – about three acres of deep and brooding water that bordered the site of the main factory. Craig's Dam, at the head of the system, was the smallest, but was silting up and full of rushes. The Island Dam was the largest and most accessible, with its wooded isle and a fairy fort among the trees along the shoreline. The Lapping-room Dam was the most picturesque, with its gently sloping shores and nesting ducks. The

Green Dam was the most forbidding and dangerous. Its sides were sheer and made of stone. The water was accessible only by boat, which was kept in an old boathouse at the bottom of a steep flight of steps. We walked, hands firmly clasped together, across the slippery planks of the sluice and along an overgrown track beside a deep and still channel filled with pond weed – the kind you could buy in the pet shop for your aquarium. At the end of the track the channel disappeared into a dark tunnel beneath an emergency overflow system for the Green Dam beyond. This was the race. I peered into its clear water in search of spricks. Annie squawked: 'Don't get too close. That's very deep water and I can't swim, you know.'

My first fishing tackle combination was a curiosity – more a toy than a proper fishing outfit. The reel was a tiny centre-pin made of wood and held a short length of line that was thinner than string but stronger than thread. It was poorly made and groaned in oil-less protest when the handle was turned. The rod was a primitive length of steel – like a stiff car aerial – and had only three plastic eyes along its five-foot length. The hook was a bent pin from Granny's sewing box. I opened the jam jar and plunged a finger into earth and moss in search of a worm. The moss helped to keep the soil damp and stopped the worms drying out, I was advised. I pulled out a small and slimy lobworm, which had innocently been burrowing in Granda's small potato garden the day before. It wriggled in protest as it was skewered onto the bent pin. Annie grabbed the waistband of my trousers as I leaned over the water to drop the bait down into the dangerously seductive depths.

At first nothing moved. It was hard to see because of the glare upon the water. It did not help that my short-sightedness would not be discovered until my first year at secondary school. Then, in Annie's shadow, I detected a slight twitch among the forest of pond weed. Tentatively, a small fish – no bigger than my little finger – edged into open water and towards the worm, which was now engaged in a fit of frenzied disco-dancing as if it was aware of the savage fate that awaited those chosen for sacrifice.

The fish was a sprick. It circled the bait cautiously and eyed it up from all angles, its gills pumping excitedly. Then it lunged like a prize fighter, grabbed the worm and spun round furiously to free it from the pin. I could feel tiny vibrations along the line and could see the flash of bronze from its tiny flanks. I lifted the rod and up came the worm with the greedy little fish still attached. Plop! – the sprick and the worm dropped off the hook, back into the water and vanished. Elation turned to tears that had to be comforted with a large hug and a hanky. 'Don't worry,' said Annie. 'There's more down there. Try another wee worm.' She deftly filled the blue bucket with water in anticipation of further success.

This time I secured the worm more tightly and dropped it into the water. Out of nowhere the spricks emerged like a shoal of hungry devils and eyed up their wriggling prize. The smaller ones held back while the big males, with their bright red chests, were bolder. The biggest attacked first. I felt the line vibrate again and swiftly hauled it up. This time the fat sprick came with it and dropped into my bucket before releasing the worm. 'There you go,' said Annie, as I beamed with pride. In the bucket, the prisoner swam frantically round and round. His home of deep water and weed had turned into a sterile world of blue plastic that smelled faintly of seaside salt. His camouflage was useless here and I sensed his panic. He was about an inch long, with a large tail and a dorsal fin armed with vicious spikes designed to deter the many predators who would make a meal of a small fish foolhardy enough to be caught in open water. I gazed in wonder at his sleek design, flashing fins and impressive turns of speed, and wondered how anything could catch this perfectly engineered little sports car of the aquatic world. His red breast throbbed with pride and anger at confinement and he demanded to be released to the safety of the shoal.

Upperlands was Annie's mill race, her family and the villagers her safety and her shoal. She was afflicted with motion sickness all her life and even the shortest journey by anything other than bicycle or on foot was a misery for the poor woman. She grew up in the village and worked in the factory all her days. Her only venture into open water was in time of crisis. During the Second World War she roomed and worked in Manchester. Her contribution to the defeat of fascism was a job manufacturing munitions. She never married, but adored children, fussed over them and spoiled them rotten with sugary sweets that were rationed by concerned parents. There were other little surprises. She once set me down a boiled egg for breakfast that cracked open to reveal it was made of chocolate inside. Her other great loves were the little birds that flocked to the garden for the titbits she provided for them, all manner of musical finches, wrens and robins. They scattered as evening descended with the choir of rooks that 'cack-cacked' a darker song as they roosted in the trees behind her house. Anything or anybody that posed a threat to Annie's carefully constructed world and her loved ones was rounded on with uncharacteristic fury. If a weasel appeared in the garden, she would rap the window and say: 'Shoo, shoo – that damned wee whuteret's back.'

Aged ninety-three she broke her hip in a fall during an electricity blackout. The villagers and the family rallied round to get her to hospital and see her through the surgery. She was unable to go home, but a place was found in a comfortable local nursing home, staffed largely by people from the village. The food was plain but wholesome, there were games to amuse the residents and walking frames were cleaned each Sunday. My sister bought a comfortable chair in which Annie could sit by the window and watch the little birds at the bird table outside. It amused me that the house was one of the grand, wood-panelled residences built by the Clarks, who had employed my aunt all her working life but failed to provide a pension. We talked of childhood trips to the swings, day trips to the seaside, the helter-skelter and the dodgems at Barry's Amusements in Portrush. She recalled long walks in summer and winters when the dams froze over. She forgot that her parents were dead and could not come to visit, but she never forgot the hunt for the spricks.

By the time the worms were consumed there were a dozen frightened spricks in the blue bucket, spinning around in desperation. I wanted to take them home and keep them as pets. Annie smiled but firmly opposed the idea. 'Poor wee things. You can't take them away from their friends.' And so the bucket was gently emptied back into the race. The spricks circled for a moment until they got their bearings. In an instant they were gone, scattering downwards in all directions, back to safety in the forest of weed. It closed around them like a warm blanket around a sick child.

# Dirty Linen

## *Martin Doyle*

*Putrid currents floated trout to the loch,*
*Their bellies white as linen tablecloths*
'Lint Water', Seamus Heaney

When I was a child, I genuinely thought I could end up in prison. It is said you can only be what you can see, and on the nightly news I saw a steady stream of working-class Catholics being sent to jail.

When our parents went shopping, my siblings and I would stay in the car because vehicles could not be left unattended on high streets – a protective measure against car bombs. The longer we were left, though, the more I began to wonder if my parents might be bombers and us sacrificial lambs. It was a strange time. And I have trust issues.

My story, like so many Irish stories, is a migrant tale. My mother is from Down and my father from Wexford. They met in the Gresham in 1962 – not the smart hotel on Dublin's O'Connell

Street but the ballroom on London's Holloway Road, a meeting place and a melting pot for so many working-class Irish of their generation.

Brendan Bowyer was playing with the Royal Showband. Thirty years later, my mother queued for his autograph at the Rose of Tralee Festival. She got him to inscribe on a card, much to my father's amusement: *Woe the day!*

My parents moved home to get married, settling first in Summerhill in Dublin's north inner city. 'John hasn't just brought you to one of the worst areas in Dublin,' his best man, a Garda, said cheerfully, 'he's brought you to *the* worst area.'

Actually, the neighbours could not have been kinder and it was with mixed feelings that my family moved north after my sister Andrea was born, to make a life in Lawrencetown, my mother's small native village.

In the literature of the working class, the rural experience is the poor relation.

In the 1970s the iconography of the industrial working class seemed a world away. Yet in a five-mile stretch along the River Bann between Banbridge and Gilford, eight linen mills had once employed thousands of workers, including my grandfather, Arthur Pat Byrne, and his sister Lizzie at Uprichard's Bleach Green.

Then, on 3 September 1920, a hoodlum home from the US shot and killed William McDowell, who was transporting wages to Gilford Mill.

Earlier that year, masked men had burned Lawrencetown's police barracks. So, before the Yankee Conlon was caught, the IRA was blamed. A meeting in Gilford's Orange Hall agreed that mill owners and their Protestant workers would turn away every

Catholic who refused to sign a form renouncing Sinn Féin. The vast majority refused. And so, out of a job, Arthur Pat moved to Rostrevor for work and Lizzie left for Canada. They never saw each other again. He couldn't bear having to say goodbye twice.

The parish priest prophesised: 'The grass will grow green over their factory chimneys and there will be work for neither Catholic nor Protestant. I might not live to see it, but some of you will.'

And he was right. But though the work ran out, one thing the North of Ireland has never run out of is dirty linen. Initially, the Troubles seemed a world away also, in Derry or Belfast, but violence stalked us too.

On 20 February 1989, Pat Feeney, thirty-two, the elder brother of a former classmate, was murdered at another linen factory, Liddell's, in nearby Donaghcloney. My mum had worked there too, saving enough to open a clothes shop.

John Michael, Pat's uncle, was murdered with two other Catholics at Bleary Darts Club in April 1975. He was with his son Jimmy, who had just won an all-Ireland boxing championship. He died with his son's medal in his hand.

The killers belonged to the Loyalist Glenanne gang, which included many RUC and UDR men. It was responsible for up to 120 murders, several of the victims from my neighbourhood. The first, in 1973, was Pat Campbell, a shop steward at the Down Shoes factory in Banbridge. It is long gone, but across the road is the F. E. McWilliam Gallery, whose bomb-blasted 'Women of Belfast' sculptures capture the terror and tragedy of the Troubles.

For much of my childhood Mum worked as a school dinner lady, which was a win when it came to second helpings. Dad worked in Goodyear – we had a glass ashtray with a rubber tyre around the rim. Dad also brought home an ugly chunk of untreated rubber, like a hunk of raw meat gouged from an animal. It felt colonial. Goodyear bailed, of course, as multinationals do.

My working-class relationship status is complicated. Trade-union leaders called in vain for peace, but the inspirational solidarity of striking miners in Britain or Dunnes Stores workers in Dublin in the 1980s was sadly lacking. For me, the most formidable display of the power of organised labour was the Ulster Workers' Council strike in 1974, when pickets, given muscle by Loyalist paramilitaries, brought down a power-sharing government and delayed peace by a generation.

The first person I ever interviewed was an impeccably middle-class Catholic senior civil servant who had risked his life to defy those strikers and keep the lights on. A hero in pinstripes.

Irishness and Catholicism were the active ingredients in my identity then, class the unconsidered filler. I took Graham Greene, Evelyn Waugh and David Lodge for the Catholicism, and digested pretty much every Irish fiction title in the local library, from Joan Lingard to Brian Moore, Jennifer Johnston and Frank O'Connor, running into a brick wall only with Breandán Ó hEithir's *Willie the Plain Pint agus an Pápa*, which turned out to be *in* Irish, a bridge too far. (I could and did study French, German, Spanish, even Latin at school, but not my ancestral language.)

Working-class writers were part of the mix too: Christy Brown, Shelagh Delaney, Alan Sillitoe, David Storey and my favourite, Keith Waterhouse, whose Billy Liar said: 'I turn over a new leaf every day. But the blots show through.' Books connected me to a more benign Britain than the benighted regimes that misruled the North.

But class consciousness was not really a thing for me, perhaps because reality belied any notion of class solidarity surpassing the religious divide. In our low-level civil war, sectarian trumped proletarian, belligerents on both sides largely drawn from the working class, divided by a common rung.

Certainly there were class-based divisions within Unionism and nationalism. Sinn Féin dismissed the SDLP as a party of schoolteachers and solicitors. The DUP painted the Official Unionists as out-of-touch elitists, the fur-coat brigade. But these differences were understood to be secondary concerns.

Home until I was thirteen was a council estate. It would have been described in the jargon of the time as 'predominantly Catholic'. That it was exclusively working class was unspoken – a given. It was named after a Unionist councillor, of course, just as the village was named after the Anglo-Irish landlord, although the latter *had* gifted the land on which the Catholic church was built.

The estate had been a big step up for most of its residents. When it was first built, to secure a house there you had to be living in a place condemned as unfit for habitation. Our most famous neighbour was Maggie Barry, a singer from a Travelling background who once shared a bill with Bob Dylan.

The houses weren't big. The parish priest once pronounced that one should sit eight feet back from the TV set. Doing so would have meant moving the settee halfway down the front path.

It was a close-knit place, with many large families going back generations. We were in and out of each other's houses all the time. When we locked ourselves out, a regular occurrence, my cousin Julie was called on to stick her skinny arm through the letter box and twist her hand up to open the lock.

There was a real sense of community, centred round the parish and the GAA. I was an altar boy. We enjoyed the perks as well as the pranks – 50p for a funeral; £1 for a wedding; and, unofficially, all the communion hosts we could eat (unconsecrated – we weren't monsters) and altar wine we could drink.

Not everyone back then could afford a car, so traders came calling in their vans. So too in summer did the mobile library, where you could borrow twice as many books as from the town library. Books were accessible in a way that theatre, even cinema, was not. Being peripheral is a disadvantage too.

Brian the Butcher's complexion was the colour of a beef sausage; the fishmonger called out '*Hernahernahern*', hawking herring as if campaigning for a future Taoiseach. Our coalman was Declan O'Dowd – my parents were so fond of him, they gave my brother Shane the middle name Declan. Our milkman was the coalman's father, Barney – we called our rocking horse after him. I was fascinated by his big leather satchel full of coins, like a pot of gold.

The Glenanne gang murdered Declan at nineteen years of age, along with his brother Barry and uncle Joseph. It is said they were targeted because they were in the SDLP. John O'Dowd, their cousin and a classmate of mine, would become a Sinn Féin Minister for Education at Stormont. Barney was seriously wounded, moving south after he recovered. I never saw him again.

There weren't many amenities. Without being prolier than thou, the playground was called the Dirt Track. Still, my childhood was Heaneyesque: blackberry picking; playing football till the light faded so the ball was only a blur; putting slack on the fire; peeling potatoes either side of a pot.

My parents, wanting the opportunities for us that they did

not have, brought us to the library every week as faithfully as to Mass – literature and liturgy. The eleven-plus exam created a new divide – streaming us into comprehensives or grammar schools. The unfairness of having your educational fate sealed at eleven is stark. Ostensibly meritocratic, the test is won or lost on a playing field that is never level, where middle-class children will always have home advantage. It was a ladder for me but a snake for many others.

Most who passed went to Catholic grammar schools in Newry. I, like my siblings and cousins, went to Banbridge Academy, a state grammar and thus effectively a Protestant one, Catholics making up roughly 10 per cent – not so much mixed or integrated then as slightly diluted Orange. I recall a teacher stopping his car in the pouring rain to send a pupil home for wearing a duffel coat, not the regulation gabardine. He wasn't the only one, but he *was* the only Catholic. Back then it was a cold house for Catholics. We were admitted but not accommodated.

Every day someone called me a Fenian or a Taig – that, for the name-callers, was the underclass. Sectarianism was not an undercurrent: it was a riptide so vicious it cannot have gone unnoticed among teachers, yet it was never addressed.

It spiked when a local RUC or UDR man was murdered, but parents and pulpits fuelled it too. It peaked with the hunger strikes in 1981, when their enemy's self-sacrifice intolerably won international support. 'Could you eat a chicken supper, Bobby Sands?' classmates chanted. 'Could you eat a chicken supper, you dirty Fenian fucker?'

The following year, on 15 March, two days before Irish people traditionally celebrate pride in their nationality, an eleven-year-old schoolboy, Alan McCrum, was killed by a car bomb in Banbridge. He was waiting in a jeweller's for a lift home, talking about his new watch, when the IRA stopped time for him and warped it permanently for his loved ones. The display clock that hung outside the shop was damaged too, its hands stilled, left frozen in time, stuck in the past.

Alienation was the buzzword at the time to describe how Catholics felt in a gerrymandered state designed to deny them their rights and identity. I felt the buzz of recognition when actor Stephen Rea admired the 'appropriate disrespect' his fellow Queen's student, activist Eamonn McCann, showed to the authorities. But I never succumbed to the nihilistic extreme of nationalism that was happy for our gutters to run red while only our rivers ran free.

In his contribution to the school history, my brother Shane, now a professor of history at Leeds University, wrote: 'The petty sectarianism of life outside the classroom sharpened my academic ambition. Repeated reminders that Catholics were stupid provoked the desire to excel, and to leave.'

My father's American boss's daughter, honey blonde and tanned, a golden girl, was in my Spanish class. My Spanish was better than hers even though she had just come from her father's previous posting in Latin America. I didn't feel competitive, however. Even back then I realised it would not hold her back. Form is temporary, class is permanent. And privilege rankles less than prejudice. A new headmaster, Winston Breen, changed things. He went out of his way to prepare Shane for Cambridge and, when his brother Harry became the most senior RUC officer to be murdered, he addressed the school on the evils of sectarianism. For me, the deepest divide was between those on all sides who supported the taking of life and those who opposed it.

My German teacher had encouraged me to apply for Oxbridge too, but I chippily said I didn't want to go to a foreign university.

My narrowed mind had narrowed my options. I got over myself and I soon got on the boat.

A blinkered Irish nationalism did sometimes express itself through sport. The village's crowning glory was an impressive GAA pitch. Woe the day, though, if you were caught playing soccer on it or, worse, cricket. The ringleader of the latter game would go on to join the RUC and be bullied out of it for being Catholic. The middle ground was no man's land. I called once for a friend to play soccer and he said that was a foreign game. We had played it all our lives. He had a Manchester United replica jersey. That's how wrong he was.

My dad was involved with Lawrencetown Swifts, and wrote the match reports for the *Banbridge Chronicle* under the pen name Coubray, the name of the field where they played. I use the term advisedly, as they shared the pitch with a herd of cattle, which meant you were lucky if you finished a match covered only in mud.

I became Coubray Junior and got a taste for journalism, as did my brother Garry. My dad kept a scrapbook of his clippings, which I read as enthusiastically as the comics *Tiger and Scorcher* and *Whizzer and Chips*. (I kept clippings for my kids, and they call me a hoarder.)

I even founded my own newspaper, the *Doyles Weekly Herald*. The only surviving copy (in truth, the only copy) is dated 16 April 1978. The title's political leanings can be gleaned from a centre spread on Margaret Thatcher, still over a year away from becoming prime minster. There is no actual text – I mustn't have pressed 'save' – but the illustrations under the subheading 'Her favourite photographs' include Willie Whitelaw, Enoch Powell, piles of banknotes and coins, Jack the Ripper and Al Capone, plus a portrait of Thatcher with a pirate's eyepatch and horns.

My grandfather Arthur Pat was another big influence. He wrote and directed his own plays and was a great storyteller. Visiting him, however, was another form of Vatican roulette. If you were lucky, you got a fireside story, a mug of cocoa and a soda farl with butter and jam. If you were not so blessed, you got five decades of the rosary, with all the trimmings.

I used to earn pocket money collecting my grandparents' laundry. Granny usually paid in silver coins, but once it was Granda, who paid in coppers, prompting me to plaintively ask Mummy whether he understood decimal currency.

My first regular job was at my uncle's filling station. When he opened he received a death threat from Loyalist paramilitaries. But he survived and prospered, even if his nephew occasionally confused orders for petrol and diesel. Catholics did not have to join the IRA or Sinn Féin to pose a threat. Seeking to advance socially or economically was subversive enough.

When I was thirteen we moved to a bungalow on the other side of the Bann. It would have been the other side of the tracks too, but the railway line was long gone. We had a ludicrously large front garden, in truth a field so full of weeds that the only cure – allegedly – was to plant it with potatoes, the picking of which was delegated downwards. If this back-breaking bending was social climbing, it felt counter-intuitive. My lower-middle-class life had got off to a very unpromising start.

Poor Shane had it worse. If there is one thing worse than lifting spuds, it is picking flax. A local entrepreneur needed labour and Mummy knew just the boy. Forget grinds. Nothing focuses a student's mind like the grind of agricultural labour.

Something *was* lost in the transition, though. My other grandfather,

Bill 'Slater' Doyle, was a roofer like his father before him and built himself a fine house. The closest I have ever come to the roof is releasing the catch on the folding ladder to boldly go into the attic.

Drawing the dole; signing on; doing the double; collecting the bru; social security – the numerous euphemisms for unemployment benefit I acquired aren't quite up there with Inuit words for snow, but speak to the centrality of the experience. The first thing I did when I left school was sign on; the same when I went to London after my first year at St Andrews. There was a precariat before the word.

My upbringing – my class background – has not completely defined me, but it certainly colours how I perceive the world and understand society. Our sky was lower, our horizons closer. Our first and only family holiday abroad was just before my sixteenth birthday. That said, we were lucky in that Daddy's parents lived near Courtown, the Co. Wexford seaside resort, and – bonus points – my aunt owned the chip shop, meaning free chips. To replicate that buzz as an adult you'd need to be a gambler in Vegas.

I saw myself as a moderate. I had a relative in the police and we played squash in the bowels of the fortress that was Lurgan RUC station. When I went to Queen's University Belfast, I played snooker in the Felons' Club on the Falls with a student whose father had been a Republican prisoner, a requirement for membership. I was an equal-opportunities sportsman. I lived near the Loyalist Village area and faced a moral dilemma when neighbours knocked, collecting for a Loyalist band. Inspiration struck. 'Thon student doesn't even understand decimal currency,' they must have said when they emptied their tin.

At St Andrews, where the heir to the British throne followed in my footsteps, I began to notice posh people. It is wrong to make fun of people because of their accent, but they were commonly called Yahs. They tied their sweaters round their shoulders, not their waists. They were loud. Even their trousers were loud.

I spoke fast and kept having to repeat myself, so I learned to speak more slowly so that English people could understand me. A public-school girlfriend insisted on giving me a cutlery lesson before we visited her parents. I was now in a world where what mattered was not which foot you dug with but how you held your knife and fork. Great.

A lecturer corrected me when I defined Limbo as a Catholic concept of a post-death state or place that no longer existed. It *never* existed, he said, in a tone that did not hide his disdain, though his came from a sense of secular, not sectarian, superiority, which was novel.

I realised I could become a different, middle-class person if I wanted. I didn't really. I turned my back on law and devoted the first decade of my career to Irish community newspapers in London – a vocation, not just a job, recognising in the Irish diaspora an even more marginalised out-group of the nation.

Now, as books editor of the *Irish Times*, I hope I bring an empathy for the periphery, an interest in the disregarded. It feels as if I have come full circle. The books that nourished me as a boy and broadened my horizons have led me to a place that feels like home.

*I am indebted to my parents, Marie and John, for, among many other things, their essays on our parish history, published in* Once Alien Here *by the John Hewitt Society. I also gratefully acknowledge the Estate of Seamus Heaney and his publisher Faber & Faber for their permission to quote from his work.*

# We All Fall Down

*Linda McGrory*

Our own house. Three words, four hearts fit to burst. Four and a half if you count the one in Mammy's belly.

The day we get the keys from the council is a Saturday. It must be. Nice things happen on Saturday. And there is no school except when there is something exciting on in one of the big classrooms that are not the prefabs.

It is drama, elocution and deportment, and it is taught by Miss Carr, who travels to Donegal from someplace that isn't Donegal, with a suitcase full of posh vowels.

The nuns must think we need our Ulster-Scots' *ayes*, *wees* and *nahs* extracted from our throats like bad tonsils and replaced with *yes*, *small* and *no*.

They hope we will stop saying: 'It's wile coul the day, so it is,' and instead: 'It's rather cold today, don't you think?'

'You'll end up in the factory.'

Mammy hated the factory but comes over sort of proud when

telling you she was good on the overlocking sewing machine before she got married. She leaves atlases about the house in case you might pick one up and see how Mogadishu sounds in your mouth.

Mogadishu, Mogadishu, we all fall down.

Daddy staves off dark thoughts of the dole with jokes: 'Warm my trousers, Ma, I'm going to the broo.'

Saturday – the dote of the seven-day week. The day you look up and imagine your whole family is safe inside a cloud. And the cloud can fly like an aeroplane, so it can, and that is great because we don't have a car.

My cloud takes us farther than any car can and we're always back in time for tea.


There's a half-dog, half-wolf who tries to hump our legs when we pass on the way to buy sweets. 'He's a banshee,' my sister says. I'm confused. 'Are banshees not supposed to be girls with long hair?' Whatever kind of beast he is, I detest and fear him in equal measure. Run.


In the new house, my big sister and I scatter like fledgling starlings who don't know how the murmuration works.

We stake claims to surfaces last touched by the chalky hands of plasterers, the carpenters' precise fingers.

The last pipe fitted by the plumber, lying on his right hip under a sink, won't be touched again for years, until it springs a leak.

Daddy lights fires where fires can be lit – the open grate in the sitting room, the butter-cream Stanley cooker in the kitchen with stubby cast-iron legs.

They have to be small, weak fires at first to temper the bricks.

Plenty of smoke without fire. The thermometer on the oven door is like a neglected clock. It becomes the single most overlooked utensil in our house, but never loses its confidence. Lumpy apple tarts, succulent roast chickens and scone bread are lifted steaming from the oven, which is always just the right temperature for the job in hand. Our first home has to be damped down of its new-house dust before we move in and colonise the pith of the place with our smells.

Our brother's arrival adds the sweet and sourness of a baby – humid nappies, warm-shortbread neck snuggles, cradle cap, Farley's Rusks and talc.

'Mind yourself coming down those stairs'; 'Stay away from the fire'; 'Leave your sister alone'; 'Don't sit on the stairs, you'll get splinters on your arse.'

My mother is an ocean of cautions. I sometimes neutralise her cautions with questions.

'Mammy, am I adopted?'; 'How do you know I'm not adopted?'; 'Mammy, do you love me?'

And when it's washing day and the twin-tub hums in the kitchen like a fat baritone warming up, the inquisition continues: 'Mammy, why is the baby's head loose?'; 'Would you cry if I ran away?'; 'Do you love Daddy?'

'We have stairs,' I squeal at my sister, as if she doesn't have eyes.

We have no stairs at Granda's and now we have fourteen. We bag bedrooms but know it's just talk.

Mammy will decide how to divvy up the two doubles and one box room with a built-in wardrobe.

As we try out our upstairs echoes that are different from our downstairs echoes, our parents name the best things about the house. A big back garden with plenty of sun; a five-minute walk to the shops; handy enough to the shore.

Downsides are cast in an optimistic light if they have home heating value. 'The kitchen's wee, but it'll be easy to heat. It's better to be in the middle, far warmer than an end house.' There are rumours about who else got a house from the council. They wonder if some of them are true. Daddy puts his hands around Mammy's waist and not for the first time she wriggles to signal not in front of us.

We eat a packed lunch standing up: Galtee cheese sandwiches, overripe bananas, Garibaldi biscuits, a flask of milked tea. Our first visit is long enough to gather about me the contented feeling of my cloud.

Long enough to imagine where we will put the new furniture that will be delivered without full payment because the shop knows we're good for it.

Houses built of need take the guesswork out of where to put tables, beds and sideboards, because there's usually only one place for things to go.

A shed that becomes Daddy's place is out the back and is even smaller than the kitchen. It has a flat felt roof, a white wooden door and not a single window.

Sheds in the seventies don't have notions.

The shed will soon have its own smells: oil, grease and damp kindling sticks, fresh grass turned to hay on sharp things; the earthiness of a bitch in heat.

Cassie, with her soft brown eyes, will have a litter of mongrel pups, the reek of her postnatal pieces adding yet another layer.

In the deep-soak of the masonry too, there's the faint whiff of Snowy the rabbit with her pink eyes and voracious appetite for pee-the-bed leaves.

Shelves will sag with odds and ends of odds and ends that will come in handy someday, along with boxes of small rusty things.

There are spanners with a nice weight in the hand, a lawnmower with a greased rotary blade, a sturdy hammer with a slimmer sibling, a doughty double act of hatchet and hacksaw.

Later, a new red strimmer will appear like an exotic bird before succumbing to the inevitable fate of functional things.

I love how the sun catches the blond hairs on the back of my father's hands and the way his gold signet ring slips sideways.

It has no inscription, but the ring honours two women: the mother who bought it for his twenty-first birthday, the wife happy for it to double as his wedding ring.

As it begins to split at its thinnest part after decades of wear, so too does my father's brain: 'Who's the woman in the kitchen?' And there is my mother clutching her forty-year-old wedding album, tatty now from attempts to prove she's his wife.

Another proof, the papal marriage blessing signed by Pope John XXIII, is down from the wall and sits beside his chair.

'There's our two names there, look see,' she says. She rings us when it gets too much.

'Will you come and tell your father who I am.'

He always seems to know his children, his blood.

It's a mercy, we say, that he's not a wanderer. Except when he goes to the house he grew up in, a five-minute walk away and a spit from the town street.

And he is bewildered when his two brothers send him back to his mystery woman: 'What's wrong with Jamesie?' they say.

We're glad Daddy doesn't leave the house in his pyjamas, like the old woman I found on a footpath in Belfast wearing her nightdress and all her worldly jewels. Along with gold chains, bracelets and rings on her fingers, she had six watches – three on each arm – and yet only the flimsiest grasp of time.

They call it sundowning. A nice word for something that's shit.

Symptoms are worse in the evening as my mother clears away the dishes from the tea. It's only two steps to the sink but, somehow, it's now fifty years.

You are thirty, perhaps thirty-five. You don't know it yet, but one day you will have a family of your own. You will be forty-seven when your first child, a beautiful girl, is born.

A second daughter, a daydreamy one, will arrive when you are fifty-one and your only boy five years from that.

After hopes and devout prayers, you will be relieved to get a pensionable job as a labourer with the council. It will keep the banshee wolf from the door.

But this evening you should be on stage with the Star Lite Orchestra, playing your piano-keyed accordion or big bass fiddle in someplace like Charlestown.

Yet, instead of the strains of 'The Garden Where the Praties Grow', there's a woman who's nearly three times your age showing you black-and-white wedding photos and saying you are the groom.

They look happy.

The man is wearing a smart suit and he's squinting into the sunshine as he holds the door of a honeymoon car for his bride.

She has on a damask silk dress with sleeves that narrow to a point on the top of her hands.

A stroke of fortune for a couple to get bright sun on their wedding, the day after Christmas.

*

Are you dreaming or is it a trick?

Could Cassie bring you back if her mongrel bones weren't already dust?

Or your old shed, if it wasn't razed to make way for a new extension, designed to keep you safe downstairs?

When it finally snaps at its thinnest part, you secrete your signet ring into a leather wallet stuffed with Padre Pio and other prayers, a faded brown scapular and a licence to let you fish the Crana River.

Let me put the ring on your finger again and watch it slip sideways as the muscles of your memory flex against the slack.

And you will come back.

You will light bright fires where fires can be lit.

It is Saturday. Nice things happen on Saturday.

# A Losty Goodbye

## *Lynn Ruane*

Lined up like they once did for dinner in the L-shaped Finglas kitchen, they say goodbye to their mother, Maureen Geoghegan. Maureen, originally from Cabra West, had reared her family of ten on Casement Grove in Finglas West with her husband, John Losty. Five boys and five girls, now men and women, each kissed their ma goodbye one last night.

Maureen whispers, 'Look after each other.'

As Maureen lay in her bed, surrounded one last time by her family as they shared stories. Opening one eye to let them know she was still there. John held her hand, and the tribe shared, laughed and loved as a family of twelve one last time.

Rita breaks the initial silence. 'Da, do ya remember lifting me to open the dresser with the blue doors, and there was a birthday cake. I was four. Ma putting on her lipstick and panstick; she'd even put it on to go to the local shop.'

Without a pause for her da to answer, Christine jumps in.

'Mother in the back hall at the washing machine. She would be mangled up to her knees in clothes. I hated that scene.' A glance to Maureen, Christine continues: 'Mam's waters going outside the local pub and me running home to tell Father, who I found in the sitting room talking to himself in the mirror.'

The other nine siblings are nodding and laughing and visibly searching for their story. Still, they allow their eldest sister to jump between memories – 'Father carrying me into the sea, dropping me and telling me to swim. He did that a lot.'

'He must have been trying to get rid of some of us... he upturned me in a rubber dinghy at sea,' says Rita.

Christine reminds her that the rubber dinghy she remembers was the inner tube from a truck tyre.

'Or the time Mother, bringing a new puppy back to Cabra in a shopping bag on a bike, told us she has enough animals, as in us. She was giving out stink cause the pup fell or jumped from the bag twice, and she had to go get it,' says Christine, as she reaches out to her ma to wipe her brow.

Rita adds that Mr Redding ran over our dog; that's how the pup came about.

'Ah, I remember Da gave me a note for school saying: *Sorry Christine was not in school, her mother had another baby and I'm up to my collar in nappies.*'

John looks around the room, slowing his glance momentarily on each child.

'What about the time Da found the baby's remains as he scavenged in the dump?' says Rita.

Everyone gives Rita a look for turning the conversation in such a direction.

Bernie, changing the conversation. 'Remember getting sent to Auntie Annie or the neighbours for a loan till payday?'

'He never passed a dump or skip.'

'Dad always picked up empty bags. He said you will always find something to put in it. By the end of the day it would be full of spuds, coal, copper – anything we found on the ground. Mind you, we needed bigger bags for the TVs,' says PJ.

'He used to bring home lots of Guinness bottles, which we washed and put a fake stamp of a harp on the label, so we could take them to the Cappagh House to get money on them – for him, not us. We used to look in the local dump for mineral bottles for the same reason.'

Again, not expecting John to take his attention away from his wife, Rita doesn't await a response. 'He brought home anything that could be used: toys, clothes, pots, wire,' she says.

'Bernie, I remember having to hang around at the corner for the loan man to pay him cause Da wasn't to know, and Rita, I remember he got me lovely pair of navy shoes with buckles, brand new, only snag one was five the other six,' boasts Christine.

There isn't a frown in the house as they remember the old times. The room is like any council-estate house in Finglas, except it looks a little smaller with twelve adults and a hospital bed inside. Luckily for the Lostys, not many of them grew beyond five foot tall.

'He is still the same, always finds a use for things... he was recycling and up-styling all his life,' Rita adds proudly, as if it's one up on the youngsters today claiming to be green.

'He used to burn the coating off the copper wire so he could sell it.' Christine only has the last word out when Rita is straight back in, typical sisters, talking over each other, but the family easily follow. 'He got sacked from a job for taking two wooden crates; he gave them to his brother, Paddy Losty, to use as cots for his kids.'

Christine says, 'That's new to me. Don't think I heard about that.'

Rita looks to her da. 'He told me that himself,' says Rita.

'Well, I always thought we were as poor as piss, but Ma had Mrs Dempsey make me a dress, Mrs Mann made me a coat, and Mrs O'Rourke knit me a jumper,' Rita says as she repositions herself on the footrest.

'Well, Ma knit for us all, Rita.'

Rita ignores Bernie's interjection. 'Ma used to knit also... she knit our school cardigans. Each had a coloured stripe: Caroline was pink, Veronica was yellow, I was blue, and Bernie was green... Christine had left school. I remember Sister Mary Louise saying how great my ma was and how lovely we looked.' Rita walks to her ma's side.

'I remember Ma had tomatoes in the press for Dad's sambos for work... one by one I ate them till they were gone. Ma went ballistic. They used to go to town on Saturday mornings; Da would say he was going to the bank; they would buy lots of fruit, veg and meat, then go to the pub, where they probably bought stuff there too, on the cheap. We were left at the mercy of Johnny and Christine. We were locked out the back and had to shelter in the coal shed if it rained. We did have the slide and swings that Da built himself from wood and lino.'

'Jesus, Da,' says Rita, 'you had done a bit of everything – delivery boy, helped your da clean the school in Cabra, and a cattleman and a trucker. As a cattleman, all you brought home was the smell of shit; you used to get drunk on Wednesdays, come home, fall on the sofa. We had to take your boots off while Ma went through your pockets for money.'

'I think Dickie Rock got him beat up for slagging him off once,' laughs Christine. Ignoring Christine's divergence to a random Dickie Rock comment, Mark says, 'When he was on the cattle trucks he brought home a full sheep and if I remember right, him and Johnny skinned and boned it in the bath tub. It was a dead one; it fell off the chute in the slaughterhouse.' He looks to Johnny for confirmation; Johnny nods and says, 'That's right.' The men of the house are quiet; nobody is sure if this is by design or just accidental that the women took centre stage.

Veronica, home just in time from Canada for one last hurrah in the Losty abode, chimes in. 'I remember the long stick he used for the cattle; it was stood in the corner of the front room behind the curtain where the TV is now, and I remember the smell too! I also remember Mom staring out the window a lot and humming. Often wondered where she went in her mind as she did that. I remember the coffee she drank was the cheapest brand with chicory in it. I remember when her sisters Ethna and Betty came to visit and how much they laughed together.'

'She was probably wondering where the hell is the father,' says Christine.

'Ma could only manage a few of us into town to see Santa in Clerys, and she would bring a present home for the rest of us. Rita was not happy with her *Sense and Sensibility* book,' says Bernie, wagging her finger at Rita. Behind Rita's head is a wall of photographs. Bernie takes them in every time she looks in Rita's direction.

'Ungrateful brat – poor Ma doing her best and not leaving

anyone out. I hopped it off the wall,' admits Rita, hoping her Ma could hear the remorse in her voice. 'Ma used to start her Christmas grocery shopping early. She kept the goodies in her bedroom, and she had about six tins of fruit put by. I punctured them and drank the juice. Come Christmas they were tins of furry mush. I didn't know they would perish,' says Rita.

'We were so lucky to have you still living at home, Caroline. Ma and Da and indeed the rest of us would be lost not to have you here keeping an eye on them. Ma loved going shopping for the family at Christmas with you – you did the research on sizes and fashions for Da,' adds Rita.

PJ, second from the bottom of the siblings, has been leaning against the door for an hour, taking in the elders' memories. Now and then he goes to the fridge in the hall to top the sisters' wine glasses up. As the evening progresses, they stop asking and just hold their empty glasses in the air.

'I remember going into Cabra, a baby in the pram, next youngest sitting on top, the rest of us hanging off the handle. All the neighbours on Killala Road waving out the windows. Mrs Merton giving us sweets.'

Interrupting Christine yet again, Rita jumps in. 'We had delivery men back then: an egg man, a milkman and bread man, and we collected the turf and coal in the handmade cart that was heavier than the fuel we were to collect. We were not allowed to leave school if we did not have a job. Christine, Bernie and me in the rag trade. I was useless and got out. The fish factory in Finglas paid well and was always looking for staff. Ma would threaten to send us there if we were idle. We were not allowed to stay in bed during times of unemployment. I was about sixteen and gotten up out of my bed and handed paper and paste and told to decorate the biggest room in the house.'

'He skinned us on more than one occasion too, when he got his barber's set out – ten haircuts for the price of none. He didn't even have to know whose hair he was cutting – we got the same cut,' says Rita, and Mark insists he might get his da to give him a haircut, as he still has the scissors. They all appear to consider this an option, with the barber's closed due to the pandemic.

Veronica takes a deep breath and gets in preparation to get everything out before Rita starts again. 'He threw nothing out; says he kept it "just in case" or, "You never know, it might come in handy." As for food, he ate everything; "Nothing goes to waste unless it goes through me" – his words,' she says. 'Speaking of jobs, he told me recently: Mom worked cleaning for the nuns and in a paper-recycling factory. Not sure when she stopped working there.'

Ann Losty, not a sibling but a sister-in-law, nudges Johnny. 'Remember you told me about Bernie climbing up the dresser in the back hall? She toppled it over, got stuck under it, and all the single records that were on top all smashed, he reckons; only one not broken was Ken Dodd "Tears for Souvenirs".'

Rita laughs her head off as she stretches out her legs and her back as if to hint to one of the others it is their turn on the footstool. 'She's lucky my birthday cake wasn't in it,' she says, her moans and groans reminding them of her dodgy knees.

Caroline, third from the bottom, but they call her 'the baby', goes to her ma in the bed. 'You okay there, Mother? Do you want some water?' She says this as she presses the wet sponge to her ma's lips.

Maureen, knowing what she wants in this moment, quickly turns her head away from hydration. Knowing her ma's agency, Caroline takes the water away.

'I remember going to school in a white skirt that had pink polka dots. I was in sixth class! I don't know why I didn't inherit one of the sisters' hand-me-downs. I remember dancing in the front room with Dad to "Save Your Kisses for Me", the winning Eurovision song for 1976 by the Brotherhood of Man,' Veronica says, as she dares move off her seat on the sofa to kiss her da on the forehead.

'If we were cold when we got in from playing, we warmed our hands under Mam's arms.' Vincent, the actual baby of the house, looks down at his feet as if to hide the emotion of the memory, or maybe the realisation that 'under Mam's arms' will be gone soon.

Christine says,'He would take some of us on the bus, give the conductor God knows how much and say, "Go ahead." In town he would stop in the middle of Henry Street, point to the sky and stare; everyone else passing couldn't resist stopping to look and he would just walk on.'

John laughs.

'I think we all remember going to the seaside in Donovan's van,' says PJ.

'Yep, ate winkles right from the shell, eating bread with dripping from the chip pan spread on it,' says Veronica.

'Bread and beef dripping with salt – it was yum. Pigs' feet and tails, cheeks, cow's tongue, tripe – not so yum,' says Christine.

'Sugar sambos,' says Rita, licking her lips.

'Da, remember you wore double denim, and ya looked like a Dick Emery character, and your Andy Warhol-print shirt – it was Heinz Baked Beans,' says Rita.

'It was Campbell's Tomato Soup,' says Christine.

'That's right,' says Rita.

As the clock passes midnight and enters 23 March, a new energy enters the room. Everyone seems to become acutely aware of their ma's movement of breath. It is near, they know it, and they direct all their love in her direction.


Two days have passed since twelve became eleven.

They drop a rose each into the ground while the wider family adhere to their two metres. No friends, family or well-wishers to accompany them back to continue their mourning. The Lostys keep their remembrance together as they settle out Ann's back; it's not long before they pick back up at the same stop on memory lane.

'Da, clearly he enjoys a corny joke. I remember him coming home one day and asked why we let the fire go out. Quick as a whip I told him we didn't, as it was home all day,' says Veronica.

'I remember me and Johnny stood in front of the parents and told how you make a baby and where they come from. We had an audience in the hall, earwigging. Johnny started smirking. He got sent out. I had to stay on my own, cringing,' says Christine.

Veronica adds, 'Think about this: by the time 17 October 1970 came around, Mom was thirty-three years and eight months old with ten children. Dad was thirty-two years and one month old with ten children.' Veronica, a fifty-five-year-old owner of a cat, blows air into her cheeks as she takes this in.

'And don't forget Da's whistle – we always knew when it was him,' says Bernie. John wanders from room to room, not knowing where to place himself.

'Yeah, he whistled, and we came running,' says Christine.

'I remember the time Ma was on the diet pills, and she was impossible to live with according to Da, so he moved into the attic, and he came through the ceiling in the boys' bedroom,' says Johnny, laughing at the ridiculousness of the memories.

'He lived up there for a while,' says Rita.

PJ stands up to get attention and says, 'Remember coming home from school, and the Special Branch raiding the gaff? They took Christine's engagement presents and Dad had to go to court; he got some back.'

'Oh, and they cut the lock on Bernie's press, and someone was in the loo – they made them come out,' says Rita.

'O'Malley was the copper,' says Mark.

'Just doing his job,' says Rita.

'They only kept his portable TV cause he had no receipt. Got everything else back,' says PJ.

'I remember Vincent scutting on the back of Da's truck and Mrs Larkin screaming after him. I also remember a guy down the road scutting on the back of the bread man's van. When he was jumping off, his pants got caught and he got his arse pebble-dashed,' says Rita.

'I think Brendan O'Carroll – Boco – went after Da to tell him Vino was on the back of the trailer.'

Ann, handing soup and sandwiches to the gang, joins in. 'I remember your da coming home after making his yearly retreat to St Rita, and he gave me a holy relic and a prayer. He said he had done the retreat for Johnny and me to have a baby. He left loads of holy pictures on the mantelpiece and PJ and Vincent took them and went door to door selling them.'

'Least you got your babies,' says Rita as she looks around the room for her da.

'Remember Dad would take a different child to the blood bank every time he went? It was a day out, all the goodies you could eat, hence we all became blood donors,' says Bernie.

'Except me,' says Rita.

Vinnie says, 'I remember I was around seven years young and it was the last day after spending a week in Butlin's with the cousins and aunts. We were all out of the rooms, waiting for our lifts home. It felt like hours, starving and with not a penny between any of the aunts. Dad arrived to collect us eventually and bought chips; those chips are the most memorable chips that I ever had. Running a close second are the chips Christine brought home after a night out when I was sleeping in a tent.'

'I also remember Johnny giving us ten pence each Friday from his wages. We got a lot for that from Chaney's van. Black Maria toffee, fizz bags, gobstoppers,' says Veronica.

'That ten pence was between four of us,' says Rita.

'Really? I remember getting ten pence for myself. Oops, hope I haven't just let the cat out of the bag.'

'I gave ten pence to each of you,' quips Johnny as he manoeuvres around Caroline, the baby, sitting quietly watching her da.

'Rita, I wonder which one of us told you there were only ten pence to share,' says Veronica, giggling like her younger self might have got one up on her big sister.

'Anyone that was working had to leave money on the mantelpiece every Friday,' says Mark.

'Yes, that was your dad's rule,' says Ann.

'And leave your bus fare for the week,' adds Christine.

'I remember splitting the ten pence between four,' says Vincent in Rita's direction, as if to show his alliance.

Johnny says, 'When I came home from work Friday, first thing you did was give Ma her wages, and pay back if you borrowed during the week, and the kids' wages on the mantelpiece.'

'And the second thing you did was start borrowing it again from Ma,' says Rita.

'Remember keeping an eye out for the insurance man? The name Jordan is coming to mind for some reason,' says Vincent, looking to Christine for clarification.

'Think he called you Fintan and was corrected by Mother,' Christine says.

'Da had an account in Mr Hips men's clothes shop in Henry Street. He paid five pounds a week and got his suits made to measure. We still have a photo of a four-piece suit, height of fashion in the seventies.' Mark elbows his da lightly in the ribs at the memory of his suits.

'Pinstripes,' says Rita.

'He probably still has it somewhere,' says Christine, gesturing to her da with her head, attempting to provoke a response. 'Ma always did your tomato soup and mushrooms for Rita.'

'And steak and kidney pies for Johnny,' says Rita.

'Ann tried the pie thing too for Johnny, but nearly blew the flat up cause she never took the lid off the tin,' says Rita.

'Your da got catering tins of tomato soup in the dump. Johnny said you all were having it for months; it put him right off it so won't touch it now,' says Ann. Johnny shows agreement with a nod of the head and curl of the mouth at the sheer thought of it.

'Same here, I hate tomato soup,' says Mark.

'The barrel of crisps! We ate them all then had hours of fun rolling about in it,' says Rita.

'That was gas fun, getting rolled down the road,' says Christine.

'I remember Granny Losty coming to live with us for a while. We fit a double bed, two sets of bunk beds and a single bed in the girls' room. Also, remember we filled glass lemonade bottles with hot water for hot-water bottles. We did have a ceramic one made of glazed pottery too,' says Veronica.

'We had to take turns sleeping with the nanny,' says Christine.

'I dressed up in my communion clothes a week after the event and called into untapped neighbours and told them my ma sent me down,' laughs Vincent.

'Those mince pies were Denny pies. They came from the meatpacker's in Leixlip. Dad walked up and down the factory with two buckets to get water for the truck, but for some reason they were full of pies. He stopped when the forklift driver told him there was a tap beside the truck,' says Mark, ten minutes after the pie story.

'We used to tie a rope on the pole opposite our house to swing on, then scatter if the Gardaí car came by,' says Rita, taking the conversation back from the boys.

'If we kicked that pole hard enough, Boco went mad as the lights in his house went out – he'd chase us with a hurley,' says Mark, going red in the face with the image of Brendan O'Carroll going mad as they messed his house lights up.

'I used to put my radio against the wooden pole, and it boosted the batteries,' says Christine.

'Remember Liam's nickname, Four Foot?' Bernie says as she returns from the jax as if she went in there to think of something to add.

'It was Four-Six,' says Rita. 'Reddins van had a raffle once for a big Easter egg. The winning number was forty-six, and the lads on the road picked him up and tried to claim the egg,' she says, with tears flowing from the endless of stream of laughter.

'Jesus, Bernie, Liam won't be pleased you knocked six inches off him,' says Veronica.

'Someone scratched Losty on a church pew, and we were all lined up and questioned, and I don't think it was any of us,' says Rita.

'Wasn't me,' says Mark.

'There were three Losty families – it must have been the others,' says Rita, as if this were the exact sentence she said at the time.

'Remember Mother roaring, "I'll hang your pissy sheets out the window for all to see or bring them to school to show the teacher." She thought the threat would stop the bedwetting. Poor Mother,' says Christine in the most emphatic way.

'Boco was a DJ at the stock-car racing,' says PJ.

'Yeah, it was with Radio Dublin. I used to cover for him Sunday mornings in McGoldrick's garage on McKee Avenue selling the Flogas – it was two-eighty a bottle,' says Mark.

'I remember going to the pawnshop with Ma, and she had a brown paper parcel. She handed it to the man and he gave her money, and when I questioned her, she told me that he was a friend, never told me it was a pawn. It was Brereton's in Capel Street,' says Johnny.

'She used to pawn her wine-and-cream trouser suit and God knows what else,' says Christine.

'I went to Chaney's van for four pints of milk once with a one-pound note, but it blew out of my hand at the counter – true story. Cyril seen this and gave me the change with the milk and told me just tell Ma to give him the one pound when she has it, but I couldn't face her, so I kept away from the van for weeks, if not months, until Cyril caught Mam coming back from the Barry shops and told her. I even remember the price of the milk: eight pence a pint,' says Vincent in a way that shows he's still a little sore for being told on.

'He's a snitch. I once threw a ten-bob note away instead of the receipt. Both were orange. She went mad at me,' says Christine.

'I'm going to miss Mom,' says Veronica.

'Me too,' says the room.

'Da, what do you think of all this?' says Caroline.

'All because two people loved each other,' says John.

# Shake the Bottle

*Jason Hynes*

I'm not sure if you can be too young to understand something. Maybe it's just that you're too young to give anything a second thought. I never questioned why shaking the gas bottle in the Superser made it come back to life. It just did. There was the same amount of gas in it, hardly any, but if you shook it hard enough for long enough, there was enough life in the heater for the four of us kids to gather round and throw our freezing hands in front of the one lighting bar. There were three bars, of course, but I'd never seen them all lit at the one time. One day, at the start of the snow, when the bottle was new, we'd had two bars on the go. But now that the snow was at its worst, there was no chance of us making it to the shops for a new gas bottle, even if our ma had had the money, which she probably didn't. We didn't really give that a second thought either.

We'd never seen snow land in heaps like it did in 1984. It was like all our Christmases had come at once. Not like those fairy-tale white Christmases where snow fell on gingerbread houses in twinkly little villages. This was real snow, on top of the car parks, and up as high as the concrete bollards. A heavy blanket of white laid down on top of burnt-out Fiat Ritmos. There weren't sleighs carrying posh women in furs around the maze of torn-up tarmac in Darndale, but there was no school and no adults on the street from one end of the day to the next and, as we soon discovered, anything could be a sleigh if there was enough ice. We turned our frozen hands to converting every bit of old rubbish we could dig out of the sheds into a sleigh. An old metal rocking horse? Bang, that's a sleigh! An upturned milk crate? Bang, that's a sleigh! And most of all, a breadboard with a piece of string tied to the front of it, and three kids sitting on top? Bang, that's a sleigh!

We adapted to our new environment with relative ease, apart from the cold that is. Almost from the get-go we'd started organising races by category, age group and distance. And, not much longer after that, the injuries had begun to pile up too. Of course, that was no discouragement. The fact that Johnner Nulty had split his head open in the 'Over-12s Downhill Breadboard' only served to solidify its reputation as the premium-class race.

But the cold, the cold was a bastard. The snow latched on to the Dunnes Stores socks that we used as mittens and formed little blocks of ice that stuck like Velcro and bit through your fingers like a mousetrap made of blades. It stung, and it burned, and it was a bastard. Your toes were one thing. If you couldn't feel your toes, so what? You didn't need your toes. But anything that was any fun? You needed hands for that. Eventually, when you couldn't feel your fingers any more, even after you'd had them stuck in your armpits for half an hour, you'd have to give up and go back inside the house, where there might be some heat. Back again, gathered around that one bar of the Superser, as our fingers turned from white to pink, to roaring red. We'd get shouted at, of course. I don't remember exactly why it was bad for us – chilblains, or shingles, or something that sounded like it was from the war. It never stopped us anyway. The sooner we could feel our fingers the better, as far as we were concerned. That was while we still had gas. The bottle was fast approaching its end. Even if we had the money, and the shop had gas to sell us, nobody was going to push a pram with a gas bottle in it through six-foot snowdrifts. It just wasn't happening. So, sooner or later, everyone had to at least consider the drastic step of lighting 'the big fire'.

Coal. Coal was expensive. It was in plentiful supply, though. The coalman and his army of urchins would drive around the estate every Friday. For the lavish salary of fifty pence each, five kids would run after the truck and knock on every hall door in the estate. Bang, bang, bang! 'Do yiz want coal?' and they were gone. They knew not to hang around. They knew, more or less, which houses had money for coal. And they knew not to get left behind. The coal truck was moving whether they kept up or not.

Even a coal truck has a hierarchy. The older lads, the seasoned pros of the game, were big enough and experienced enough to jump up onto the bed of the truck as it moved from one cul-de-sac to another. This did come with the added responsibility of beating the head off anyone else who tried to do the same. You see, wherever the coal truck went, it was followed by another group of kids. Kids with biscuit tins, and buckets and coal shovels, and every one of them was out for coal. Anything that spilt from a bag, anything that slid off the moving truck and, occasionally, anything they could grab without getting the head beaten off them. They weren't collecting the coal to sell it. As soon as they could fill whatever container they were carrying, they'd bring it straight home. That's what they'd been sent out to do. No one's ma let them leave the gaff with the good coal scuttle for no reason. It was a job. You weren't just sanctioned by your oul' one to do it. She made you do it.

But the rules of engagement were clear. You weren't to rob anything. You could pick up anything that fell on the ground, but you weren't in any way to encourage that to happen – yeah, right! The other 'rule', of course, was 'don't scut on the truck'. Now, we were never supposed to scut on anything – cars, vans, the ice-cream van – but of all the things we were not to scut on, the coal truck was the most forbidden scut of all. All along the edge of the coal truck were little metal hooks. They were there for tying stuff down with ropes – not that they were ever used for that on the coal truck, but that's what they were there for. The story, according to the mas of the world, was that, without noticing, you'd get your jumper caught on one of these hooks. Then, when you tried to jump off to abandon your scut, you'd be stuck on the hook and dragged along behind the truck. You'd be done for, pinned to a ten-tonne wagon by a £3.99 polyester-mix jumper. We paid them no attention. We'd torn enough holes in cheap knitwear down the years to know better.

As it happened, nobody was interested in scutting on trucks in the snow anyway. We were only interested in getting pulled along behind them. We grabbed on and slid across the icy ground on our flat shoes like we were floating around the estate. The coal round was chaos; the coal round on ice? Well, it wasn't Disney. Whether you were there to grab coal or not, you were there to grab hold of the side of that truck. All of us, every kid for miles around. Kids you'd never seen around your area before were dragged there in gangs, like a net of scruffy sardines, sloshing from side to side as the clanking diesel lorry skidded through the corners and then dragged them back out again. At every stop the coal truck made, it picked up more kids than it offloaded coal. In the end, I don't think even the kids working on it knew who was part of the crew and who wasn't. The truck driver himself had long since given up on trying to chase them away. He paid little attention to the kids that actually worked for him at the best of times. Right now, all he wanted to do was get his round finished so that he didn't have to deal with 'another Jaysus child this day'. That was not going to happen.

Gumpo was a nice enough youngfella. He was eight but acted a lot younger. If you were posh, you'd probably call him naïve. We'd say he was the kind of youngfella you could easily convince to post a shite through a letter box. Let's say he was easily led. If there was a gang of kids hanging off the back of a truck, you could be guaranteed he'd be one of them. Actually, that's not exactly true. If Gumpo had been hanging off the back of the truck, then there'd have been nothing to worry about.

Sliding on ice is pretty fail-proof, so long as you have ice. But ice is inconsistent. It gets laid down as randomly as snowfall. It gets churned up by cars. It gets broken up by kids with hammers, so it's patchy: a patch of ice, a patch of tarmac, and if you hit a patch of tarmac while you're sliding, you're not sliding any more, you're stopping. That's not so bad if you're hanging off the back of the truck. You'll be dragged forward and fall head first to the ground. But there were kids everywhere. They were hanging on to the truck from wherever they could find a space. They were all over the back of it and all the way up along the sides, grabbing on to those dreaded little hooks. Gumpo was one of those kids. He'd found a hook that was near the back wheels. It was just in front of the back wheels. And when Gumpo hit a patch of tarmac, that's where he was thrown.

When I was younger, I had a football that had been signed by the Irish footballer John Devine. He'd opened the Summer Project with his Miss Ireland girlfriend, and I gave him my football to sign. He wasn't too happy about it, or at least he pretended to be unhappy about it because it was a Liverpool FC ball and he played for Arsenal. I really had no idea who he was or what the significance of the two teams was either, but to me, it made that ball irreplaceable. One day the ball got kicked under a truck. It rolled straight between the rear wheels and got wedged there. I ran after it, and when the driver saw me, he stopped. I stuck my little arm between the wheels, rolled my hand into a fist and banged as hard as I could underneath the ball to free it. Eventually, the ball began to move, and I got it back. It was a bit flat, though. The impact had squeezed about half the air out of it, but I got it back.

Gumpo was a goner. We were not getting him back. As soon as the truck driver felt the bang, he stopped. He was covered from head to toe in coal dust, and still we saw his face go pale. He grabbed one of his older crew and shouted at him to go find someone with a phone to ring an ambulance. The kids began banging on the doors of all the surrounding houses. Gumpo's friends were despatched to get his ma. They ran as fast as they could through the ice and the snow but, the truth is, it didn't matter how fast they were. It didn't matter how fast the ambulance got there either. Gumpo was a goner.

Rumours of what was happening in the hospital went from chattering oul' one to chattering oul' one. From time to time we'd get curious and creep our heads around the crack of the door to hear what was happening. We were overhearing the facts and taking in none of the meaning. Mostly, we just sat in the living room, in front of a Superser that now had all three bars lighting. We definitely didn't understand why or how that came to be, but we never gave it a second thought. Two days later, the snow melted.

# The Hoping Machine

*Eoin McNamee*

**#1 The patience of the working class, Summerhill Social Welfare Office, Dublin, 1986**

We're signing on and entitled to rent supplement and waiting in the queue to go into an office where an official will hand me a cheque to give to the landlord. The man sitting beside me is carrying a rusted steel fence post. It has been taken from the ground with most of its concrete base intact. Every so often he lifts it and lets the concrete footing strike the floor. He says he's had enough. We've always dealt with the same official and we all know the reason for the delay. He writes out the cheque from a binder and signs it. Then he starts to ornament his signature. He doesn't say anything. Minutes go by. He adds tails to the letters, serifs. The signature starts to become ornate, esoteric. You feel that he is taking something essential off you and adding it to his signature. This can go on for an hour. The fact that there is a kind of aesthetics involved makes it more difficult. Outside the man with the fence pole lifts it and sets it back down on the ground again.

## #2 Photographs of the working class, Newry, 1976
Troubles-era monochrome prints. The drizzled-on streets, bullet casings on the ground. War debris, the metal frames of burned-out buses, uncovered bodies in the streets. The children are urchinish, smudged. The photographers come from France and Germany and England. The frame of the photograph places you inescapably in a set of assumptions. You are somehow to blame. You are somehow complicit in your own destruction. This is someone else's vision of who you are, ready to be fed into what they want to say about you. We look furtive, semi-defiant, enlisted against our will to someone else's cause. Everyone's a witness against themselves. Susan Sontag said that 'photographs cannot create a moral position, but they can reinforce one', but it feels as if these ones create and reinforce.

## #3 Home-movie footage of the working class, 1976
We're watching Super-8 footage on YouTube of people from the Northern towns of Warrenpoint and Newry who have crossed the border on their holidays. They're in Panavision colour, the film taken by ourselves for ourselves. The children are wearing shorts and striped t-shirts. Their young mothers are in sundresses and bikinis and are vivacious. The men have sharp haircuts and Ray-Ban sunglasses. The sun dazzles. The men and women are frankly beautiful and of their time and of ours, the film stock muted by time to the colours of sun-faded beach clothing come across unexpectedly in the back of old presses. There is sadness

in looking at those who were young and now are old but it is a melancholy they can lay claim to for themselves. They are beautiful and complicit in their own beauty. This seems more like the way we held ourselves; we had our own hands on the camera, our own eyes framing us, and we were somebody else.

## #4 Experience of the working class in other countries, 15 October 1895, Butte, Montana

The Pinkertons are out on the Anaconda Road. There's ten inches of snow on Rogers Pass. Men's breath hangs in the air. Six masked men knock on the door of Nora Byrne's Steel Block boarding house and ask for room 32 where union organiser Frank Little is staying. They drag him behind a truck out to the Milwaukee Road where he is hanged from a frosted railway trestle, his body broken. As they take him down a murder ballad's being written in East Copper Street, in the area known as Dublin Gulch where Irishmen from Warrenpoint and Newry sleep after a shift working in the deep shafts. At the Butte Daily Post a headline's being written. *Masked Men Take Agitator Out of House to Death.*

## #5 Definition of the working class by Karl Marx

'The distinguishing characteristic of this class is their inability to obtain unhindered access to the means of production for purposes of satisfying their material needs.'

## #6 Secret language of the working class, Monaghan Street, Newry, 1941

A tram carries working women from Bessbrook Linen Mill into Newry. The design of the mill is based on Jeremy Bentham's panopticon, a unified design of prisons, factories and schools, where the watched become their own watcher. Oppression and enlightenment in the same model. My grandfather stands at the junction of Railway Street and Monaghan Street. He is selling silk stockings to the mill girls. What service to longing. What service to secret desire. The girls used sign language to communicate in the mill because of the noise. They spell out the word for *work*. They spell out the word for *love*. He goes home by the ship canal designed to access goods from the industrial interior. The canal is laid through farmland so that it looks as if the seagoing coasters are sailing through the fields and are suspended in a reality of their own where the bare ground is navigable.

#### #7 Housing of the working class

Dublin, January 2019. It's bitterly cold. Wind driving the weather up the Liffey. Cruel winter. We're on the number 13 bus. A woman with an end-of-her-tether look to her smacks a needy little girl on the hand. She has two other children with her and a young man who walks up and down the bus on some patrol of his own, as if he knows they're behind the lines and might never get home. She sees us looking and feels she has to explain. She says they're homeless and have been given accommodation for the night but they have to wait until 10 p.m. to access it. She points to the little girl, who has spots of red high on her cheeks and a cough. She's just out of hospital, she says. They get off the bus in the sleety rain and dark at Thomas Street. The little girl blows kisses to us.

#### #8 The flight of the working class, Gdańsk/Warrenpoint, 1976

You met him in Poland and you fell in love. You were pregnant.

You obtained the necessary papers to bring him back to Ireland with you. The shipyards in Gdańsk were aflame. You were blown like feathers under the giant cranes of the shipyard and of history. You paid the captain of a coal ship for passage to Waterford. You were ill on the sea crossing, the grey waves, the bile, you couldn't leave your cabin, *your baby*. When you docked you were in Warrenpoint, which was not the designated destination of the ship. You were on the wrong side of the Irish border and in the wrong jurisdiction. It was a scab ship, a blackleg ship, a blockade-runner hired to help break the British miners' strike by landing coal secretly, and it landed you, pale, sick, wrung-out. You waited for them to come on board and send you back to Poland.

### #9 Sentences written by the working class, Dublin, 1987

I'm working in Coláiste Dhúlaigh, which is a large secondary school in the suburb of Coolock. There are ten boys in your class. They are classified as ESN, which means 'educationally subnormal', and deemed illiterate. There is in fact nothing wrong with them, except that they are poor and have been neglected by the system. We got them to write short sentences. I'd take the sentences home and type them out. The act of typing made their words start to look like other words. Newspaper words. Book words. Lyric words. One boy from Darndale started to write poems. There was something there, a wild twist, some fugitive knowingness in his work. The day I finished he was to bring them in so I could show them to a publisher but he lost them on the way to school. He looked miserable for a minute then dismissed it. There were worse things that could happen to you.

#10 Vengeance of the working class

The 1907 Newry and Warrenpoint lockout led by James Fearon and James Larkin was a forerunner of the 1914 Dublin lockout and part of a greater labour movement in the dock cities of the Mersey and the Clyde. The strikers were defeated and humiliated by the Newry-based shipping company J. M. Fisher. The company insisted that the strikers surrender their union badges and then nailed the badges to the desk in the company's reception area where the men could see them as they queued for daily stevedoring work. In 1972 Fisher's vast yard in Newry was bombed and burned to the ground and the rusting badges and the humiliation they represented were consumed by the incendiary night.

#11 Defence of the working class, Newry, 1943

My grandfather spent the 1930s as a Pavee in the Welsh mining villages, selling household items from a suitcase on the back of a bicycle; the same villages whose mines were closed and destroyed by the strike-breaking coal ships from Poland. Thousands of people, including my wife's family, left from Warrenpoint to work in the copper mines of Butte. The men of the Belfast shipyards and engineering works who stood side by side during the 1907 lockouts became the sectarian mobs who expelled Catholics from the shipyards during the pogroms of the 1920s, and the defending of the working class falls to the man with the fence post who will take on the official with the dreaming pen.

#### #12 Resting places of the working class

At his own request Jeremy Bentham's body is preserved in University College London. His body is stuffed with lavender, straw, wool and cotton.

My grandfather is buried on the mountain above the valley where ships sail through the dreaming land.

Frank Little is buried in the paupers' section of Mountain View Cemetery, Butte. On his gravestone is written: *Slain by capitalist interests for organizing and inspiring his fellow men.*

# The Trellis

*Kate Burns*

She had been dead for twenty years, he for fourteen. Strange how in recent times I had found myself looking back, searching for them.

Rubbing the goosebumps flat on my arms as the sun dipped behind the coal shed, I remembered another yard, another shed, a skinny little girl shivering in her big sister's cardi. Hiding from her mother in the darkness and wishing that her father was home from his shifts on the buses. The memories began to rise like old colour slides flickering on a viewer across the surface of my mind.

Glencairn, Mountpottinger, Ballysillan, Ligoniel, alien but familiar names conjured up as I visualised my younger self in that coal shed and remembered too the long summer afternoons spent on his bus. How he would take me with him to the depot and lead me up to the front seat on the top deck. My legs hardly reaching the floor as my pants gradually stuck to the hard seat that boiled in the sun below the big window. I was always fascinated at this other world outside that window, beyond Andersonstown and the Falls

Road. Up as high as the treetops, under the sparking electric poles of the old trolley bus, the slow steady pace gave me time to absorb all of life outside and below. He was downstairs, dispensing tickets, rattling the coins in the worn leather satchel. I was safe. I always felt safe with him.

It might have been the everlasting sweet pea, leaning forward off the trellis, tangled and heavy, laden with its pinks and blues, that brought me back to my childhood days in Andersonstown all those years ago. Or maybe it was her voice, the totally unanglicised southern Irish brogue, pure and undiluted, despite almost seventy years of living in England. I suspect, though, it was the distinct colour of her eyes, a colour you felt you could dive right into and come up feeling cool and refreshed. Perhaps though, it was all those things. She is my mother's sister, after all, and there was I, sitting beside her in her garden, filled with a quest for retrospective understanding, meeting my mother's sister for only the third time in my life.

My aunt broke from our conversation intermittently. At times she would pick up the watering can, spraying a pot plant here and there, as she stretched her arthritic bones and plucked at a deadhead on some shrub. In her mind she was back on the farm in Leitrim, recalling her early life before the fare would arrive from an older sibling already in work across the water, and it would be her turn to leave. In time, the seven surviving siblings would settle in England or Canada or the USA, but my mother went no further than Belfast. She would never talk about her early life, in fact she wore secrecy like a suit of armour, and we, her children, knew not to ask, not to pry. In contrast, my aunt, who bore a striking resemblance to my mother, unleashed her stories of the past with unhindered ease, her words flicking off the pages of the history book that was her memory, wanting eagerly to be read.

My childhood story was one of little surplus, but it was luxury compared to the story of my mother's own early life, unfolding now through the voice of her younger sister. The baby of the family, she was born as her mother died in that little farm cottage. No doctor in attendance, the eighth daughter and ninth child of my grandparents. How my grandfather managed, being left to bring up all those children and run a farm, is unfathomable to me. I suspect, though, that the inner resilience, strength and survival instinct of a working-class family had much to do with it. Certainly, I and my sisters were raised with a cast-iron belief that families are always there for each other. It was an impenetrable fact, an intergenerational bond of solid rock.

As we sat together, each of us immersed in our childhood memories, what came back clearly to me was an enduring sense of my mother's anxiety, my father's quiet strength, and the love of two devoted parents who struggled to give us everything they never had. I could see my father's shirt, wet and pasted to his back with his own sweat after a long evening shift in the bar, where he worked extra hours to supplement the family income. I could hear the tapping of my mother's anxious footsteps while she paced the floor, waiting for him to come home, as the hours moved on past midnight and his dawn shift on the bus approached.

Those were the days before the Troubles descended upon us, before his bus would be hijacked, his colleagues killed, and he would endure beatings and threats, working on regardless, as the city routinely erupted all around.

That afternoon, as the sun sank and I grew colder, I shivered with a sense that perhaps I was an intruder, with no business looking into a past that my mother had kept securely hidden. Her tight-lipped secrets maybe masked a pain she did not want revisited. Here was an unfamiliar version of my mother as a young woman who enjoyed a cigarette, who was known by a family nickname I had never heard of, who fabricated her age to make herself older so she could leave the farm early and gain employment. Armed with a letter of introduction from the local priest, she travelled north on her own with only limited education and little knowledge of life beyond the farm. We celebrated that false birthday until her death, when the real date was revealed on an official document. Somehow, around 1939, she had got herself 'digs' with a lady on the Cliftonville Road, a job in a city-centre café, and lived in North Belfast throughout the war years, until she married my father in 1948 and moved to Ardoyne.

How different her childhood must have been from mine, and how privileged she must have felt we, her children, were. How hard it must have been for her to adapt to city life without the support of her father and sisters. The glimpse my aunt gave me into this other world showed it to be a harsh one, clothed in hunger and the daily grind of chores. Washing clothes in a river; fetching water from a well; bringing cattle to market; smashing stones into gravel for extra income; and walking miles to chapel or school along country lanes in the unforgiving Irish winters, to be met by authoritarian priests and teachers. Listening to the story of my mother's childhood, I recognised the source of her sheer determination to push us through education, her scepticism of the Church, and her fearless challenges to our teachers.

Finally, I understood the periodic outbursts of anger that overtook her and sent us children fleeing in all directions, fearful of the cane that hung ominously from the bleeding Sacred Heart who saw nothing, his eyes forever turned skyward.

Her frustration and outbursts alternated with her abundant loving care, and her anger, once spent, was quickly forgotten. The pressure of paying bills and feeding us all flowed steadily and constantly throughout those years, but we never truly absorbed her concerns. We could not have understood her angst and her fears.

Despite all this, we never felt disadvantaged. We were turned out shining for Sunday Mass, our scalps sore from sleeping on the tightly tugged rags that twisted our hair into springy coils. Home-knit cardigans and jumpers were our reward for patiently holding up yarns of wool while she rolled them into balls ready for knitting. My mother would work magic with only a few ingredients, keeping us fed with her broths and stews, her apple tarts and breads filling the kitchen with smells that will always be evocative of home. Sometimes boiled eggs and potatoes had to suffice, or 'spud and milk', as we children called it. A big pot of rice with a dollop of jam kept us going on cold winter days. There were no chickens in the yard, but whenever a chicken was bought, she had no reticence gutting and cleaning it, covering the Formica table with layers of newspaper and chasing us with its severed head.

The house was cold, but the living room always glowed with the heat from a coal fire constantly lit, warming the water as it roared up the chimney and heated a back boiler. On winter mornings we would waken to the magical fern patterns on the inside of the single-glazed windows, and huddle together under the candlewick bedspreads for warmth. She was always the first up. The school uniforms already draped on the clothes horse around the fire, the oatmeal bubbling in the pot. We would dash downstairs and dress at that fire before the biting cold penetrated our thin bodies. I had thought it was a sparse upbringing until my aunt revealed to me a new understanding of that concept.

My father, by contrast, was a constant calm underpinning the passion of my mother. He was the love of her life, my aunt said, and she spoke of him gently, as if the character he possessed deserved reverence in the memory. He took out a mortgage on the house that they loved, never missing a day at work until he underwent cancer surgery in his fifties. On Thursdays his pay packet was given over to my mother, while we children waited eagerly for the Cremeline caramels he brought home with his wages.

I loved to sit on the bar of his bike and feel the wind in my hair as we headed off to visit my paternal grandfather in the lower Falls. He would take us on adventures during the school holidays and on weekends. The number 11 Whiterock bus to the Hatchet Field on the Black Mountain was always a favourite. There in the springtime we would gather armfuls of bluebells, the cut stems sticky and dripping, wilting and limp by the time we got home and presented them to our mother.

Often he would walk us through Musgrave Park to the railway bridge to wave at the trains, and feel the power of them roaring beneath us as they sped towards Lisburn or the city centre. Some of our adventures were kept hidden from our mother, like the times when he took us to the bar where he worked, perhaps to collect a wage or just enjoy a pint. We children, hidden in a snug, relished the reward of a split bag of crisps and a glass of orangeade, or sharing a bag of chips from a nearby café. We knew instinctively that her disapproval of this would land us all in trouble, and not a word was ever said about it on our return home.

It was surreal watching and listening to my aunt as she chatted on while lovingly tending her garden. In our shared company, my aunt's memories and mine entwined, merged, and breathed life into my parents once more. Slowly I began to appreciate how the sisters had both needed to transport something of the farm and their childhood into their adopted urban life. The hedgerows they had grown from slips, like the country lanes, provided a boundary between them and the outside world.

Behind these hedgerows they grew vegetables and flowers, potatoes, rhubarb, roses, lilies, an abundance of everlasting sweet pea, and much more. Behind it grew their children, flourishing in the legacy of love, resilience and survivorship, handed down through the hard-working generations who went before.

That evening as I left my aunt, I felt humbled and grateful for her revelations, and for the family and the childhood days that shaped me so much more than I had ever realised.

# Excerpt from *Lost, Found, Remembered*

### *Lyra McKee*

*The following piece is all excerpted from the book Lyra was working on at the time of her death:* The Lost Boys.

Many people have grown to dislike the use of the word 'war' to describe what happened here. The term 'the conflict' became a more acceptable alternative, even if it made a thirty-year battle sound like a lovers' tiff. It's got the ring of a euphemism, the kind one might use to refer to a shameful family secret during a reunion lunch. Part of the argument was that the victims felt calling it 'war' gave legitimacy to terrorist groups and their volunteers, allowed them to view themselves as soldiers – either in the cause of saving Ireland from British rule, or of saving it from those who wanted to save it from British rule.

But we were to be the generation to avoid all that. We were to reap the spoils and prosperity that supposedly came with peace.

In the end, we did get the peace – or something close to it – and those who'd caused carnage in the decades before got the money. Whether they'd abandoned arms (as the Provisionals did) or retained them (like the Loyalists), they'd managed to make a ton of paper. We got to live with the outcome of their choices. But before I tell you about how my generation got fucked over, I should probably talk a little about how the war started in the first place. You probably know this story, or parts of it, but let me tell it to you in my own words, because the answer to the question depends on who you ask and how far back you want to go; and so my own take matters.

Northern Ireland was created in 1921 after the southern twenty-six counties broke away from British rule, following the Easter Rising – a rebellion – five years before. The North of the country had a solid Protestant population who considered themselves British subjects and wanted to retain the link with the UK. So the rebels got their twenty-six counties, which would eventually become known as the Republic of Ireland, and the UK got to keep the remaining six. This would have been a perfectly satisfactory solution were it not for the sizable minority of Catholics left stranded there on the wrong side of the new border.

The Catholic civilians didn't protest much. They'd been all but abandoned by the rebel leaders in the south, so they might have settled down and integrated well with the majority. They were native-born, after all, and British rule was the only rule they'd ever known. But in their newly created country they were abandoned by London and left to face bouts of violence and discrimination. Protestants received preferential treatment in the form of housing and jobs, a status quo actively encouraged by the Unionist politicians of the time. The likes of the Harland & Wolff shipyard, which sat at the edge of East Belfast and built the *Titanic*, employed Protestants almost exclusively.

My friends and I would argue about this all the time.

'I don't remember my grandparents having any money. They lived in poverty with an outside toilet.' We were in a grimy Wetherspoon's near the edge of the student district in South Belfast, sandwiched between the city centre and the road that led to the William of Orange mural. Most of its clientele were working-class Prods. With the bus station and Queen's University nearby, it drew in its fair share of tourists and students, too. Three decades before, whatever establishment it had been then, it wouldn't have been safe for me to be there, drinking among a bunch of tattooed Loyalists, especially with such an obviously Gaelic name: 'Leer-rah'. The pronunciation would give me away instantly. In fact, it still wouldn't have been safe for me to go into a pub in a Loyalist stronghold. This place, though, was a geographical no man's land that anyone could lay claim to, and the Prods, tourists, students and I drank together amiably enough, lured in by the promise of cheap food and booze. I'd been visiting Spoon's on and off for ten years, first as a student and then into adulthood and the world of work; while I was definitely better off than I had been, journalism did not a luxurious lifestyle fund. Besides, it was a neutral venue for meeting Will. Like mine, his name gave him away – William was usually a name reserved for Prods. We could have met near my place; the area I lived in was becoming slowly gentrified, with a mix of Protestants and Catholics moving in, but the local pubs still retained their more hardened clientele – people who'd supported the IRA and would have bristled had they thought there was a Loyalist in their midst. The ex-prisoners themselves, those who'd actually been in the organisation or one of its splinter groups, were much more relaxed; they'd probably have bought him a pint. That could have been said of ex-prisoners in general; it was always the armchair commandos who were the rowdiest. Will was from the east of the city, but I felt too nervous to venture into one of the working-men's pubs there. So Spoon's it was, barely a two-minute walk from the city centre and a halfway point between us. 'How were your grandparents any worse off than mine?' We'd had this argument before – always in Spoon's.

'Because yours were given jobs,' I said. 'And housing. Look at what happened in Caledon.'

Caledon was a tiny village in County Tyrone, near the border with the Republic of Ireland. There, in 1967, a family called the Gildernews had decided to squat in a house in protest at discrimination against Catholics. The house had been granted by the local council to a single nineteen-year-old Protestant woman, who happened to be the secretary for a Unionist politician. The Gildernews' protest led to the organisation of civil rights marches throughout the province. It became a movement, drawing inspiration from the campaign across the water in the US. It was one of many signs of discontent before the Troubles began.

I reminded him about 'one man, one vote', too. Under Unionist rule in the 1950s and 1960s, only ratepayers and their spouses could vote in elections – owning or renting multiple properties entitled you to multiple votes. Since Unionists fared better in terms of jobs and housing, these rules favoured them.

'That was bad for my grandparents as well as yours!' he replied. 'They didn't own more than one house.'

I hadn't considered that. Catholics in 1960s Northern Ireland had had legions of grievances. They'd since been remedied but, still, that sense of resentment had been passed down through the generations. We – their descendants – were no longer out protesting. Instead we sat in pubs with our Protestant friends and bitched at each other about the things their 'side' had done to ours, and vice versa. It was nasty but kind of irresistible, like picking at a scab.

We should have been worrying about the future, not the past. The prospect of a harder border between the North and the South, as a result of Brexit, was looming like the shadow of a TV villain. The peace we'd enjoyed for twenty years was fragile at best. Even after the signing of the Good Friday Agreement in 1998, it had taken some time for the interface areas – where Protestants and Catholics lived on either side of a dividing road – to feel less like a war zone. The old tensions would return every July, when the Orange Order marched down the Crumlin Road, much to the chagrin of residents in Republican Ardoyne. Peace was an acquaintance rather than a friend. But we were alive and more likely to die by our own hands than somebody else's. I didn't know which was worse, but nor did I want to go back to those days and find out.

Even this, though – sitting in a pub, arguing with a friend from the other side of the peace wall – was an incredibly middle-class thing to do. Neither of us were born middle class; we grew into it. We'd both grown up in what were euphemistically called 'deprived' areas. Deprived or disadvantaged were just polite ways of saying 'shithole'. If you lived in one of those areas and never managed to escape, it was unlikely you had friends from the other side to test your beliefs against. In recent years, youths from Ardoyne, a large Catholic area, and the nearby Protestant enclave of the Shankill had met on cross-community trips and befriended each other. They would travel back and forth on visits. It was welcome progress, but the two communities were still fundamentally segregated – living in separate areas, going to separate schools. At a grassroots level, community workers weaved miracles and brought them together. At a political level, though, there was a lack of will to do that. For the bigger parties, playing on tribal fears was still the go-to strategy for getting voters to turn up at the polling station.

So how did the conflict begin? The point is this: if you asked someone from Will's community how the war started, they would blame the IRA. The IRA had wanted a United Ireland, they'd argue, and they were determined to get it at any cost. They would bomb, kill and maim if they had to – and they'd done so, with gusto. The Unionist community only had the police and the army to protect them. And, some would add, terror groups like the UVF and UDA.

If, on the other hand, you asked someone from the community I was born into, you'd get a similar answer but with the roles reversed. In that version, the IRA were the protectors of the Catholic population, guarding them from all manner of evils: a mostly Protestant police force with corrupt officers; British soldiers who shot civilians on sight and rounded up young men, interning them without trial; Loyalist gunmen who roamed Catholic areas, often at night, and picked victims at random.

Which side was telling the truth? The most honest answer was that paramilitaries had killed both innocent Catholics and innocent Protestants.

The weirdest thing, though, was this: if you spoke to an IRA-supporting Republican – someone who wanted a United Ireland – they would list every injustice visited on Catholics by the army, the police, the Loyalists and the British state. They would never mention that more Catholics had been killed by the IRA than by all those other factions put together.

UVF/UDA-supporting Unionists (known as Loyalists) would give a similar – but, again, inverted – answer. They would list every Republican atrocity, murder and injustice, but the names of innocent Catholics who'd been slaughtered – and, in some cases, those of Protestants – would never pass their lips.

As for me, I would say that the Troubles began partly because the IRA spotted an opportunity. In the 1940s and 1950s their armed campaigns had failed, mostly due to a lack of support from the Catholic population. By 1969, though, tensions were spilling over, with Catholics being burned out of their homes by Loyalist mobs. They heard rumours of the same mobs being assisted by the police, who were mostly Protestants themselves. The community was developing a kind of Stockholm relationship with the Provos – too afraid to stand up to them but depending on them for protection too. And by 1972 the Parachute Regiment of the British Army had killed over two dozen innocent civilians in Belfast and Derry, in the Ballymurphy Massacre and Bloody Sunday. This had only reinforced the Catholics' fears and made them more dependent on the IRA. Decades later Sinn Féin would claim the Provisionals' campaign had been about securing equal rights. But that was a lie. In '69, I reckoned, some of their leaders probably fancied themselves to be like the 1916 rebels and believed they could score a coup, forcing the Brits to the negotiating table. Similarly, the leaders of the terror groups emerging from the Protestant community thought of themselves as the defenders of the province. No one

– not the Brits, not the Loyalists and not the IRA – expected the Troubles to last thirty years.

The motivations of the foot soldiers who joined the groups, though, were often simpler than any of this suggests. I'd go to interview fifty-something ex-prisoners, covered in tattoos but ultimately softened by decades of three meals a day and lights out at 8 p.m., and leave with a different image: of the frightened sixteen-year-old they'd once been. When you were a working-class kid with no money and no prospects and feared people more violent than you, nothing made you feel as powerful as a weapon in your fist.

That seemed to be how the IRA and the UDA and all the other groups sucked recruits in: fear. As the war dragged on, it became about other things. Money. Sex. Greed. Power. Being senior in one of these groups came with status. Women threw themselves at you. There was the risk of prison, but if you avoided that, there was more money than you could imagine – particularly if you operated near the top of the organisation. An ex-Special Branch officer once told me how, in 1985, he'd observed a UDA brigadier and Provo leaders in a bar in Belfast city centre – the Capstan in Ann Street. They were negotiating the carve-up of building sites. Back then, everyone from builders to shopkeepers had to pay 'protection money' to whatever group was running the area. If they didn't pay it, they couldn't work there. It still happens now, even in peacetime. The lower Newtownards Road, a Protestant area, was pocked with shuttered windows, the remnants of small businesses that couldn't afford the regular payout to the Loyalists.

So it wasn't just ideology: it never is. War was a business, and nothing proved it like collaborating with the enemy to make money.

Of course, the back-room deals of the officer class wouldn't have been known to the average volunteer. Later, some of those who'd been ground-level troops in the IRA would speak out, feeling like the years they'd spent in prison had all been for nothing. They viewed the peace deal as a betrayal. What had been the purpose of it all, if the end point was going to be an armistice? Some met with their counterparts in the UVF and compared notes, trying to figure out who or what or how they'd been fucked over. Had it been the plan all along – to sell out? With hindsight, some of them believed it had.

# The Night of the Wake

### *Michael Nolan*

I was pacing the length of my room reading an excerpt from a short story I planned to read at a book festival in Castlebar the following day. I hadn't packed. I hadn't washed the clothes I planned to pack, and every attempt I made to organise my thoughts around what I would say during the Q & A ended with me throwing my hands up in the air and whining horribly through my teeth: *Fuck this. I can't. I just fucking can't.*

I hadn't published a lot of work, after all, and the few things I had published were, in my mind, painfully mediocre compared to the bodies of work the writers I would be sharing the panel with had produced: one was an established author with ten books under his belt, the other an emerging writer with a lot of hype behind her, and deservedly so. Insecurities aside, the idea of speaking in front of a paying crowd about anything to do with writing had me clawing the walls for a way out. Then I got the phone call.

Gerard's ma had died. The funeral was in two days.

It was like my abdomen had been punctured with a needle and the air was slowly leaving my body. In my hand, the excerpt from the short story I had printed off the day before. I folded it up and dropped it on my bed before picking it up and bringing it with me into the living room. There was more brightness in there, more air. More sunshine to drink in those afternoons I would sit at the desk I had placed in front of the bay window and work.

I thought about Gerard. The few images I had of him were more distinct because they were painful, and it was through this prism of pain that I remembered him when we were kids. He was obsessed with Lil' Bow Wow, and later, Eminem. He had a VHS tape of the *Up in Smoke* tour. We fast-forwarded to the bits where women showed their tits and hit pause, play, and pause again.

'Fuck me, look at them,' we said.

His home life was an anomaly in that most of the people I knew who came from single-parent families had single mothers, single aunties, single big sisters, because there was nobody else around, the common denominator being that somewhere along the way the men in our lives had gone. For Gerard, it was his mother. Rumours she had taken off with another man trickled down to us through overheard conversations late at night, when our mas gathered around kitchen tables drinking bottles of vodka they had bought using the money they were supposed to pay the window cleaner with the week before.

'Poor child,' they'd say. 'How's he going to cope?'

I looked out the window. Sunshine streamed along the tree-lined street. The trees themselves had been losing their leaves for the past few weeks now, and the birds, twittering as they did around the next-door neighbours' front garden, were hiding away to moult.

I had never felt so far away from where I was from.

During my early twenties, when I first graduated and couldn't get a job, I would often find myself back in the company of the people I grew up with. We would sit around a table with the big light on and gurn at each other until we ran out of things to say, then I would stagger through the afternoon blearily home. Between those two- and three-day sessions, I would attend poetry events in town. Book launches too. I would hang around the smoking areas of bars with people who spoke about literature like they did about everything else, like they were connoisseurs. It was while being around these people that I became conscious of my own working-classness, in a way that had less to do with the disparity of material wealth than the more refined cultural tastes they seemed to carry around with them almost second-naturedly. I didn't know much about the music they were into, or art, and the cultural references that were alluded to all the time and with more irony than I was capable of keeping up with went completely over my head. This forced me, consciously or unconsciously, it's hard to tell, into making certain cultural adjustments: I learned how to alter my behaviour, my mode of speaking, my frame of reference, even, depending on where I was situated, and in whose company at any given time.

This was during a period of my life when I was profoundly embittered by how little my circumstances had changed even with the level of education I had acquired. Nobody in my family had made it through secondary school, and there was a certain amount of expectation on me, as the only one who had, to do well for myself, in the most material sense of the term. I had no illusions – accruing actual material wealth was as unlikely an outcome in the trade I had chosen as it was for my older brothers in painting and decorating. My conception of making something of myself therefore became equated with some amorphous and deeply misguided idea of accumulating the embodied forms of capital I would need to succeed in a world that was defined by those who regarded themselves as possessors of legitimate culture: the middle class.

The only way I could think to do this was to distance myself from the place where I was from, the people I had grown up with, and set my sights firmly on the only consistent ambition I'd had since that first time my ma's best mate, Mary, showed me how to type my name on a typewriter. Slowly, painfully, and with more than one wobble along the way – within a year of graduating, I was sentenced to 200 hours of community service for hitting someone a dig in the mouth outside a house party on Tates Avenue, knocking him unconscious – I worked and saved enough money to move to the other side of the city, which was twenty minutes down the road from where I was from, but may as well have been another world.

There I found a place to live, in an area where my university friends lived, where the streets were wide and lined with trees. I settled into a life I had fantasised about for as long as I had known that if I didn't stop taking gear, and partying, and running about with the kind of headcases who seriously considered joining Óglaigh na hÉireann* – just so they could rob the drug dealers they owed their wages to – I didn't know where I would end up.

---

\*    Óglaigh na hÉireann was the title taken by a dissident Irish republican paramilitary group. The organisation started carrying out attacks around 2009 and was formed after a split within the Real IRA.

\*

The coffin had been placed in front of the living-room window. The blinds were closed, and on the floor around the coffin, dozens of Mass cards had been arranged neatly, from largest to smallest, with several framed photographs of Gerard's ma smiling happily among them. In the corner of the room, on the armchair at the foot of the open casket, Gerard's da stared into the space above the wooden box. He was wearing a red jumper with blue jeans and a pair of black shoes that had creased around the toes, and his hair, which was long and grey down to his shoulders, was starting to thin. Nobody seemed to notice he was there. He looked very alone.

I had a card I picked up in the garage on the way. I had scribbled my condolences while the taxi driver waited for me to fork out the sixteen quid his meter showed – the stop at the shop had cost me an extra quid, which I was happy enough to have paid now that I could see that the people who had arrived in front of me had come with a card of their own. They handed theirs to Gerard's big sister, Ciara, who was standing in the doorway between the living room and the kitchen. She looked tired and agitated. I told her I was sorry for her loss and she ran her hands through her hair.

'Gerard's in the kitchen,' she said.

The kitchen was brightly lit. Three women who hadn't taken their coats off were squeezed around the table with a bowl of crisps they had cordoned off and were eating one after another without looking at where their hands were going. I waited as Gerard finished what he was doing with the empty cups he had lined up in front of the boiling kettle. He glanced at me and it was like he had made eye contact with someone he was passing on the street, and then, with the slowness of a pebble sinking to the bottom of a pond, it clicked.

'Well, Mick,' he said. 'What's happenin'?'

It had been eight years since we last saw each other, and although Gerard's face registered surprise, it wasn't the surprise of a person who had assumed we would never see each other again, and it hit me in the stomach. The debilitating sense of loss that came with comprehending for the first time the extent to which I had closed the book on our friendship while he, being the one who had not been able to go anywhere, whose existence remained fixed to the place that each of us, in our own way, had tried our best to get away from, had merely turned down the corner of the page. Pleased as I was to see him, and touched as he was by the gesture, the fact that I had chosen his mother's death over the innumerable traumas he had suffered long before his eighteen-month stint in Maghaberry, which culminated in him being put out of the country by the same men who left him breathing shallowly through a punctured lung one night, when he was trailed down an alleyway yards away from his da's flat, hung like a dead weight over every word we exchanged. It immediately quashed whatever hopes I had of us falling back into step with one another, even just for a few minutes – our lives had diverged too thoroughly, the distance between our realities was too remote. But we weren't completely foreign to each other: we saw in ourselves some semblance of who we were when we were kids, and that was enough.

'Do you want a cup of tea?' he said, and I said no, I was all right. One of the women sitting at the table said, 'Who's he?' and Gerard chuckled and said, 'It's Mick. Mick from down the street.'

His other big sister, Christine, stopped in the doorway leading into the living room and stared at me with an expression that was, as ever, one of utter disdain. Her natural stance was to always assume that whoever she was talking to, regardless of who they were, had some kind of problem with her, and everything she said seemed to be an attempt to get to the bottom of what that problem was. Being subjected to this degree of scrutiny from somebody with Christine's reputation could be a coldly intimidating experience, especially for someone who had known her for as long as I had, since I was a child. She used to sit with her best mate Donna on the green electric box across the street from my house, waiting for my big brothers to come home from work. They would call me over and tell me to tell my brothers they could get their holes any time they wanted, and they would cackle.

'All right, Mick?' she said.

I smiled – she flashed a tit at me once, when I was fourteen. She and Donna got their nipples pierced and thought it would be funny to see how I would react.

'Well, Christine,' I said. 'How's it going?'

Christine stared. The kitchen seemed to constrict.

'My ma's dead, Mick. How the fuck do you think it's going?'

I tried to apologise and take it back, but Gerard slung his arm around my neck and said, 'Shut the fuck up, Christine. He's just trying to be nice.'

When I first moved to the other side of the city, I lived alone. It was the summer, the sun was out, and when I wasn't hanging around my friends' front garden, admiring the plants and the flowers, the little cold frame they had built for their seedlings, I spent my afternoons sitting at my desk in front of the bay window, making the most of the time I had now that I didn't have to work – I had been accepted onto a fully funded PhD, the payments for which appeared in my bank account like a miracle at the end of every month.

I did what any twenty-eight-year-old in my position would've done with all that money coming out of nowhere, and spunked it on alcohol and takeaways. No routine, certainly no getting out of bed before midday, I regressed into a kind of pseudo-student lifestyle, with plenty of early-morning walks home from somebody else's house, only now I didn't feel as bad about what I was doing. The people I was drinking with talked about literature, after all, and politics, and they had heated discussions about all sorts of things, but mostly poetry. When the dust finally settled after locking horns over whether or not Kim Kardashian's Marriage was as innovative as people were making out, we would dance, and because there was only a few of us left at that stage of the game, you could hear our shoes scuffing across the lino floor.

Occasionally, that curious discomfort. The terrible yearning.

I could be walking along the shopfronts, glancing through the windows of the various food places lining the road at the top of the street – the taqueria, the gelato place, the French restaurant – and suddenly there would rise to the surface a powerful longing that was not unlike the sensation of walking along the promenade while on holiday in another country, and thinking, in a strange and abstract way, that where I am now is nowhere, a fantasy world where nothing exists but the brochure-like landscape, where real life is played out elsewhere, beyond the façade.

I had become intensely nostalgic, homesick even, to the point where I began to spend an unhealthy amount of time late at night moving through the places where I grew up on Google Street View: Twinbrook, Poleglass, Areema Drive. The whole of west Belfast became a stadium through which the imagery of my childhood and adolescence could be re-experienced from the safety of the desk I had placed in front of the bay window. And it was while sitting at that desk during those nights I couldn't sleep, when my dreams were imbued with the guilt of having disconnected myself so completely, that I began to realise that no matter how obsessively I searched, I was no longer the person whose image I was desperate to find inhabiting the space I had once moved so naturally through, and I never wanted to go back.

Not knowing how I was supposed to be in the eyes of the people around me, and the expectant dread I had become familiar with years before, when I first started going to poetry events in town, was something I never thought I would experience while surrounded by people who were from where I was from. It was like I had stepped out of myself and was looking in, and what I saw was a world that was irreconcilable with the person I had become. Whatever plans I had to go for a walk around the estate and see what it was like seemed suddenly ridiculous to me, concocted as they were before I had taken the time to consider how sentimentalising the place I no longer belonged to would only serve to perpetuate my estrangement from it. And the chances of someone seeing me walking forlornly around the estate, especially now that the wake was carrying on into the night as late as it was, were too high for me to risk it.

All that was left for me to do was to leave. I had shown my face, I had paid my respects, and although I didn't get to talk to Gerard as much as I would've liked, I knew that my urgency to reach out, to reassure myself that my existence within this world had not been forgotten, wasn't enough to justify my staying any longer than I already had. The difficulty came with actually leaving. I hadn't been able to present the version of myself that corresponded with how people at the wake that night saw me – it was impossible to when I didn't know what they expected me to be – and I didn't want their lasting impression of me to be the wrong one, so I hung around the periphery of the group, taking the odd can that was handed to me from the case that had been set in the middle of the back garden. And it was there, while I was listening to some fella talking loudly about money somebody else owed him, that Gerard's da asked me for a light.

I didn't smoke. I told him this and he looked at me as if from across a busy road.

'You don't remember me, do you?' I said.

Again, the pebble dropped. The moment of recognition.

I used to watch from my bedroom window as he walked across the street with a black bin bag filled with clothes my ma had given him for Gerard, usually around Christmas time, or at the start of the summer. She took pity on him, and she admired him for being one of the few men she knew who would do what he was doing, as a father, which was as much an indictment of the patriarchal slant of the world we came from as anything else. He was a quiet man, with an accent oscillating strangely between Scottish and English. It seemed to amplify his loneliness. He didn't really mix with anybody, and the only time you ever saw him was late at night, when he came out onto the street to find Gerard and take him home to his one-bedroom flat on Aspen Walk. The most recent news I'd heard about him was from my ma, about a year before, when she had, for some reason, decided to paint a portrait of Che Guevara for him. He was keen to talk about that now, and about my ma in general, who he described as one of the good ones, a real diamond, he said, and I agreed. She was.

From there, the conversation moved on to what I was doing with myself, the things my ma had told him I was writing a few months before, when she bumped into him outside Tesco, and how brilliant it was to see me doing as well as I was at university.

'Your ma sent me a story you wrote, but I couldn't open it...'

He wanted to talk to me about the aspects of my life I had instinctively supressed the moment I stepped into the wake that night. I knew that part of the reason he wanted to do this was out of a sense of pride he felt at seeing a kid he knew from about the estate overcoming the odds that were stacked against us from the very first day we entered primary school. And the odds *were* stacked, but for some more than others: I hadn't so much overcome these odds as benefited from a slightly different set of circumstances than many of the kids around me. My ma, although a single mother throughout most of my childhood, married a man who had a decent job as a satellite engineer, installing Sky and RTÉ aerials, and that provided enough income to allow us to live more comfortably than we would've done otherwise. And there was the move we made away from Poleglass, one of the poorest areas in Belfast, with one of the highest crime rates and highest rates of unemployment in the city, which came early enough in my life to give me a better chance.

Perhaps he was hoping for some kind of reprieve, some distraction from the circumstances of the wake. But I blanked him. I turned away, pretended to be engaged in conversation with somebody else. And the look on his face, the slight wobble in his voice as he tried to catch my attention, his bony fingers fumbling with the feg he struggled to roll.

'Your ma was saying you're back at university.'

'Still at it, aye. How's it going with you, anyway?'

'That's great, son. God, that's brilliant. What about the writing stuff?'

'Aye, it's going. It's going grand. It's just—'

I laughed. I said something like, 'It's good to see you again, Seamus,' and moved across the garden, where I stood for a moment in the shadow of the coal shed, the roof of which we used to climb up onto when we were kids, and ordered a taxi home.

# More or Less

*Paul Dunne*

Through the sitting-room doors, I can hear Mam tapping out the beats to the dances, as if she's on screen in a sparkling dress too. That familiar jingle starts up; it's the ad break in *Strictly Come Dancing*. She watches it every Saturday night, alone, because I can't stand reality TV. I don't understand why you would choose to watch an obviously fake reconstruction of 'reality'. Is working-class life so shit that you want to fall into a fake one? Although is there any difference between me repackaging our lives into turning pages, and the twisting bodies of a ballroom dance? Is one any more 'real' than the other?

Mam tip-tap-tips her way into the kitchen, reliving childhood memories and far-off flamenco fantasies she once had, and asks me:

– D'ye want tea?

– Eh... yeah g'wan.

I'm at the kitchen table, in the same spot where I studied so diligently in the build-up for the Leaving Cert. I haven't 'left' anything yet, though. I'm still at home, in the same bed, studying at the same kitchen table, six years and one and a half degrees later – as Mam often hints at.

We have a strange way of communicating: she doesn't listen, and I get carried away easily; she uses her 'posh voice' when she answers the phone, and I curse constantly in front of everyone, especially her; we tend to talk around each other. Somehow we get by, more or less.

She starts to fill the kettle from the tap but stops and turns to face me.

– So, what happens after all this then? Are ye qualified?

Here we go again. We pick up the same conversation we've had for six years now. I know my lines and she knows her steps. I hope we'll get somewhere this time, like I've hoped every time.

– Qualified for what?

– I dunno. You tell me.

She wants the maths of my life to add up squarely, but I'm dealing with words now.

– Tell ye what?

– Ye finish the master's – then what?

– I just keep writin'.

– There's no job after?

– No.

She fills the rest of the kettle, taking her time. I take some deep breaths, preparing. We both know what's coming. We've danced this dance too many times. I'm tired of our bloody *paso doble*, and I wish she was too.

She clicks the kettle on, its rumbling like raucous applause as we both enter the bullring-cum-dance floor from opposite sides.

I don't want to go there again, but we're circling each other. And that circle is getting smaller and smaller.

– What about teachin'?

– I wanna be a writer, not a teacher.

– What about a job in an office? Like – as an editor? Or an intern?

– I wanna be the one sendin' in the scripts, not readin' them.

She's quickened the pace of our circling. I can't tell if she's following my lead or I'm following hers.

She breaks the circle, stepping forward, calling me out.

*Appel!*

– Ye can't just work in a bar for the rest a' your life, Paul!

– No, I won't. But I'd kill meself if I ended up stuck behind a poxy desk in a fuckin' office! Seriously – I would!

– All right! Calm down…

The kettle clicks off. Our *promenade* has reached its end, but we're not finished. Far from it. We're both just warmed up now.

She throws the dregs of her last cup of tea down the drain. It's probably her fourth or fifth half-cup today. She only ever uses the one mug all day, and she never uses the fancy ones on the kitchen counter. I wonder if I only notice these things because I'm a writer and I'm always looking for the details, or because we're family and we know more about each other than we would ever want to.

She fishes my favourite mug out of the back of the bottom press, the one with the ridges and the chip in it that she always hides behind the rest of the Delft. She fetches tea bags from the faded Lyons tin. That tin is probably older than I am and is one of the only worn things she keeps around the house, though it's always kept inside the press, never on the counter.

She fills our mugs with boiling water, swirls the teabags around, and dumps them in the compost bin. She adds a drop of milk to hers, turning it from black to dark brown. I take a slightly heavier splash – a soft beige. She struts across the room, handing me my mug before crossing her legs, marking her formation.

We're facing each other now across the kitchen table, yet hand in hand too, in some metaphorical dance. Anticipating each other's next step.

She steps first.

Tentatively.

Honestly.

Attempting to bridge the gaps between us.

– Would it not be better to get inside first? Like – inside the industry – and with a bitta income too?

I move with and around her. I don't know who's the matador and who's the bull; it wouldn't be our dance if we both weren't trying to lead the other.

– That's just a distraction. I'll lose track of what I'm workin' on. I don't wanna end up as one a' those people.

She breaks formation, calling me out again, curious.

– What people?

She can't help herself.

And neither can I.

– People who 'have a book in them' but never get it outta them. People who put scripts in drawers as if they're gonna write themselves. People who don't even realise that they've given up.

She sips her tea and runs her hand through her hair, buying herself some time. I'm glad of the air but I dread her response.

Suddenly, she swirls around me, taking the lead. The dance isn't meant to work this way. She dares me to follow.

– Ye'll have two degrees. Ye can't just keep pullin' pints for minimum wage n' tips… Would ye not even consider teachin'?

– I've not been workin' for six years to end up as a fuckin' teacher or in a bleedin' office!

– And ye've not been studyin' for six years to be a barman either!

We swivel and swirl ferociously, *chassé* after *chassé*, on the verge of falling over each other. Our voices echo around the house, probably next door too. We both realise this, so we stop for a moment.

Foolishly, she still clings to that idea of me standing at the top of a classroom that I expressed long ago to appease her insistence that I have a backup plan. Foolishly, I fall into anger at that fake dream every time, even though I know she'll always bring it up, even though I know it's never going to happen.

She drains her mug, rooted to the spot, tapping her toe against the kitchen floor to a beat I cannot discern. I run my hand through my hair without even thinking about it. All I can think of is how I have to remember this specific moment, how moments like this are painful and necessary, how I'm always halfway on the page before the moment's even passed, and how I have to be a writer even when it's hard and especially when it hurts.

We pause and pose; this is our *highlight* now. She rests her weight entirely on me but keeps one foot firmly planted on the dance floor in accordance with the rules, in accordance with our rituals. We are equally uncomfortable, yet equally committed to the dance. I am my mother's son, after all.

The crowd, and I, draw breath. The standstill gives me a moment to think.

I think of the pain in my wrist. Is it my writing? Or her rheumatoid arthritis that I may yet inherit? Is that why she didn't pursue dancing seriously? Why wouldn't she let herself dream? Why won't she let me? Can we even afford to dream, living the lives we do?

I think of a dinner I had with a friend's investment-banker father recently, where he refused to let me pay my portion of the bill, even after much insistence. I think of how he described his slight embarrassment but swell of pride hearing his daughter read her intimate poetry in front of an audience. I think of how the only thing Mam has read of mine – a personal thank-you note in the preface of my undergraduate dissertation – made her cry. If I could, would I swap parents? If I did, who would I be then?

I think of the six hours I spent watching ballroom dancing videos on YouTube – and the unknown amount of time I spent sitting at my desk – so I could try and frame an intimate conversation like a Spanish dance using French terms, to dubious success. I think of the forty hours she spends working across three jobs each week – compared to my cushty part-time bar work, which contributes only a small fraction towards our house – to keep the mortgage ticking and food on our table.

Maybe we could have spent all that time getting to know each other better. Maybe I could sit in on the odd episode of *Strictly*. Maybe she could read one of my stories. Maybe we'd be closer; though that wouldn't be me, or her either. We are who we are: similar but different, more or less.

Slowly, I place her back onto her feet.

Softly, she takes the lead. She asks:

– OK. Explain it to me all again.

I take up her request and diligently run through my well-practised speech and steps about agents, publishers, advances, book deals, and everything else I hope to see in my future. A future I want her to see. A future I hope she will have a part in, whether she wants to or not, whether she realises it or not.

Our circling has slowed to a stop.

She stares at me with a look I haven't seen before.

– So, you'll be... self-employed?

After six years, we aren't dancing any more. This is something different, something new. I'm not a matador, nor she a flamenco dancer. I think we are starting to see each other as we are and who we could be. I'm hopeful, but suspicious too, because I know what we can be like.

Warily, I reply.

– More or less...

I think more or less is all I'll ever get with Mam. I think she's shown me how to work both hard and smart to get by, because there is no other way where we come from. I think that's what fuels my ambitions to be a better writer tomorrow than today. I think she's a good mother to me, even though her love often feels like iodine on open wounds. I think I could be a better son in spite of everything I'm trying to un-inherit. I know that we love each other. More or less.

# Are Ye Going Out Tonight?

## *Claire Allan*

All the world's dramas – all its losses, gains, grief and joy – are played out in the chairs of hairdressers where generations of women sit side by side and chat to people they've never met as if they've known them all their lives.

These aren't ridiculously expensive salons with upselling on luxury products. There are no stick-thin receptionists acting as gatekeepers for stylists, with unconventional hairstyles and edgy body piercings.

These are the hairdressers in the heart of working-class areas. Where pensioners can get their blue rinses done alongside the wee girls getting their curls in for their First Holy Communion. Where you can find a lady getting her hair cut and coloured for a family member's funeral, sitting beside a bride having a trial for her 'big day' look.

It's where roots are touched up, cups of tea are made, and no conversational topic is off limits. Where there is an unspoken understanding that what is said in the salon stays in the salon. Women can offload their worries, fears and most embarrassing moments without fear of judgement or reproach. Instead they find themselves cradled in understanding, amid the scent of ammonia and hairspray.

Where someone offers to take a run up to the shop and take a list of buns that customers and staff might want. A wee cream finger. Or a turnover. Or a 'Just get me a banana. I'm back at Slimming World'.

Where a collective groan of recognition sounds above the hairdryers and the sound of the water running into the basins.

'Did you know a banana is worse than a Mars Bar?' someone says, and a debate kicks off about how best to lose half a stone before the 'big do' in a fortnight. A back and forth of wit and banter follows.

'I've a frock bought from the internet. I'll have to wear the suck-me-in knickers and not eat for a week before it. Even then, I'm not sure I'll be able to sit down.'

'Wear flat shoes, then. So your feet don't get sore.'

'Flat shoes? Are you wise? I'll have my highest heels on if it kills me.'

A cackle of laughter follows. Everyone understands.

The merits of fad diets, slimming clubs and their various leaders are discussed at length. Someone mentions colonic irrigation and someone else asks, 'What in under God is colonic irrigation?'

'They stick a hose up your arse and wash all the badness out.'

'Jesus Christ,' the response follows. Someone blesses themselves at the very thought.

'No one is seeing my arse. Even if Tom Cruise walked in here right now, my arse would stay hidden.'

An old lady, who looks as if butter wouldn't melt in her mouth – with her beautifully white hair set in curlers – shocks everyone by declaring: 'I've had twelve wains. One more person seeing my arse won't make a difference. Half the doctors in Derry have seen it.'

There's talk of the now-forgotten practice of pre-birth enemas. Younger mammies, and the wee girl who is brushing the floor while periodically rubbing her expanding belly, pulls a face at the very thought.

A social history of home births and midwives with blunt razors dry-shaving pubic hair plays out amid the locks of hair falling to the floor. Of coming home to a three-bedroom house, where nine other children lived, three to a bed. Each of them bursting with excitement to see the new arrival. A tired new mammy. A hard-working daddy. Families who see raising another child as no burden. 'Just throw another spud in the pot for dinner. It will be grand.'

Children reared in hand-me-downs that have been handed down so many times no one remembers where they started off or who owned them first.

The trainee thanks God she's having her baby now, when she can rest in a birthing pool between contractions and not have to keep quiet because there are five wains asleep in the next room who will be a nightmare to deal with if they waken. She has saved up and got the best of everything for her new baby. She's even held a baby shower.

The buns and bananas arrive. While the woman on Slimming World eats a banana, she isn't able to stop sneaking surreptitious glances at the cream-filled pastries. She questions whether or not she actually does want to be thin after all, but she is buoyed by the encouragement of her fellow women.

The wee girl having her hair done for her First Holy Communion fidgets in her seat. She's wondering how many more kirby grips are going to be slid into her hair. It's a long day and she's tired already and her mammy is up to 'high doh', hoping they'll get back to the house in time to get changed into their fancy clothes and out to the chapel in time.

Someone else walks in. It's reminiscent of the scene in each episode of *Cheers* when Norm walks in. Everyone stops what they are doing to say hello. This woman is as much a part of the fixtures as the chairs and the basins. She arrives at this time every week for a wash and blow-dry. It's more than a trip to the hairdresser's for her. It's more than making her hair sit just the way she likes. It's her social life, her time out to chat and laugh and drink tea. Her daughter drops her down, and her husband picks her up after. She only ever misses one appointment a year, when she is on her annual holiday to Santa Ponsa. She has been going to this same hairdresser for fifteen years. Seen people come and go. Heard stories of illness. Of joy. Of fear. Of hope. Of friendship and family. Because no one is 'just a customer'.

Everyone's story plays into everyone else's sense of self. It's a place where we consoled each other during the worst of the Troubles. Where we celebrate together on high days and holidays. Where we while away wet Wednesday afternoons, the windows steaming around us, the smell of shampoo clinging to our nostrils.

It's where we can sit and listen to the gorgeous cadence of the Derry accent. Conversation trickling like water. All life and all experience coming through the door, being offered a seat and a cup of tea.

It soothes and it heals. Grounds us in the now. It reinforces a sense of belonging. It is so much more than just getting your hair done.

A microcosm of the best of us: the support, camaraderie and community that runs through our blood. Everyone is equal in the hairdresser's chair.

# Where Turkeys Fly and Horses Race

*Alison Martin*

In the run-up to Christmas the turkeys would literally walk out of the shop – and the bigger the woman (because it had to be a woman in 1990s Finglas; these were gender-rigid times), the bigger the turkey.

It was an ingenious plan, if a little unhygienic. It was not for the faint of heart or the weak of calf muscle. Like those turduckens that would later become popular (a chicken stuffed into a duck, stuffed into a turkey), this was a multi-bird affair. A woman with as much grit as a gizzard would stand over a frozen turkey fresh from the freezer and hoist it under her seasonal dress of choice, between her thighs and out past the security guard of Dunnes. That the shop had been doing a roaring trade in XXL undergarments at the same time of the 'Flight of the Frozen' was surely no coincidence.

If, as my mother used to say, sitting on a wall would give you a cold in your kidneys, I dread to think what incubating a frozen turkey would do. I didn't ask. The turkeys crowned around the corner from the store, for safe delivery to their new homes.

Around that same corner was the betting shop where I worked, on and off, from my teens until my mid-twenties. I worked in bookies across the Northside and the inner city, but the one in Cardiffsbridge was where I spent most of my Saturdays as a late teen; part time during the school year and full time during holidays. At the time, betting shops were not the sanitised, glossy affairs they have become, for the most part, these days.

Just like my hair back then, they were a bit wayward and full of colour. They were heaving, pulsing, smoky behemoths full of shouting and roaring – mostly at the horses and their jockeys on-screen, other times at the board marker who marked up the odds, and other times at us: the staff behind the counter.

Everyone smoked at the time, inside and outside the counter – all except for the asthmatic assistant manager, who tapped out of the relentless relay of John Player Blue batons being passed along the rest of the staff. The longer the race, the better it was for us smokers; a three-mile, five-furlong race meant you could have a full cigarette and even throw in a couple of sips of tea if you were lucky. And yes, it was always Lyons teabags: we were Dubs, after all.

Behind the counter we were shielded from any would-be robbers and the odd flying pencil by a bandit screen, which had enough space between the countertop and see-through screen to carry out our transactions: bets and money being the main thing. Sometimes a sound customer would surprise us with chocolate or drinks. Minerals only. No turkeys.

From the till you could see the length and breadth of the shop – there were no blind spots. This was to prevent robberies, as well as drug-dealing or other behaviour of a dubious nature that might raise eyebrows and/or hackles. On the right from where we stood was a single row of stools under a short counter with betting slips and pencils, and to their right was a line of newspaper racing pages pinned to baize that ran perpendicular to a bank of TV screens.

In front of the TV screens was a podium, where board marker Alan made an unlikely performer, using his sleight of hand to whip up and down sheets of odds. Outside of work, he was big into the dogs and would spend his free time and money caring for his own. A fairly unassuming guy, who shared the wiriness of the greyhounds he adored, he was nonetheless territorial about his area. Give a man a podium and watch him rise. And when he is settled at just the right height, see how his legs are whipped unceremoniously from under him. To say Alan was long-suffering wouldn't do justice to the amount of flak he put up with from his colleagues in search of a bit of banter/entertainment. One Monday morning the assistant manager gave him a Lotto ticket to check in the nearby newsagent's; she had bought the ticket after the Saturday-night draw and filled it with the winning numbers – partly testing if Alan would come back to the shop if he thought he had a winning Lotto ticket burning a hole in his pocket. He did. Another time, he was given one of the dud notes we had been duped into taking and asked to go around to the shop to get us messages. Alan returned with a red face and a mouthful of expletives for us instead.

As a rookie cashier, learning the names and cost of the different bets was tricky at first but made slightly easier by their names – an Alphabet was twenty-six bets (two patents, one Yankee and a six-fold accumulator). Given that my own gambling history consisted of the odd 'tipping point' machine on holiday and spinning the wheel at a sale of work, it took a while to get my head around the likes of the Heinz (fifty-seven bets, just like the brand's '57 varieties') and the Super Goliath; the biggest of them all, with eight selections and 247 bets.

Every newbie gets the short straw, and every Saturday morning at 10.30 a.m. I was greeted with the familiar rasp of a 'How are ye, love?' and around twenty dockets filled with skinny lines of 10p each-way bets, the top one dusted with fag ash from a cigarette as omnipresent as the glasses on the face of Mrs O. Her husky voice belied her diminutive stature; she was a five-foot racing compendium, with as much knowledge and as rough around the edges as the *Racing Post* that stood on a lectern in the corner of the shop.

Coming in from the outside, by a short head, was another regular; every afternoon a hand would appear at the counter like Thing from *The Addams Family*, followed by a turned head. This was a former neighbour who thought he could twist himself out of recognition. He was afraid I would recognise him, but obviously not afraid enough to stay away – or risk a back injury. He needn't have worried. Customer confidentiality was always respected: when wives came in asking if we had seen their husbands, for example. And if the husbands weren't in with us, there was a good chance they were in the Cardiff next door: a pub whose Saturday-morning trade would be the envy of any other local on a Friday night. It was where we went for a drink after work; it was where we went to get cigarettes, and where we went to get change.

'Give us the money or I'll ram this in her head.'

It was a Tuesday morning and I was sent for change. The shop was quiet – there were only a couple of punters and the racing hadn't started yet, so there was no commentary apart from the guy who had his arm around my neck and a pencil poised for my jugular. He and his accomplice rushed the counter when I was walking out through the metal door to the shop floor. They didn't get much; we didn't get much for our trouble either – the price of a pint next door, which partly was to deter against any staff getting in cahoots with robbers.

'Do you remember what they looked like?' asked the Garda.

The truth was I didn't. The truth is that when somebody has something to your head, or is pointing a gun at you, you don't have time to think. And I couldn't see what the guy who had me by the scruff of the neck looked like.

At such times, the fear starts saturating you to the point that your body and mind reaches an adrenaline overload you think you will never experience again. Until the next time.

The next time it was Grand National Day and another shop in the same chain of bookies, where adrenaline was running high – among the punters, among the staff. British racing's showcase event was the highlight of the year, with Cheltenham being a close second. The Irish Grand National was and is a big deal too, but there was something special about the Aintree National; the stakes were higher.

From the minute the door opened, punters filed in – from the young novices to the old nags.

'I'm not sure if I filled this in right,' the newbies would say, passing over free bets from the newspaper folded into dockets written by everyone from their grandparents to the woman next door. The bets at the time were usually for £1 or £2, but one year the Chinese customers got a boost with free bets written in Chinese in the paper. If memory serves right, they were £5 and it wasn't long before word spread to their Irish pals. The takeaway from that was that you can never underestimate a punter – Irish or Chinese.

'Ah, it's just good to take an interest,' a nice old dear said before whipping out the sharpened pencil keeping her bun in place and changing her stake from £2.50 each way to £5 each way. This was followed by a quip about being 'last of the big spenders' and a quick shove of change back into her bra. How she managed to keep her coins inside the bra I will never know. It would have been rude to ask.

The excitement crackled through the shop. The manager, Mai, was a veteran of the trade – her Donegal lilt at odds with the brash live commentary coming direct from Liverpool to Dublin West. Then there was the settler Sinéad (who manually settled the bets with a calculator, a pen and a small computerised ready reckoner), and cashier Phyllis. Then there was me, bracing myself. There was a till charged with taking Grand National bets only and that was mine. It was a poisoned chalice: the bets were simpler but the queues were longer.

We took it in turns to have our lunch in the kitchenette at the back of the shop. It had enough room for a stool, a fridge, a press, a kettle and, as standard, the microwave – all mod cons. It was later in the afternoon before I went for what is now called a 'comfort break'. Back then it was simply called a piss. And so I found myself hovering over the toilet bowl like my mother always told me to (apart from at home). The race was three miles, five furlongs – it would be long enough to go to the toilet, wash and dry my hands, and if lucky, spark up a cigarette.

So there I was, marvelling at how I was in what would have been the perfect turkey-smuggling stance, if I was that way inclined, when a roar went up.

There was nothing unusual in that – it happened every Saturday when a favourite won or a horse unseated his rider, or when some chancer called Derek came in with a universal remote control and started switching the channels off mid-race.

One of the customers would usually shout: 'Do that again, Derek, and I will shove that remote so far up your...' But Derek wasn't in that day.

The door handle started cranking up and down as fast as it could go without coming away from its frame.

'Stay in there, Alison, stay in there,' shouted Mai. I froze mid-flow. I felt like peeing myself, so I was in the right place. And then my legs started to tremble; not entirely unusual at the time as, until my late twenties, I was visited by the odd bout of the shakes when I could have done without them – usually when drinking water at interviews, or pouring hot tea, or on a couple of dates (which was probably why there wasn't a second).

'We're OK, you just stay where you are,' came Mai's voice from outside the door – not directly, but closer than the counter.

The roar outside was flattened by a gunshot and a thud, followed by thuds and squeals this time; metal on metal and bodies on floor. My hands were shaking so badly that it felt like an age before I could zip up my trousers. At that moment, I was more concerned that whoever was behind the gunshot was going to see me in Penneys' finest.

What a way to go. I could see my passing on the next day's *Evening Herald* flash before me (because I was unlikely to make the broadsheets with such an unladylike demise, am I right?): 'What are the odds? Cashier killed in bookies' loo', 'Garda bid to flush out cashier killers', etc.

I didn't say anything. I couldn't. When the noise faded, my boss Mai was at the door again: 'Alison, come out, we're OK, you're OK, come out.'

I opened the door slowly and she gave me a hug. Sinéad and Phyllis came out from the kitchenette, where they'd hidden when it all kicked off.

Behind the counter was covered in glass and betting slips. The place was in smithereens. The bandit security screen had made a mockery of its name. The gunmen had shot it down by caving the frame. Nobody had seen what the robbers looked like. There were three of them, all in a uniform of jeans and balaclavas. Customers had thrown themselves on top of each other in corners like mini-scrums. We offered them tea – I didn't pour.

When the Gardaí arrived, they took fingerprints from inside the counter – the dusting for prints was nothing like I had imagined and lacked the drama that I would enjoy a few years later watching *CSI*.

The Gardaí asked questions but I didn't have much in the way of answers.

'Why did you go to the toilet when you did?'

How do you answer that, my friends?

On top of being shook, with good reason this time, I felt bad for leaving my colleagues and friends in the lurch in their time of need. Thankfully the only damage was structural.

Sinéad broke her heel running into the bathroom, so she was given the price of a pair of shoes from head office as compensation;

the rest of us got the then norm of a price of a few drinks. Incidentally, my hands didn't shake when pouring *them*.

But perhaps the most daring and mysterious betting-shop heist didn't involve anyone at all – well, anyone visible, at least. One night, the then manager of the Cardiffsbridge bookie's was walking home from the pub with her husband when she saw the shop safe in the bus shelter, for all the world looking like it was waiting on the no. 40.

Needless to say it got a one-way ticket back to its rightful home, but the curious thing was that whoever had taken the safe, which was impossible to lift manually, had emptied its contents and locked it again. The culprit or culprits were never found, and like all good stories, it soon grew legs – just like the turkeys around the corner.

# Geepads

*June Caldwell*

The first day I bled, armed men took over British Home Stores on O'Connell Street in Dublin, stopping the traffic. It was Saturday 2 May 1981. I was eleven years old, en route to Brendan Smith's Academy of Acting. They were H-Block activists protesting the hunger strikes happening in the Maze prison in Northern Ireland, three days before Bobby Sands died. A youngfella shouted, 'Jesus it's De Ra, g'wan ye boyos!' An old woman barked: 'Pack of bowsies!' Other passengers stood up to get off. The trickle between my legs was warm. The 19A bus had come to a halt directly across from BHS – now the site of Penneys – and crowds were gathering on both sides of the street. I sat with my hands pasted on the window frame, staring out at the commotion. There were more protestors dangling from the lower shop windows, holding banners bearing slogans. One of the men who'd made it to the roof wore a balaclava and was holding a gun, which terrified me. The canoe-wedge of bleached wood pulp was beginning to catch the hairs at the sides of my legs, as it wasn't stuck on properly. I couldn't bring myself to get off the bus because the oozing was getting worse and I was panicked there'd be visible stains. Eventually, I think, the army or bomb squad showed up, and my bus pulled off.

Earlier that morning I'd called my mum into the box room. 'I think I've cut myself,' I said, yanking my nightdress up to show her maps of sticky burgundy on my thigh. She disappeared and came back with a sanitary towel, unpeeled the adhesive strip, then shoved it crookedly into place. 'You're able to have a baby now, all grown up.' I already knew about jam rags, geepads, your friends. I knew about brown-paper bags before they were associated with political corruption. Newsagents wrapped sanitary products at Olympic speed under counters out of sight every day of the week. They were burrowed into the arms of nod-and-wink mothers and squirrelled away separately to the rest of the shopping. Back on home turf, they were hidden immediately. My sister was nine years older than me. I'd witnessed her rustling in the wardrobe late at night, where used towels were allocated a temporary mausoleum. A gangly girl at school got her friends two years before me, at age nine. She was instructed by the teacher not to panic the rest of us by describing period cramps or other delicate details, but she did in the playground straight afterwards.

I knew, without knowing what it really entailed, that it was on the way. Feelings of revulsion as well as flagrant excitement surrounded the whole shebang. Being part of a body-seeping, crimson-goo league of gentlewomen. Power. Currency. Fertility. Or something like that. Being old enough to technically 'do it' but making sure to also never contemplate it, or you'd end up like such-and-such who went off in the shade of night and was never heard from again, or who ended up mad in Manchester, or incarcerated behind a very high convent wall in Limerick. To know that a part of your body might be a threat to the moral labyrinth out there was pure mystical. Though in reality it was no joke: in 1985, on the brink of the morning-after pill being available for the first time, a girl in our school was hauled off to a Magdalene laundry in Cork, to have a baby. When she returned we weren't allowed to ask a thing about it. Instead, and rather inappropriately, we followed her around watching her intently as if she were an untouchable film star straight off set.

A few golden rules with my mum when it came to all things menstrual and its by-products: never, under any circumstances, call sanitary towels 'geepads' in front of her (offensive and common); never dispose of them in an ordinary household bin. The dogs on the street could potentially get at them and terminally mortify us. She'd fetch them herself every month from the dark crevices of the wardrobe I shared with my sister and take them to incinerate in the open fire when the men of the house were absent. 'It's what everyone does,' she said. Dublin, then, had one of the highest smog levels in Europe, Ballyfermot being named as the worst due to housing density and the fact that it was surrounded by factories. My father came home from work early one day, saw the pads curling and popping on the fire, and said, 'It smells like Auschwitz in here.' He'd been a refugee from the Blitz in Coventry. 'He wouldn't know what they were,' my mother said, reassuringly. Finally, never be mad enough to flush one down the toilet; plumbers were expensive, and there was no way in hell she would endure the embarrassment of *all of that* if the pipes jammed.

I'd familiarised myself unwittingly with sanitary towels years before, when I opened my dolls' hospital on a brass drinks trolley we kept in the dining room for guests that never came. My patients were given a hospital bed (slice of trolley) and each allocated their own individual mattress. Pulling the thin strips from the back of my sister's stash of geepads, I fashioned a new mattress onto each doll's back, and laid them flat for optimum comfort. Even the 'Chinese Sindy' my mum bought me for Christmas in 1977 in Moore Street – which wasn't a real Sindy because she couldn't afford one – was gifted a snug cushion while waiting for the nurse to do her rounds. Teddy bears got special treatment, and were allowed to use them as parachutes or duvets, the latter only newly on the scene in Ireland to replace traditional horse blankets on beds.

Actual tampons never made it over our threshold, even though they were off doing their thing in the world since 1931. They were outlawed by my mother and were taboo for a lot of Catholic oul' wans overly concerned about decency. Nothing to do with the dioxin levels, which were even worse than those in disposable nappies. Nor the possibility of tragic early death from the barbarous effects of toxic shock syndrome. Stranger stories instead made the rounds: girls who went horse riding with tampons lost their hymens in country lanes. Sanitary towels had a hermetically sealed purity in comparison. Like the newspaper ads said: *Soft, Absorbent, Antiseptic ... Southalls' Original Sanitary Towels ... sold in sealed packets to ensure purity and absolute freshness.* Girls who wore them were pure and fresh too.

In the early eighties, at least where I was in the north Dublin suburbs, showers or fancy tap attachments that would assist with a thorough cleanse weren't a going concern when you had your monthlies. I didn't know to wash myself regularly at all. There were no clear instructions for how *not* to smell like a butcher's counter at closing time. Modern semi-ds like ours, built in the late 1950s, had a bathtub, but a lot of houses still didn't have showers to practise more economic modes of washing. We didn't have a fridge until I was eight, and I was the youngest of five kids, so I can't recall exactly when we got around to installing the rickety wall-mounted shower. A lukewarm bath once a week, if you were permitted to switch the immersion on for longer than an hour. The bathroom was shared between seven and was nearly always occupied, and there was no lock on the door.

In my mum's time toilets were outdoors in brick sheds in back gardens. The art of body bathing was transacted in public swimming baths or else, as was more customary, women or girls 'topped and tailed' at kitchen sinks with carbolic soap before heading off to school or work. When the moon pulled again on fragile interiors a month later, it was clothing rags that were used as makeshift sanitary towels. Tied with string inside giant knickers; washed out by hand afterwards for reuse, or even as hand-me-downs.

I was shocked to find out (eventually) that sanitary towels were invented in the early 1880s. The first advertisement for geepads appeared in the *Irish Times* on 2 May 1885, accompanied by 'testimonials from medical men' as a permission-type go-ahead for women to use them. Femina were available to buy 'in all good chemists, drapers, and department stores' by the time my mother was a haemorrhaging teenager in the late 1940s. I'm guessing sanitary products may have been a perk of the comfy class, but an unreasonable extra expense for working-class women during the post-war ration years that lingered.

When I had my periods, I smelled terrible. I may have been a free bleeder without realising it, a hippy movement that had started in America almost as soon as I was born. What started as a reaction to toxic-shock syndrome from tampons soon grew into a protest platform to highlight the lack of affordability of sanitary products by purposely bleeding in clothes. It posed the fundamental question, 'Do we really need to apologise for our bodily functions?' No matter, I lacked the foresight to bring a change of pad with me to school. If the towel got too loaded to the point where my skin was chafing or I could smell myself in the classroom, I'd tear the pad off in the toilet, roll it into my pencil case, and bring it home for the ritual torching. Crumpled toilet roll was a convenient solution, but you couldn't use it for too long or it'd give way and leak onto the back of your school uniform. I also once bled onto a Flintstones sock for the entire duration of a three-hour state exam. In the early years of secondary school, during assembly-type gatherings in the main hall, you could smell the metallic tang of collective blood. And yet no one discussed periods openly. My sister's experience a decade before sounded even worse. 'There were no stick-on pads when I started – you had to wear a belt to hold it in place, akin to a chastity belt. I was handed five pads in total for five full days of heavy bleeding. It was humiliating and stressful.'

Only once at school did someone dare say something that was menstrual-applicable. During the solitary sex-education class we were ever made to sit through, a girl from Swords raised her hand to ask, 'If you're wearing a tampon, can you be raped?' Rather than answer the question straight out, the session was cut short by forty minutes and we were allowed off school early, which was a first. Friends in other schools would tell me later that they had experienced the same bland sex-education diatribe before the Inter Cert. Not only did it involve a sex-by-numbers 'when a man loves a woman and after they marry' sequence of what young girls could expect ahead, but it included a horrible video of a late-stage abortion – complete with indigo foetus – which traumatised to the desired effect.

As twelve-year-old girls, whose spiky hairdos were fast replacing pigtails and plaits, we weren't confident or unrepressed enough to normalise the tiny chaos happening within our bodies, or the body politic that was pulling it along. If someone puked or collapsed with period cramps, they were sent home alone with a teacher's note as the rest of us giggled and felt relieved. Not like today, where there's a clear sense of pride and increased openness about the female body: the delights of Mooncup and 'get them up there, girls' TV marketing. There's even a regular Menstrual Hygiene Day. Or the likes of Míosta, an Irish initiative, facilitating workshops at universities to get rid of the stigma surrounding periods.

Yet, as a country, we are still not doing enough to tackle 'period poverty' in the purse. In 2019 England, Scotland and Wales introduced schemes to distribute free sanitary products to tens of thousands of schoolgirls. Campaigners highlighted the fact that schoolgirls were forced to miss days at school because they could not afford products. Two in five girls had to rely on using toilet roll to manage their period. Some were forced to use socks (like me) or newspaper. Northern Ireland has also upped its effort to supply free sanitary products in at least some settings. Derry and Strabane District became the first local authority in Northern Ireland in 2018 to offer free sanitary products in some of its public buildings. Stormont too, the site of governing power in Belfast, wants to make them available at Parliament buildings in a pilot scheme. What the Irish government has done (to date) is set up a committee to talk about what needs to be done. Girls aged between twelve and nineteen, in a survey, said they had experienced issues paying for sanitary products. Free sanitary products in public buildings is a stated starting point by the committee, and a commitment to work with other EU states to have VAT removed on all sanitary products.

Our gloss-yellow school toilets back then didn't boast sanitary accessories or vending machines on walls. There were no slimline bins lodged at the side of toilet bowls. Bins that I used to think were air fresheners when I'd spot them in hotels as a young kid, when my parents took us on Sunday afternoon pub crawls disguised as family outings. I'd bang those small bin lids up and down, making an awful racket, and relish the weird synthetic pong.

Geepads did make the news on a few occasions when I was a teenager. Reports on coastal water pollution; rubbish being dumped on Dollymount beach; complaints from the Prison Rights Organisation (PRO). Like Sunday 3 June 1984, when thirty-three women, including a nun, were arrested in the Phoenix Park, campaigning for nuclear disarmament. They'd been singing 'Give Peace a Chance' when the Gardaí closed in. Three women were given two sanitary towels between them during the short incarceration that followed. A month before, an 8 per cent tax on tampons and sanitary towels as part of a clothing tax was hastily lifted by Finance Minister Alan Dukes, following multiple complaints. Fianna Fáil TD Mary O'Rourke said she found it extraordinary that an item that all women would have to use for nearly forty years of their lives should be taxed: 'To classify them in the same bracket as hats, t-shirts, headbands and bracelets is insulting.'

Twenty million sanitary protection ('san pro') items a year sold in Ireland at the time, with a market value of IR£9 million. Categorising them as a 'clothing accessory' was horribly disingenuous. (There is zero per cent VAT on sanitary products in Ireland now, except for menstrual cups, which still carry a 13.5 per cent reduced rate, along with condoms.) Aside from the financials, if menstruation was mentioned at all, it was usually in a medical context, and nearly always by a man. An interesting opinion column by Dr David Nowlan talked about the different monikers – from 'the curse' to 'flowers' – all kinds of cultural customs and variations. 'In Egypt and Mexico, words were used to imply a state of ill health or pain, such as "being unwell" or "having the blues". In other countries it's referred to as a "visitor". In Britain, the familiarity of an old friend "Charlie" or "Archie" [men's names?]. While in Jamaica, young girls are taught about growing up using the analogy of "flowers" and "bees".' In Ireland, inanities about young girls and periods were routinely dished out, usually from the gobs of sleazy aulfellas in smelly pubs or mates of my older brother: 'If she's old enough to bleed, she's old enough to breed.'

Once I managed to blag a half-price school trip abroad, only made possible by a last-minute cancellation and a bingo win of my mother's. Sixty of us, to Paris, with four teachers, for three whole days. Kids who couldn't afford the yearly 'big one' had to make do with dreary trips, like the one I'd already done the year before to a quarry in Co. Kildare, to learn about geographical differences in layers (or strata) of stone. This trip would be my first time on a plane and my first to Europe. We stayed in a no-star hostel in the centre of Le Marais. Call it a melatonin and cortisol party or just bad luck, but by the time we got to our shared six-person dormitory, I was bleeding profusely.

Years of soaking up my mother's neurosis of not disposing of dirty pads in public meant that daily, whether on our way to marvel at the al-fresco pipage on the Georges Pompidou Centre, or to gawk at bad caricature artists in Montmartre, my attempts to shove geepads in public bins on the street failed. I'd completely lost my nerve. At Charles de Gaulle Airport on the way home, I shuddered when I saw the customs officers pulling over some of my classmates in front to check their luggage. I saw only one way out, flinging myself on the ground, barking like a dog. One of my party tricks I did to amuse boys I was interested in. It quickly turned into a security alert, with Miss O'Connor – who already disliked me for refusing to do Honours Irish – going to great lengths to explain I had an unusual sense of humour and was a 'creative' kind of girl. I was banned from further trips, but left that school a year later to head to another that taught better subjects and was a bit more progressive.

One of the most excruciating incidents of my teen years was still a year or more away. By then I was a music-obsessed mod: cropped bob, button earrings, Fred Perry polo shirts, tight Sarsaparilla jeans in pastels or pure white, which cost a bomb, and winkle-pickers you could only get in Simon Hart's shoe shop on Henry Street. We'd waste every spare moment hanging around with other Sixties fanatics in the city centre. Days squandered at the Pillar, a statue in the middle of O'Connell Street dedicated to James Larkin, the founder of the Workers' Union of Ireland. Mods would pull up on scooters, and we'd all look stupidly cool and flirt. Two nights a week it was down the sticky-carpeted stairs into the vault of Bubbles disco on Fleet Street, with its red-and-black décor and newfangled ultraviolet lights that showed up every speck of dust. This fella I was really into was a proper scallywag: great sense of humour, massive brown eyes, Robert De Niro swagger. You had to be high-end gorgeous to make it into a doorway with him late at night, where he'd work your lips numb over forty minutes before the last bus home. He sauntered across the dance floor, tapped me on the shoulder, smiled the smile, and said, 'You've blood on your arse.'

I always carried a spare after that. I found out years later he'd been involved in 'the movement' and was probably at British Home Stores the day of the H-Block protests. Though he would've been thirteen, preened to roar, and comfortable in his own skin.

# Improper

### Riley Johnston

An improper noun is a common noun: a person, place or thing. A proper noun is the name of that thing. Its identity. And identity is important to us.

*What school did you go to?*

It's a question we in Northern Ireland dread. We know the intention. Nine times out of ten, the answer will signal religious affiliation, class and intellectual ability. For those enquirers, the name of our school is a summary of our identity.

I went to an all-girls grammar school on the Falls Road, Belfast, and I loved it. However, there have been times throughout my life when I've been coy when asked the question. I had to win a place by sitting a transfer test called the eleven-plus. Although formally abolished in 2008, a version of the assessment still exists today. A place in a grammar school is considered a symbol of middle-class propriety and some parents will spend hundreds of pounds on tutors to ensure their child gets a place in a school with a ribbon on the blazer.

In my primary school there was very little tutor intervention. In fact, there wasn't much teacher interaction either, save from the odd past paper thrown at us when the other half of the class were at the swimmers. It kept us busyish and provided satisfactory evidence that we were being prepared, as was the requirement in the early 1990s.

There were nine of us from my primary class who passed the exam, and eight of us applied to the same grammar. I remember seeing the class suddenly carved up and learning something about my peers that had never occurred to me before. My friendships changed as I found myself belonging to a clique.

I couldn't wait to don the dowdy pinafore and beige knee socks, and imagined myself walking into a building full of other bright, beaming girls full of zealous pride. I learned quickly, however, that to beam proudly or, in fact, show any emotion other than disdain was seriously uncool. For some of my schoolmates, getting a place in a grammar school was an insult to their pride. Groups of surly girls bemoaned the privilege and spoke dreamily of all the *real* fun they could have in the secondary schools.

And those from the secondary schools were insulted too. On the bus, they called us snobs and painted our uniforms in Tippex and stuck compasses in our backs. Our woollen blazers provided adequate padding from the stabs but not from the onions that hit our heads or indeed the eggs they pelted us with. I was unlucky enough to be a victim of the eggs. Even with a careful wash at a launderette, the colour ran and the blazer came out a glaring shade of magenta. It lost a layer of wool too and looked skinned and shiny. I was scundered wearing it, like an embarrassed dog that had its coat shaved for summer. My parents caved and bought me another. Though, given the extortionate price tag, it had to do me for the remainder of my time in school – four more years – and therefore was several sizes too big. I never grew into it.

I had the audacity to play the trumpet. In school, I hauled its black fibreglass mass about corridors, banging into other girls' legs, wishing it was more compact. Every edge of the rectangular box was emblazed with 'CBSM', so I could be under no illusion that it was my own instrument. I was lucky. My friend had also borrowed one from the School of Music and her case was held together with her dad's belt. The trumpet was in no better shape, and she made the wise decision to pack it in and play a tin whistle instead.

The journey home from school was often a trial. From 3.25 p.m. until 3.50 p.m. I stood outside the Royal Victoria Hospital waiting for my bus. On regular days, we all had to be vigilant and on music days, I was even more so. Occasionally, boys from another school would come to torment us. Forgetting they'd sisters themselves, I suppose, they would arrive like the cavalry, charging at us. If you were deep in conversation or perhaps unlucky enough to be standing at the end of the line, you might only discover their arrival when your ankle-length skirt was hauled up over your head. Others might have seen them approach but were too afraid to stop the contents of their school bag being flung out into the road. I was hyper-alert, always. I'd have nightmares of my trumpet being taken and thrown out among the cars and buses. I had a strange attachment to it. Who knows why, since it wasn't mine and, as I found out years later, was barely more than scrap metal in a decent, sturdy case. I guarded it nonetheless, terrified of it being taken and brutalised by hoods.

On the bus it caused havoc, needing a seat of its own. There may have been overhead compartments, but no one used those. You might as well have handed over your possessions to the hoods directly. If the bus was busy, I had to rest it on my knee, and it sat upright in front of my face, and other kids laughed and taunted. A girl in my class had played a French horn in primary school but gave it up when someone on a bus asked why she was carrying a toilet around. Faced with similar humiliation, talented girls quit their instruments to save themselves the ordeal of hauling the box on the bus and inviting abuse.

I lacked the self-respect and discipline to apply myself to schoolwork. I'd coasted through primary school, won some awards and got by without having to try, but grammar school was a different environment. I was just like everyone else and, wary of upsetting the surly girls, I was careful not to shine, lest I draw their scorn. I spent my A-level years hiding in an unused music-practice room, pretending to various teachers that I had a lesson. Sometimes, if I got bored, I'd go for a dander round the school. It was a beautiful place: stone steps leading to panelled corridors and mosaic floors, all soaked in the history of other girls' experiences. It had a grandeur that we were encouraged to be proud of, and we were. The grounds were equally beautiful and were once described by our principal as 'an oasis on the Falls'. And it was. When the British Army ran through the grounds, we felt exhilarated. We hung out of the sash windows from the eaves of the old building and looked down on the intruders in our walled oasis, feeling safe in our cocoon.

I felt at home in that place. Maybe a little too comfortable and definitely too curious, and this took me on explorations to places

I shouldn't have been. I was fascinated by the convent that was installed above our classrooms. A whole other world existed there. The daily smells of food were often our only hint that a community lived above ours. Cabbage and fishcakes. We were convinced that's all they ate. I wanted to know for certain, so I'd gather friends and go to look. On a few occasions I found myself being the target of a chase from a nun who caught us snooping. I hid under pews in the school chapel or under desks in the library at the top of the school. Beyond the odd nun in pursuit, no one else came looking for me when I was supposed to be in lessons. 'It's *your* A level,' we were told sometimes when we failed to do what was required. The onus was on us. Maybe it was the grandeur of the setting or the years of coasting and getting by, or perhaps just blissful ignorance. Whatever prompted me to languish there, it did me no favours later on.

Since leaving I have been asked what school I went to and a few times my answer has been followed up with, 'But that's not a proper grammar, is it?' I'd blush, feeling, as the speaker intended, inferior, wracked with my own regret at having scraped through my A levels with barely adequate results. It was a preposterous yet frequent enough question. I had to sit an exam to get a place, as did my peers. So why wasn't it a proper grammar?

I often pondered the basis for this mindset. Was it that my school did not participate in rugby tournaments? Was that the measure of proper grammar status? Was it that it did not have an address in a leafy, tree-lined part of Belfast? Was it because we were Catholic? Not daughters of landowners, businessmen, doctors, lawyers or even teachers? Is it because we were all girls and no matter how many times the school encouraged us to believe we could be anything, society decided that we could not? Mary McAleese, then President of Ireland, visited our school. She was a past pupil. This promoted a surge in our feelings of self-worth, but once out of the cocoon, we were faced with a judgemental world.

It was years later that I learned what a proper grammar school was. It was about the same time I realised I was working class. At university I tried to mix with people. The more I did, the more challenges I encountered: questions about where I lived, assumptions about my religion, and horror at my accent and my swearing. I tried to adapt, because every authority I met told me they were right and I was wrong. When I began teacher training, I had to try even harder. With no relatives in the profession, nepotism wouldn't secure me; no Sunday school teaching experience to prove my goodness and, of course, I had a tendency to pronounce words in a way that some peers thought was 'wrong', 'common' or 'too Belfast'.

Early in my career I taught English in a proper grammar school. It was my third year of surfing on temporary contracts. I felt like a failure; I was exhausted starting over in different schools and by the relentless begging for a job. The school was the type that had its name mentioned on the illustrious rugby schools' reports, ribbons on their blazers and a wake of past pupils eager to drop its name unnecessarily into conversation. The principal at the time would not thank me for revealing that the school itself was packed with working-class children. I felt an immediate connection to them. They often obscured themselves to avoid having their accents mocked and expectations adjusted for them. I remember two boys in particular who were like a comedy double act. They had intelligence but modesty, and a humour and zeal borne out of hardship. It struck me then that they might be stripped of this character in future years, forced, like me, to conform to someone else's notion of propriety.

In the same class was a pregnant girl who had the airs of a middle-class upbringing. The school hadn't told me about her, as they should have, and I guess they hoped I wouldn't notice, being that my contract was short and I would be moving on soon. Indeed, I didn't notice, being disinclined from surveying a child's stomach area. She walked into my classroom twenty minutes late one day. The weight of my responsibility flooded me. Twenty minutes; a child who was meant to be in my care was elsewhere without my knowledge or permission for a whole twenty minutes. I enquired. She snapped at me. I pushed further and she flung the weight of her entitlement in my face.

I was called to the principal's office later that week. As I entered, I realised that a stage had been set. A solitary chair had been placed six feet from his desk. His posture was courtly behind the desk and, as always, he was draped in an academic gown. He took long pauses between sentences, savouring every bit of his power; a smug smirk formed at the side of his mouth as he spoke, slowly, so I would understand. He was not ashamed of the negligence of his staff in omitting the detail about the pregnant girl. I was not worthy of this information and he did not apologise for having shocked me with the revelation as I sat in the centre of his oak-panelled office.

*She said you made her stand.*

He had notes, filled with youthful anger and resentment that he was eagerly passing on to me, unfiltered.

*But I didn't know. They were all standing. The activity required it.*

My responses were disregarded.

*She said your language isn't appropriate and I quote...*

Years of mockery for my words and accent culminated in that room. I was accused of being aggressive, a familiar code for those of us raised in working-class communities who are used to directness.

*We don't speak like that here.*

It was his morning's work; a rehearsed admonishment punctuated with the odd flash of that benevolent smile men like him afford us when they wish to pretend to be kind. The ordeal lasted longer than necessary and, satisfied with himself, he sent me on my way to think about my need of adjustment.

I met his son years later in a bar. Despite an age gap of about fifteen years, he had the gall to flirt with me, by telling me I had nice teeth (I don't), then chastised me for not accepting his compliment. Unsolicited, he then began to recite his A-level results and I laughed. He was a proper grammar-school boy: full of ego and steeled with the unyielding belief that academic awards were tantamount to a personality. No doubt he would have told me my grammar school wasn't a proper one, had I given him the chance.

Proper or common, the labels are loaded. Some people have tried to make me feel ashamed of my identity. My vulnerability has forced me, at times, to surrender to the murky world of propriety. But seeing what was on the other side of that smokescreen gave me the confidence to take myself back out. Today, I pronounce 'butch' like 'such', not 'mooch', as feels natural to me. If people ask what school I went to, I tell them emphatically and feel relief that I was spared the snobbery of the so-called proper grammars. Hindsight furnishes me with retorts and retaliations no longer available to me and some episodes haunt me too often. I've even wondered about the principal's son. I want to know what profession he patronised, whether his A-level results got him a date and if he ever learned how unremarkable he was to be proper.

# Begging From Beggars

## *Jim Ward*

'You could use a pumice stone to get rid of it,' Maurice advised. He was referring to the nicotine tan on two fingers of my right hand, the only sort of tan I could afford. It was a damp, black night in Galway and we were walking back from the pub – sober, I might add; we could only scrape up enough funds for a couple of pints each. I had a job interview the following Wednesday and was worried about these brown marks going against me at the interview. They had, by now, reached my fingernails. Employers, especially the multinationals, took a dim view of anyone with a social life that didn't reflect positively on the firm.

The streets were deserted, a Sunday night in winter, and the wind rattled the hoardings of the shut shops. Late-eighties Ireland. It would be what seemed like my millionth job interview since I'd left college the previous summer, with each one holding my breath in hope, each time winded by reality. Some of my classmates had got jobs in DEC – the Digital Equipment Corporation – the mainstay employer in Galway, the town's saviour. The rest emigrated. I had long ceased to be interested in a 'career'; I simply needed a job. DEC didn't want me for some reason; I did say it was the late 1980s. Recession. For some.

Though if you read the papers, you'd read about Dermot Desmond and financial services, Tony Ryan and GPA, the wonders the cutbacks were doing for economic confidence in Ireland. I had an engineering degree and was on £18.45 a week on the dole, a king for a day. Only, dole day was Thursday, so how come I was coming from the pub on a Sunday night? Well, Maurice, who was training to be a solicitor and practically as skint as me, took me for a couple of pints to pep talk confidence into me before Wednesday's interview. For a position in a local multinational. By this stage, many's the train I had taken to Dublin and buses further again, for interview after interview, only to get the polite but chilly standard letter.

Funny, I thought, how you must sell yourself to employers. They are not philanthropists as Charlie McCreevy, a future finance minister, would tell us. Enhance your CV, bullshit your achievements, prove your worth. A whole industry has built up on the back of this. It's a form of prostitution, the hiring process. My old man would tell me how as a nipper he'd watch stout farmers feeling and sizing up the *spailpíns* lined up in Eyre Square, selling themselves for a day's labour.

I had done well, the first of my family to go on to university. But after graduation I found I had to survive in the cannibalistic environment of cutback Ireland. Same old story – *cruacás na hÉireann* (the old hardship of Ireland). A recession brought about by government cutbacks in public spending to offset the profligacy of the now infamous 1977 Fianna Fáil Manifesto. These austerity policies now continued despite the same Fianna Fáil being returned to power on a platform pronouncing: 'Cutbacks hurt the old, the sick and the handicapped.'

I very soon became convinced of the truth behind the executed 1916 leader James Connolly's assertion that in capitalist countries, governments are merely committees for the rich, but kept this to myself. After all, look what happened to Connolly. It also heightened an awareness of events that would repeat again and again: in times of economic distress the ruling class would unite and the poor pay for the excesses of the rich.

In those days of seemingly hopeless alienation from work and any meaningful role in society, my distractions were smoking, drinking (confined to Thursdays), films on TV, music and books. Capitalism had spawned consumerism as a mechanism to feed it. Globally, Thatcherism and Reaganomics had taken root, the unions put in their place. Yuppies carrying Filofaxes crowded the sprouting wine bars, and on television, Harry Enfield's Loadsamoney, a self-employed tradesman character, sang about waving his wad at the blokes in the gutter.

The wide disparity in wealth between the haves and have-nots grew from what it was in the much-maligned but misunderstood 1970s. The seventies had public-service strikes, power cuts and overcrowded and seemingly underfunded police precincts, as TV's Kojak in his 'downtown' New York precinct showed us. It was, however, compared with, say, the excesses of *Dallas* and *Dynasty,* a shoddier but much more democratic and egalitarian time. As always, in Ireland, we were spared these wealth disparities till later. I had noticed, on bus journeys to various job interviews, the odd Irish version of J. R.'s 'Southfork' scattered around the countryside. I remembered the comments of the late C. S. 'Todd' Andrews, author of *Man of No Property*, a founding member of Fianna Fáil as well as a leader of many state companies, who said that 'class in Ireland was merely tuppence ha'penny looking down on tuppence'. I wondered. If anything, the lyrics of Leonard Cohen's 1988 'Tower of Song' made more sense, singing about the rich having their channels in the bedrooms of the poor and a mighty judgement coming.

Then there was Fianna Fáil Tánaiste Brian Lenihan, who in the sixties once described himself as a socialist, saying that Ireland was too small a country for class politics. You got that back then, a sort of social democratic tinge in all Irish political parties, something to do with our collective history. Why even the Blueshirts, Fine Gael, had a social democratic wing, the 'Young Tigers' of the sixties, who eventually rallied around Garret FitzGerald. This was a result of some sons of prominent Fine Gael politicians (FitzGerald himself and Declan Costello) waking up in the 1960s and acquiring a social conscience. Instead of joining Labour (they couldn't, because of their history obviously, join the more *de facto* social democratic Fianna Fáil), they produced the document *Towards a Just Society* and tried to change Fine Gael from within, culminating with a motion at the 1968 Ard Fheis to change its name to the Social Democrats. It was firmly dealt with. Fine Gael, like Thatcher in Britain, was not for turning.

So, I'd sit home at night, smoking affordable roll-up cigs, no job to go to bed for and, like a god, view the world's actions through late-night television, though unlike a god, having no input into making them happen or improving my situation; the proletariat works for others, not itself. A Generation X-er before the term was popularised. Channel 4 had great late-night discussions. I became an *After Dark* junkie, supplementing my education.

The Reagan-Thatcher revolution of the eighties reversed the post-war progress made by unions and the democratic left of centre. The bright future was cancelled. The new future was to go back to an ill-defined set of values. For Thatcher, Victorian *laissez-faire* economics and welfare privatised to begging from regulated and unregulated charities. For Reagan, it was a continuation of his 1950s Crusade Against Communism, which viewers on black-and-white television sets were invited to subscribe to. This, now in colour and for a wider audience. After all, he was 'the Great Communicator'.

At home, Fianna Fáil Taoiseach Charlie Haughey's megalomania was presented as 'pragmatism'. Strange that once the carpetbaggers hijacked Fianna Fáil, this once idealistic movement, whose founders had fought a civil war on word-splitting principle, became classed as 'pragmatic'. At least the press, for once, approved of his change of direction. Box ticked for him. What did I say about Connolly's insight about governments in capitalist countries?

Well, the Brits had Page Three, the football and Bananarama to distract them in their media. Not that I wasn't distracted as well, alternating my reading between the *Irish Times* and the *Daily Mirror* – I was, I convinced myself, well balanced, though both papers, for differing reasons, caused me understandable frustration: Conor Cruise O'Brien in one and Maria Whittaker in the other.

So, back to my impending interview. Maurice, it seemed, had a shrewd strategic head. He reminded me of the opening scene of *The Godfather* where the characters are paying their respects to the Don, presenting him with their requests and all. He suggested I attend the constituency clinic of the local government TD the next day and tell him straight I needed his help in getting this job and if he could use any influence to swing the interview, not only would I be eternally grateful but I'd actively help him get re-elected next time. Isn't that the way it works? Clientelism? We clinked our pint glasses in agreement over this plan.

Wednesday came; interview managed. At home my father asked me shyly how I'd done – he had given up asking me obvious questions ages back, just as I had less and less confidence and self-esteem following endless rejections. I felt I'd done well. I had, I thought, a round in my revolver, what with a politician behind me. In fact the meeting with the local TD went fine. They always do. Firm handshakes and smiles. His official letter arrived a month later – 'I will of course help you with this matter … I have made representations on your behalf…' Too late.

The week following the interview, a letter arrived. I knew before opening it I hadn't got the job; it had the same standard appearance of so many before. Frustrated and powerless when I read it, I crumpled it and tossed it in the fire. My old man said forget about it, and with the wisdom and the vexation of a man who had earned an honest living all his life and could see this opportunity slowly passing his son by, he told me, 'Forget selling yourself to these cowboys and their politicians and lackeys – you'll only end up as bad as they are. Give it up – you're begging, you're begging from beggars, begging from fucking beggars.'

He was right. We are all treading water trying to stay afloat, eking an existence. Without universal solidarity you can rely on no one. Whatever about back then, there's no such solidarity on the horizon today. No one owes you a life in the *mé féin* world of neoliberalism.

I learned that back then.

Oh, by the way, I hadn't the guts to let Maurice know at the time that I had never even heard of a pumice stone – 'twas far from them I was reared.

# Four Green Fields

*Danielle McLaughlin*

If this were fiction, I would probably decide that the story wasn't mine to tell. 'Working class' wasn't a term I associated with my rural North Cork upbringing in the 1970s. I didn't think of myself as belonging to any other class either. My father worked as a clerk in the offices of the Irish Sugar factory in Mallow and was a trade-union member, but I don't recall being aware of class distinctions, or of the language or politics of the workers' movement when I was young. Then again, I was an odd child who spent much time inside her own head – not always a fun place – or with books and animals. I had a tendency to immerse myself in certain things to the point of obsession, while remaining blissfully oblivious to others. I do recall once, when I was about ten, asking someone if our family was working class and not getting a satisfactory answer. Having grappled with a plethora of definitions in the course of writing this essay, that person now has my sympathy. I'm not sure that I have a satisfactory answer myself.

I grew up with an eclectic mix of language, a soup of vocabularies and narratives. Myriad rebel songs, for instance: 'Come Out Ye Black and Tans', 'A Nation Once Again', 'Some Say The Devil Is Dead', 'Follow Me Up To Carlow'. I have a memory of singing 'The Men Behind the Wire' at national school and being puzzled when it wasn't well received. My paternal grandparents, who had a small farm, also owned one of the six pubs in the parish and my father, as a young man, was lead singer in a folk band. I travelled on the bingo buses with my aunt and there I learned a whole other set of refrains: two fat ladies, key of the door, all the twos, top of the house, sweet sixteen with its wolf whistle. My Hiberno-English was scattered with words from the Irish language, to which Enid Blyton added such phrases as 'jolly good feast', 'my word!' and 'oh golly'. I knew nothing about Jim Larkin or lockouts, and all I could have told you about James Connolly was that the British sat him on a chair to shoot him in 1916.

My baby years were spent in rooms above the pub, but when my parents got a housing grant, they built a bungalow on the farm. I grew up among bogland and wildflowers, streams gloopy with frogspawn; in the evenings I took a gallon tin to fetch unpasteurised milk still warm from the cows and carried it across the fields to our house. For all its bucolic loveliness, country life was unsentimental. I remember sitting on a gate with one of my brothers singing goodbye to a bullock that was off to the abattoir. The bullock was blond and stocky, and we'd named him Charlie Bobby, 'Charlie', I'm guessing, being a mishearing of Charolais. Later, during my first year in secondary school, he would become the first in a long line of dead animals to feature in my stories, though there was to be a gap of decades before the others emerged. I remember my English teacher, Miss Higgins – and yes, it was Miss, I was no more familiar with the concept of Ms than with the concept of the proletariat – praising the story lavishly. In March 2020, almost forty years on from writing that story, I gave a reading for International Women's Day from my short story collection *Dinosaurs on Other Planets,* published in 2015 by the Stinging Fly Press. I was very touched when I saw Miss Higgins come in and take a seat, and afterwards I had the great privilege of signing a copy of my collection for her.

I had lots of books growing up, including many in the Irish language: *An Tíogair a Tháinig chun Tae* by Judith Kerr, *Amhránaithe Bhremen* by the Brothers Grimm. I read most of the Enid Blyton books, and I also remember reading *Anne of Green Gables, Little Women, Black Beauty* and *Treasure Island,* among others. Alongside some of the books I still have from my childhood are books that belonged to my mother when she was a girl. Like most Irish women of her generation, my mother didn't get to go to college. She had a job in local government but was required to give it up because of the Marriage Bar.* Her father, my grandfather, was the local schoolmaster. He's dead many years now, but last year, at a family wedding, I learned that he used to write poetry. One of my fondest memories from national school is of him reading aloud *The Flight of the Doves* by Walter Macken, one chapter a day.

At seventeen, I filled out my CAO form knowing that I would most likely be offered my first choice, law, and also knowing that, most likely, I wouldn't be accepting it, which was how things played out. These were the years before the abolition of third-

---

\*     The Marriage Bar required women in public sector jobs to give up those jobs when they got married. It was abolished in 1973.

level fees, the Ansbacher years, an era of 'only the little people pay taxes', when corruption, unemployment and emigration prevailed. Fortunately, the legal professions offered other routes to becoming a lawyer. I did a secretarial course for a few months and then got a job with Cork Corporation. At night I did a BA degree at University College Cork, and as soon as I graduated, I resigned and went to Dublin to do a one-year diploma in legal studies in Rathmines and afterwards, sit the Law Society entrance exams.

I live now in the same parish where I grew up. Here, when we talk about the 'upper parish' and 'lower parish' we mean altitude above sea level, the windswept hilly side of the parish having its own microclimate. Children of the parish attend school together, regardless of what their parents do for a living. There are no townlands that are considered to be more desirable postcodes than others. Which isn't to say that there aren't inequalities in rural society, or differences in access to opportunities, just that I'm not sure they can be usefully categorised or addressed using the same social stratifications as for urban centres. More and more these days, I find myself wanting to explain to people that rural Ireland is still a real place, that it didn't stop existing when someone in Spencer Dock got to the last page of their John McGahern novel.

Nowadays, since I'm a lawyer, albeit not currently practising, when the question of class arises, I tend to slot myself into the 'middle class' category, since that, apparently, is where lawyers belong. It's handy to know which box to tick. So does this mean that I've changed class? Or is that what I always was? All I can say is that I've changed in umpteen ways over the decades. I think most people who know me now would be surprised to encounter me in a pub singing 'Come Out Ye Black and Tans'. But I don't know that

I'd file any of those changes under 'class'. This strikes me as the kind of answer my ten-year-old self would have deemed unsatisfactory.

It's likely that at least part of the reason the politics of class struggle didn't gain much traction where I come from was because for hundreds of years most of our energies were expended on issues relating to our colonisation by Britain. The Famine, for instance, brought devastation, and trauma that lasted for generations. In the ten months between November 1846 and September 1847, 1,400 people from my parish died. For context, our current population is approximately 2,700. I try to imagine half of my neighbours dying in the space of less than a year, their bodies piling up on roadsides, in ditches. Then there was the War of Independence, the history of which sat quietly on the edge of my every day, because on my grandparents' farm was the ruin of a house that had once belonged to an Anglo-Irish family and was set on fire by the IRA. I have happy childhood memories of searching its yard for the remnants of hand grenades, and – after it had come to house pigs – delighting over litters of pink squealing *banbhs*.

During the War of Independence, our parish was an IRA stronghold. It was only in recent years that I discovered a connection between the parish – and my family – and one of Ireland's most famous short stories, Frank O'Connor's 'Guests of the Nation'. In 1921 a British Intelligence officer called Major Compton-Smith was held hostage by the IRA in our parish on a small farm in the Boggeragh Mountains. In the evenings he would be brought from a shed into the house, where he took his meal by the fire with the family, talked politics and history with the men guarding him, and sang songs with them. After eleven days, he was taken outside to the bog, given a final cigarette, and shot. In a letter written in the hours before his death, Compton-Smith gifted his watch to the IRA battalion commander who had ordered his execution, a distant relative of mine, saying, 'I believe him to be a gentleman.' Frank O'Connor fought in Cork during the War of Independence. His mother, Minnie, was from our parish, and it has been suggested that 'Guests of the Nation' was inspired by the execution of Compton-Smith, though I'd no inkling of this when I read the story in school.*

After the War of Independence came the horror and trauma of the Civil War. It's not difficult to see how anyone who tried agitating for class struggle in our part of the world in the decades following might have got short shrift.

I'm glad, I think, that I wasn't really conscious of class growing up. Sometimes being oblivious to things has its advantages. If I'd been aware of class distinctions, I might have believed that certain things were not for me. Law, for instance. Looking back, I can see that I never countenanced not becoming a lawyer, a belief that strikes me now as ludicrously naïve, and in no way grounded in an objective assessment of the facts. I remember attending a career guidance talk once that was given by a young barrister. Barristers are often portrayed via lazy stereotypes as high earners. While there are indeed a small number of established high earners at the top of their careers, the reality for most is years of precarious, badly paid work, with many ultimately having to drop out because they can't afford to continue. Anyhow, this barrister stood in front of us that day and declared that his advice on becoming a barrister would be not to do it. He went on to say that he knew he could tell us this,

---

* I am indebted to Saoirse Ní Shiocháin for her research on Major Compton-Smith and in particular her essay in *History Ireland* magazine, September/October 2018.

because the students who really wanted to would go ahead and do it anyway. It strikes me now that while this in no way answers the question we came in with – the one about class – it's the sort of answer I might well give to someone who asked me if they should become a writer.

# The Things I Had Forgotten – A Memoir

*Elaine Cawley Weintraub*

The term 'working class' is not widely used in County Mayo in the west of Ireland, where social status always depended on land ownership and education. To be landless was to be destitute and so, a hundred years ago, when the Irish War of Independence raged, the focus here in the west was on the demand for land distribution. This was the home of the Irish National Land League exerting desperate pressure on the ruling classes to give us land. The colonial system of the 'big house', which owned every humble field and could end the tenancy whenever they chose to, had fuelled a burning hunger to hold land free of rent and free of favour. The lessons of the Great Famine were well learned, and to hold the land and make a living from it was a mantra that all rural Irish people learned as children. With independence, everyone got their land, but for big families on smallholdings that meant that it was understood that one sibling would inherit the land and the others would emigrate or hire themselves out to some other, more affluent farmer. The land so well loved and nurtured might well be poor bog and in great need of fertilisation, but it represented the heart and soul of the faithful who tilled it, harvested it and fought for it with a passion that no other love could compete with. Working class is a strange term in this context, because to work this land was an act of worship, though it was back-breaking and often poorly rewarded.

We tend to think of the definition of working class being in some way an urban situation, and that rural areas are a more bucolic and essentially healthy environment. In fact, the grinding poverty and the lack of basic amenities in rural post-colonial Ireland made life very hard for the big families struggling to flourish and survive. Poverty should not be romanticised but it should be remembered, and even though rural Ireland today is unrecognisably affluent, there is a 'race memory' that motivates many Irish people to help others. In June 2020 the Navajo Nation in the United States, who are struggling mightily against the Covid-19 pandemic, publicly thanked Ireland for their contributions to the Nation's Go Fund Me campaign. The Navajo Nation's attorney general, Doreen McPaul, noted: 'There has been a staggering outpouring of support from Irish people and people of Irish descent sending donations.' All Irish people know of the story of the Choctaw Nation's donation sent to Ireland during the Great Famine. This empathy with those who are struggling is a very vital part of the Irish psyche.

There were no jobs in Ireland. There had been no Industrial Revolution in the western part of the country, and jobs were few and far between. As a child I was very familiar with the notion that everyone left to make money to try and sustain the life at home. I recall uncles and cousins heading out to England each August to pick potatoes in Lincoln. Reflecting on those days, my cousin Mick told me that: 'We got one pound a week and we had to send ten shillings home to Ireland. Daughty Brogan, the postmistress in Knockmore, would bring the envelopes for the families to Mass on Sunday morning and everyone would notice if someone didn't get an envelope. It was hard enough work there. They would have you pick the potatoes and then go through them when you went to get them weighed, and throw any smaller ones out, so you had to start again. They put us all sleeping in a barn together and it was very cold, but what choice did you have? There was just enough money to buy a couple of pints on Friday night and a packet of cigs, but you had to make sure that you saved enough to buy a new suit so that when you went home at Christmas you had a nice suit and people thought you were doing really well in England and you wanted them to think that you were a "big man".' Those were the stories told around the fire, and the lessons were taken to heart.

Emigration, both seasonal and permanent, was the reality for us all. I remember the train from Ballina in the west across the country to Dún Laoghaire, where we were herded onto the boat to Holyhead in Wales, the first step of the voyage from the rural west to the big, bustling cities of England. We called it the 'crying train' because at each station along the way, weeping passengers boarded the train while the families watched stoically from the platform, only to subside into storms of sadness when the train pulled out. The boat from Holyhead was memorable too, as we sat on our cases on the floor because every seat was taken while the boat rocked and rolled. Spilt beer and vomit perfumed the air and floated across the floors. Staggering off the boat with too many cases, we boarded another train for a journey of introduction to our new world. I can hear the metallic voice of the announcer now: 'The train from Holyhead stopping at Chester, Warrington and Manchester Exchange is leaving from platform six.'

If it is hard to define what social class I was in Ireland, I have no such problem about my status in England. We joined the working class who sell the only thing that they have: their labour. We traded the parish pump for the gasworks and the building sites. There were problems with that dislocation. The young men who had left Ireland seeking a better life found themselves living in boarding houses with other lonely men, far from all the cultural support they had known. Life was working hard, and the only community was the pub. I dreaded Thursday nights when my father had been paid at the job and spent some hours in the pub before returning home. We did have ambition, but it was a uniquely Irish ambition of that era. The children were to be educated to work with clean hands, hopefully as teachers. Nobody thought of themselves as future captains of industry or investment bankers. We did not know those people. We were firmly aiming at more modest targets. We were immigrants and we were outsiders learning a new game plan. The values we heard expressed around us were not ours and I remember being so confused about that, until my mother explained the situation using the analogy 'When in Rome do as Rome does and when at home do as home does.' I am not sure she was right, but it was a coping device.

Though we were members of the urban working class, we did not feel connected with that identity. We did not share their patriotic support of England's imperial role or their interest in the royal family, and any confusion we had about who or what we were was clarified for us by Margaret Thatcher's government, who made it very clear to us that we were outsiders and suspect. This was the time of the Troubles, and the television screens bombarded us with pictures of bombed-out buildings, young boys throwing stones at British soldiers and nightly violence on the streets of Northern Ireland. The image portrayed was of the Irish as terrorists, and though this was a war in which we played no part, we too were considered alien and potentially violent. It was an image to which we could not relate, and which did not resonate in any way with our sense of who we actually were, and yet we were aware that all Irish people were vulnerable during the time of the bombings in mainland Britain. When the outrages happened in Guildford and Birmingham, we understood that those accused may or may not be guilty.

We were, for the most part, Catholic-school educated, aspiring for advancement to satisfy the modest ambitions of our parents' generation. We congregated in the same areas together and celebrated Irish culture in the pubs and clubs, where we felt welcome and supported. Within our Irish community there was competitiveness and envy of those who had achieved success, and in some strange way there was a prejudice against those who did not adapt at all to the dominant culture. It is a feature of oppression to internalise the prejudice and to be ashamed of those who seem to conform to the stereotype. Those who lived their lives as they had in rural Ireland were usually viewed as foolish and it was widely felt that they would not be able to survive in the UK. I recall my father often saying: 'There's more to life here than whistling to the dog and taking care of the few sheep. You need to be a wise kiddie for this country and forget the Connemara talk.'

The overt anti-Irish prejudice that swept the country during the 1980s forced me to re-evaluate what it meant to be Irish in the UK. I took pride in staring right back at the immigration official who welcomed my obviously American husband who was entering the United Kingdom from Ireland, but who stopped me. The official apologised to my husband for taking me out of the disembarking line. I recall his words: 'I am sorry, sir. You are obviously American, and you are very welcome into the United Kingdom, but what about her?' That experience of being singled out as alien and suspect has been an important experience for me. It has given me empathy towards all those people all over the world who experience this hostility. In many ways it has shaped the person I am. Being Irish meant something different. It meant being vulnerable, but it also meant I shared a story with the people I had always known, and that I knew, from my own experience, about oppression, but I drew strength from the community stories that gave me pride in my Irish identity. Being a member of the working class means that you have no understanding of how to approach the structures of power to advance yourself, but being a member of the Irish working class in the UK meant that you did know that those structures existed, and you knew that they did not operate in your interests.

Ireland in the 1980s was a country in recession with a sectarian war raging in its Northern province. The key to advancement was education and emigration. Education would free us from the old, grovelling sense of inferiority that had to be grown out through the coming generations as their education gave them access to the world. For the child with talent there was a path forward, but for those on the cusp of the old world and the new, it was hard to shake the old shackles and confidently manipulate the new world. I shared the anxiety of my generation, pursuing education to insulate myself against the constant fear of failure and leaning on my family and neighbours, who were part of the stories and traditions that define us. I moved forward to the new world with one foot firmly rooted in the past. The new Ireland, where an educated population have challenged the orthodoxies of my youth and created an inclusive, secular community, is underpinned by memory and characterised by a cultural inability to accept individual praise. Accustomed as we always were to the group identity, we do not value individual attention, and any compliment paid is likely to be deflected with an immediate disclaimer. To the comment, 'That's a nice dress you have, Kathleen,' my neighbour immediately replied, 'Oh, it was half price in Penneys.' God forbid we would consider ourselves worthy of owning a full-priced dress. Compare that to the burning pride that people have in the west of Ireland in their county football teams and in the nation of Ireland, and the ease with which they analyse their government's actions.

Reflecting on my life as a member of the working class in rural Ireland, I see the strengths and support that identity gave to me. I remember the struggle and I remember the poverty quite well, but I try not to draw a romantic picture of not having enough. I still have a book I received from my mother for Christmas when I was ten years old. It was treasured, not only because I loved the book, but presents were rare. More importantly, I have the strong identity that I learned throughout my childhood and the common language of my ethnic and cultural group. There are daily reminders of words that I had forgotten that I knew, and the ease with which I can suddenly remember their meaning speaks to our shared history. A neighbour recently told me during a conversation about badgers and foxes invading his sheep field: 'Badgers are different. They are real hokers. They hoke up the whole field. Foxes might use one of their old holes or if they do dig, they would only make two holes.' The word 'hoking' brought back a flood of memories of the old days when the rural Irish poor flooded to England and Scotland to dig the potatoes each year. They were known as the tatie hokers.

There were hard times and there were times of great laughter, music and storytelling that I have brought with me in my travels through the United Kingdom, and later the United States, and which have sustained me throughout it all. We carry ourselves with us wherever we go and see the world through our own cultural values. Ireland has taught me well about pride in all that we are and have achieved, and to recognise the struggles that others face each day. In my own village here in Mayo, our neighbour, who is a farmer, wanted to go as part of an Irish Farmers' delegation to Ethiopia. The village raised the money and he made connections and was able to work with Ethiopian farmers. Reflecting on that experience, he commented: 'I didn't know much about what they were growing but I knew poverty when I saw it. We saw enough of that here when I was young. I wanted to help and do what I could because we have been in the same place.' I think he speaks for us all. We remember how it was and the struggle that we had, and we reach out a hand.

# Choose Your Fighter

## *Marc Gregg*

The first time I ever experienced the embarrassed stinging flashes of having my masculinity questioned was when I was playing the game *Tekken 3* with my older brother. I was leaning over our top bunk and he was in the bunk below, and we were deciding who we'd use to beat the digital shite out of each other. Ryan picked his favourite fighter, Paul Phoenix, an all-American muscle-bound hero who was as macho as he was deadly. In turn I chose Ling Xiaoyu, a highly evasive Chinese schoolgirl martial artist with a crush on the brooding main protagonist.

When my six other siblings and I played against Ryan in a video game, we would never really be able to hold a candle to his skill. But *Tekken* was *my game,* and I made sure he knew that. I may not have been able to flick around corners and gun down soldiers like he could, but put us onto the streets of Shanghai and I could throw down like the best of them. Round after round we would play against each other, and each time Xiaoyu would be posing in celebration of her achievement with a massive grin on her face, and the words *YOU WIN* plastered on the TV screen. Mr Phoenix, however, would be crumpled in an exhausted heap on the ground, fairly bested in combat by the effervescent young woman.

I heard the controller hit the floor and leaned over the side of the top bunk to see my brother's head in his hands, exasperated that his skill had failed him.

'Why the fuck do you always pick the girl characters?!'

Even though he swore, and Mum and Dad didn't allow us to swear, I could tell there was no malice in his question. I suddenly realised there was some aspect of what I had done that was shameful to him. What was wrong with picking the girl characters?

They're all just as useful as the male characters and, furthermore, I was the one controlling her, so he couldn't be embarrassed because he was beaten by a woman, could he? The heat of triumph would dismiss this criticism as the bitter grumblings of a sore loser, but his question seemed to follow me, and was asked countless times by my friends growing up, no matter what game it was we played. Only now the question wouldn't be for the sake of curiosity and exasperation. It was a scalding-hot brand wrapped in barbed wire used to discredit my victories and scar me with my failures.

'I just think she's cool...' was always my sheepish reply.

High school brought with it a more solid understanding of how it was I differed from other people my age. Our school was one that had always suffered from the debilitating middle-class anxiety that a large portion of their student body came from working-class backgrounds, so they went out of their way to attract as many better-off families as they could. When they succeeded in obtaining one of their golden geese, those parents who might donate sums of money to the school or serve on PTA boards, they'd make sure their gilded offspring would be awarded as many opportunities as they could get their hands on, leaving the rest of us to fight among ourselves for whatever was left. My younger sister, who would later go to the same school, despite being one of the most academically gifted children in the country at the time of her eleven-plus testing, was initially rejected on the grounds that her disability would cost the school too much money. Of course, they had already made more significant and more expensive changes to accommodate a child from a much wealthier family years before, no questions asked. It took considerable fighting from my parents and the senior staff of her primary school, as well as threats of airing out their discrimination to a local newspaper, to convince them to change their minds.

The teenage years was when the differences between boys and girls became clear to us, and it was then I sensed there was a feeling of betrayal among my male peers at my reluctance to take part in the rituals that ensnared us. I had never realised that we were meant to be fascinated with the form and function of bodies, both our own and especially those of girls, and to an extent I was. But my own body had always had nothing more than a loose association with my spirit and, looking at the others as we would change for a sport that I would inevitably be bad at, I realised my body wasn't like a boy's body either. Our nakedness revealed not only our bare skin, but the terrifying realisation that I craved to both be and have something that was entirely outside of the realms of possibility for someone like me. Boys were collarbones and wide shoulders and biceps, golden or porcelain skin with barely a blemish daring to cross their solid frames. And what was I? I had neither the strength of masculinity that the boys had, nor the softness of femininity I could see in the girls. I was the painter's dirty-water pot, a collection of all the unused colours of God's creations, and they were the illuminated gallery pieces to be photographed in silent awe by tourists. My body became a clear visual indicator that masculinity wasn't just something that I could fail at, it was something that I was biologically barren of.

High school continued to be a soul-crushing experience for me and my friends, and by the time I had entered sixth form I was determined to leave for brighter lights and a bigger city. The educational, social and political institutions that surrounded me seemed suffocatingly small, and every day was an exercise in parading about, a colourful parrot boy who squawked whatever it was people needed to hear from him – some days being more convincing and melodic than others.

I had somehow managed to fall into singing at school, and despite being a latecomer to music compared to my peers, who had been taught since childhood, the choirmaster and the singing teacher thought my voice had promise. They were a husband-and-wife duo who were incredibly kind and compassionate towards me my entire high-school career, and they even gave me a bursary for free singing lessons, among other such generosities. From then on, I pursued singing as if my life depended on it, and slowly, over time I began to realise that my voice was to be my ticket away from the judgemental eyes that seemed to follow me wherever I went.

I had my heart set on London, and my parents' objection to me leaving the country stung at the time. They had raised me to believe that if I worked hard and buckled down, I could do anything, but now their concerned glances at each other whenever I talked about how cool London was going to be felt mocking and cruel.

Looking back, however, I could hardly blame them. I was just one of eight children in my family, and we had never had money floating around. Now their third oldest, who had never really shown an interest in music until two years ago, was suddenly about to jet across the ocean to study *opera*, of all things. None of us had ever even seen an opera before, let alone sung in one!

In an attempt to understand this new passion, my parents came to almost every one of my concerts that they were able to. I remember acting coolly embarrassed when my mum wailed in the front row of my first performance, and even though I had to endure the brotherly teasing I received from my peers, I was secretly thrilled to have moved her in this way. She and my dad would attempt to piece together the lives of long-absent cousins and distant relatives to trace back where this alien ability came from. I had never felt there was anything particularly impressive about my vocal ability – if anything, there remains a naivety to my performances – but the way they spoke about my voice that night felt like I had gifted them something unique and precious. For the first time in my life I felt like I had become someone remarkable.

The performance alone wasn't enough to convince them that I should gallivant off to London. I had always sensed in them a wariness at the idea that talent itself could lead to any sort of financial stability for working-class people, and ultimately, I think they were right. We had been raised on the idea that work was something that you did passionately but suffered through, and the decadent world of opera must have seemed worlds apart from the more practical work both my parents had toiled at themselves.

At the time, their disapproval felt glazed in a thick layer of disbelief in the power of my talent and work ethic to even get me to London in the first place, but now I can see that their discomfort came from the fact that they knew I didn't have the financial backing to infiltrate London or the world of classical music. They didn't have the means to fund any of this adventure, let alone repeat it for any of their other children, and classical music was something they knew next to nothing about – except that people like us were actively discouraged from participating in the first place.

With thanks to three different bursaries, I was eventually able to study in London, but disaster struck in my second year when my largest bursary was axed by the government, grinding my studies to a halt. I was to come home that night via coach, then ferry, then taxi, then train, then car, as we couldn't afford the plane ticket to fly me home at such short notice, and I couldn't continue sleeping on my friend's sofa any longer. I remember the commuters who walked past in their business suits glaring at me, this ugly fat boy covered in snot and tears as he cried loudly on the phone to his dad in the queue to board a Megabus in Victoria Coach Station. My father desperately tried to convince me to take the university's offer of accommodation that was £180 a week and we would 'make it work', but we both knew it wasn't possible. I could hear his heart break for me over the phone, and I knew he felt responsible for not being able to help me achieve this dream. In turn, I was ashamed that I had acted so arrogant and untouchable that I had disregarded the advice of the two people who loved me the most and potentially jeopardised our family's already fragile financial stability.

Not being content with one crisis, I thought, *Well, sure, what's one more?* and decided to finally come out as queer to my best friend, who I had been not-so-subtly in love with for the past two years. 'Queer' was one of my new London terms, and something that my friends from back home, and my parents, to whom I was forcibly outed much later, would misinterpret as gay, but I knew that it wouldn't faze someone like him. For the record, I don't think confessing your deeply repressed feelings for the first time in your life via text at 3 a.m. on the ferry from Holyhead to Dublin is necessarily the best idea, but for a nineteen-year-old whose whole world had just dissolved in front of their very eyes, what's another shame thrown on top, sure?

It didn't go as well as I'd hoped. He was kind and said all the right things, but he didn't share the same feelings that I had, and when I eventually returned to university later that year after my bursary was reinstated, we had countless altercations that eventually ended in the destruction of the friendship altogether. Nevertheless, I think this pivotal moment of my life set in motion a lot of the healing work I had to do, and it allowed me to start disinfecting the noxious ideas about my class and sexuality that were rotting me from the inside out.

My friends were paramount in showing me a way to lay down all this baggage I carried with me. I remember we were sitting necking cans outside our university library at one in the morning, buzzing from the high of cheap music and cheap alcohol, when a man approached us for seemingly innocent conversation. Aimee had broken off the tab of a can of Red Stripe and attempted to slide it onto Finnuala's slender finger. The man had been given one of our cans and was gulping it down when Aimee would grab Finn's now decorated hand and turn to beam at him.

'Look, we're getting married!'

We were all laughing and discussing the details of this hypothetical wedding between our newly betrothed friends when the stranger eyed them both suspiciously and said, 'No, you aren't. Lesbians aren't real. You just haven't found the right men yet.'

Back home I was used to homophobia like this, so in honesty I didn't think much of this open disrespect of both myself and the several other queer friends I was with who had just heard the same ignorant sentiments that I had. I laughed and tried in earnest to engage him on why he was wrong, failing to identify that what this man really wanted was a fight.

I turned to face Finn, and her expression, normally bright and warm and inviting, had sunken, barely concealing a fury that was bubbling intensely beneath the surface. She was lightning, snatching back the can she'd given him moments before, and tipped the entire remaining contents over his head.

'Fuck off, mate.'

She is ashamed of that flash of anger to this day, but in one swift motion she had undone so much of my own self-hatred. It felt like she was saying: *You don't have to take disrespect, Marc. They are wrong and you are right. You are sacred and you are true, and so am I.* She said so much with so few words, and I don't think I would've been able to carry on the days without her unbending will and protection.

*Why the fuck do you always pick the girl characters?!*

To this day I'm still unsure, but I would go back and tell my brother this: *Who fucking cares how you win, so long as you do.*

# Maisie, Lila
# and the Two Jacks

*Angela Higgins*

The closely built estates, with rows of pebble-dashed two-storey houses that gave a haven to former tenement dwellers and housed the workers from Rowntree's, Jacob's, Guinness, Capital Tea and the railway yards, are sprawled wide in suburbs close to the city. These houses, shared by grandparents and grandchildren, mothers, fathers, aunties and uncles, hold histories of generations of workers from those factories that fed the people with sweets, chocolate, biscuits, stout, jam and other groceries.

If a drone, had they existed then, flew over the neat rows built after the war years, gathered around big greens and tidy parades of small shops (the greengrocer selling biscuits by the pound; the pharmacy, butcher and hardware shop), there would be aerial photographs of long back gardens full of fresh-grown vegetables, fruit, clotheslines, makeshift swings, and the odd chicken. The tenants would be visible, bent like the characters in the Millet prints of gleaners and peasants saying the rosary, which often adorned the sitting-room walls, over spades and rakes after their long day's work in the factories and shops, growing food for their families and loving the joy of their blooming flowers. This was a triumph in which people were housed in their own homes, as complete families, with their own door keys. Nana, my maternal grandmother, a laundress when she was younger, proudly polished her lovely brass doorknob and scrubbed the granite step every Saturday till they gleamed. She lived where the streets were named for the rural mountains and ranges – Mourne, Slievenamon, Keeper, Galtymore. The landscapes once familiar to people who brought their rural skills to the city. She was a great one for elbow grease.

In another part of the sprawling working-class suburbs there is an area with streets named after the Irish patriots – O'Leary, Kickham, Emmet, Bulfin, Connolly. If our drone were to home in on one particular street, the pristine gardens with their own fences would be visible. These houses did not have the long back-garden allotments, but had sheds, and pigeon lofts, and dog runs. One house, my paternal grandfather Jack's, had two sentinel evergreen lime-green *Griselinia littoralis* clipped and poised rigidly outside the yellow front door, which only opened for funerals or guests, and never for children. We secretly picked and folded the leaves till they split into tiny crumbs. My lost, depressed grandfather's topiary, an image of perfection, square and pristine, matched only by the weed-free flowerbeds containing measured-out dahlias and red salvias. The regularly mowed lawn, perfectly edged, never touched by child's footfall or football. The sharp edges were measured with the same gift and attention that his painted signs received when he worked as a painter and signwriter in the railway yards.

This house is covered in brown pebble-dash, its original lightness coloured by the atmosphere. The pebble-dash has many sharp edges. Scraping knuckles down the passage at the side, which was the entrance prescribed for kids, and around the corner the perfectly self-built shed, with a corrugated roof, clapboard sides and high windows, leaned against the back wall. The door looked onto another perfect lawn surrounded by a corrugated fence, which kept the world at arm's length. There was the sunny seat where only the head of the household sat in the sunshine, warding off the cats with a washing-up bottle and reading the *Herald* each evening while taking a John Player Blue.

Through the door, the bikes were on the left. There was one for everyday, one for Sunday runs and one for spare parts. On the other side, the perfectly organised workbench: pots of paint in rows and clean paintbrushes in their glasses and tins. This shady place reeked of a mixture of creosote, iodine, kerosene and tobacco smoke. My dead grandmother's old mangle, source of much fun when we helped her with the washing on visits, sat unused in the corner. The kitchen window in the original back wall above the bench, cast a little electric light on that tenebrous, gloomy shed. It was my grandfather's domain.

To get to the kitchen, we went up the step and passed the toilet without a wash-hand basin on the left, to the old back door, and ascended to my grandmother's old realm, where her clean dresser stood proudly adorned with blue-and-white-banded Cornish pottery and her navy flowered pinny hung ready on the hook. Later, when we moved in, this became my mother's place. The kitchen table covered in oilcloth – site of the breakfast challenge of trying to read the back of the folded *Irish Times* upside down in one or other of the alpha male's hands as they read at the breakfast table.

A bath with a cover that served as a worktop stood along one wall, while the geyser, the source of all hot water in the house, the sink, and the gas cooker took up the window wall. Generally, hot baths were taken in Nana's house, when we dropped off her shopping. She had a proper avocado bathroom. Sometimes, too, we went to the Iveagh baths on Saturdays. Every child for a ten-mile radius was sent there for a swim and a wash. In good times, my father piled all the children on the road into the station wagon to go there and treated them to aniseed balls afterwards. The time of that car, which lasted about four years, was a good time, when my dad, who was called Jack after his father, had interesting work, and we could go on holidays and picnics.

The hall stitched the kitchen to the rest of the house. This hallway was created when my parents moved the family from that lovely seaside town, near the mountains, to be close to the city and to look after the old man. On the right, a small sitting room. Upstairs there were three bedrooms. A bunk room for the boys; Grandad's room, which was never seen; and the front room, linoleum-floored. The faint tang of iodine and smoke came from the middle room and became stronger whenever my mother had to deliver a tray of tea to the room.

The front room contained a double bed and a locked wardrobe, and was 'L' shaped, with my bed around the corner, overlooked by a tall, built-in press. This was filled with the bags and bags of fabrics, old clothes, bright threads, wools and braids that were the materials of one of my mother's several trades.

These parents of mine were the children of the workers, offspring of the children of the revolution, who set out for the hopeful newer suburbs buoyed up by regular salaries, permanency and mortgages, and working as teachers and unpaid housewives. Mine returned to their roots so that my mother could care for the elders on both sides.

Moving back in to his father's house after his mother died, my dad redesigned it a little, and they redecorated it, and we children adjusted to a very different world. My mother worked non-stop. She went to the Ladies' Club. She started a playgroup for local children and ran the Summer Projects. When Dad left his civil-service job because he didn't like the politics, too proud to take the dole, he looked for work through friends and contacts, read, and took long walks, sinking into his first depression. Mum went to work in a shop in the city centre, trading luxury goods to American tourists and exotic international visitors visiting the sites of the ancient university. She loved to tell their stories when she got home, and she loved recounting all the little dramas of the day. She travelled to interesting places by association with her customers and the beautiful and sometimes tacky craft in the shop.

She stood all day in the shop, and two evenings every week she gathered the energy to go to the vocational school to teach sewing, coming back inspired by her students. When she left school, she worked in the same tea company as her father, and learned her trade as a seamstress at night, paying for classes. She mass-produced funky leatherette tote bags and cushions for fundraisers and garden fetes; made costumes for every dance school performance and Ladies' Club musical, stitching like a madwoman with her head down on evenings when she wasn't teaching. She needed to work in a shop and teach to make sure the family was fed and dressed.

When the dishes were washed and put away, that sewing machine was on the table, her foot on the pedal, guiding it through the gears, the whole household vibrating to the creation of long seams, and listening to the fitting, shaping, connecting, problem-solving and pressing. Sometimes she went on and on while the household slumbered, not because she had to, but because she couldn't draw herself away – 'I'll just do one more seam, and then I'll tidy up.' The joy of completing another item driving her on, but still getting up for work the next morning, uniform neat after a stand-up wash in the kitchen.

The small house was a place of no hiding. Sometimes it rattled and shuddered with the raised voices of adults. For us children, my grandfather's rule was that we 'must be seen and not heard' while in the house. There was an air of bitterness, and tension about lingering and present histories unknown to us children.

Every week there was a shopping trip on foot, after the car and the job were lost, to the bright new shopping centre to get the family shopping, then Nana's shopping, and to sometimes have a bath at hers. There were two statuesque spinster sisters, Maisie and Lila, who lived near Nana, and who carried a mystique for us. We were slightly scared of them, but curious too, although much too shy to talk to them or ask about them.

Mum used to go to the Bull Ring for her fabrics. The market was a treasure trove, piled high with rolls and rolls of many-coloured materials, and all kinds of threads, bindings and ribbons. It could be quite scary, crammed as it was with all the expressions and yarns of the people who lived around, shouting and roaring to buy and sell at the best rate. One day, after a visit to Nana's, we took one especially satisfying trip there on the number 21 bus, full of chatty women in headscarves and old characters in overcoats threatening to shoot us all down, and my mother seemed very happy. We came home on the bus loaded down with large black bags full of yards and yards of blue-and-white polka-dot cotton, pink-and-white floral lawns, and lace, buttons and ribbons, soon to be rattling through the Singer at a ferocious pace.

Immediately after that visit, Mum got to work, first pattern-cutting on the clear table, then sewing into the night, the fabric feeding through her hands, rippling and surging in folds. Her clever fingers constantly sensing into it, feeling for tautness or slackness or what was just right, and not too tight. Feeling for changes in the rhythm or vibration that might indicate a knot or a need for new bobbin thread, making little mechanical adjustments to keep the old Singer singing nicely. Adjusting the presser foot and adjusting the pressure of her foot on the pedal. Sometimes her variable mood was clear from the sound of the sewing machine.

I watched from the doorway to the kitchen, with its gently curving arch, a decoration installed when that hall was built, woodchip walls rough under my fingers. Night after night the sewing machine rattled, sewing long, long seams that went on for ever, her foot on the pedal gradually building to a crescendo, the needle hammering up and down, each stitch a means to an end.

'Why are the dresses so big?' I asked. There seemed to be no one she could measure these against, and they looked so shapeless when they were held up, stitched seams perfectly finished and pressed. 'Maisie and Lila are very big women,' she said. She worked so hard making those dresses and more, sewing with intent until they were complete.

That house shook with her energy and continuous work in service to her extended family and community, not as a maid in a fine house like her own mother – this was the seventies, after all. Shirley Conran and Germaine Greer had crossed the threshold. She never stopped advising, fundraising, making, helping, working, constantly creating as the needle stitched on day after day into night after night, and living a life of constant work and occupation. She had this drive, gears rarely changing, only stopping to have a little think to solve problems for a neighbour, bring meals upstairs to my grandfather, who had become less energetic, or chat to a little child. The bags of fabric in the tall press never got smaller. The press, bursting with stuff, sometimes flowing out to avalanche over my small bed, muffling the noises from the rest of the house. In and out of shorter and shorter periods of work, my father sank further into depression, made worse by economic recession. Lifting out of it sometimes to educate us children in news, history, religion and art, and tell us about whatever he was reading at the time, taking us for long walks, never breaking stride, through the city at night, discussing stuff. The rows and fights got worse, and we left our grandfather's house.

In the hospital, years and two or three house rentals later, this working woman who fought desperately to keep a roof over her children's heads, food on the table and power in the cables, now silenced and weakened by illness and anorexia, sought desperately to tell me something important.

Clearing their last home – in a charitable trust – after she died, we found the reason why. In another tall cupboard there were size 12 stilettos, man-sized women's underwear and dresses. I wondered whether those dresses – polka-dot and lawn, large, pretty dresses – were for Maisie and Lila at all, or whether they were for my dad, who was now languishing where he could not express himself at all.

I felt her years of pain, financial strain and shame deeply, their secret lives grating and scraping like the pebble-dash through everything else they tried.

# Nostalgia

## *Rosaleen McDonagh*

Roads and motorways, traffic jams, congestion and fossil fuels, frustrated drivers moving from lane to lane without warning. There are four lines of traffic approaching the motorway. M4, the M11, M6 or M8. My route is towards the west, Sligo. Nostalgia kicks in. Being on the road was very much part of my childhood.

In my car the rain is pelting across the windscreen. Struggling to find the button for the wipers. Loud beeps from other road users add to my stress. The torrential rain makes the colours of the traffic lights blurry. Lowering the radio, struggling to centre myself. My peripheral vision is propelling me to look left. There is a roof, higher than the wall that's supposed to hide it. For a moment, my attention is diverted from the traffic, the road and rain. The entrance of a site is exposed. Emotions conjure up inside me that bring me back to a place where once was home. There's a tear trickling down my cheek.

*

That tear is for memories of hot days. Sitting at the entrance of our trailer with the door open, the smell of my mother's home-made bread. The sun making it difficult to see across the site. The tear also renders up the fear of when the site was raided. Five o' clock in the morning the sound of police sirens. Bursting into the caravan, looking for stolen goods, tax and insurance, drugs, firearms. They pull my brothers and my father out of bed. Trousers and boots, no shirt. Made to stand in the middle of the site alongside thirty or forty other men and boys of various ages. The women and children, including my mother, are terrified. Two emergency response police burst into our bedroom. My sister and our smaller siblings, some of them infants, are frightened of the guns and uniforms. One of the guards pulls me out of bed. My sisters tell him my legs don't work. It's too late; they pull my resistant body and I fall to the floor. The chaos outside has gone quiet. The young man in uniform stares at his colleague, then turns his eyes back to my curled-up, twisted feet and hands. He's not sure whether to offer help. His colleague has already reached for my body. This frightens me more, lying on the floor of the bedroom in our trailer. A third officer arrives and calls his two comrades. They walk past my mother. The men are arrested. Two hours later, in dribs and drabs, they come back into the site in clusters of four or five. Nothing was found; all tax and insurance related to our vehicles were in date. By midday the media has got hold of the story. They expected the raid would expose criminal activity. Later in the afternoon my father had the radio on. We're all gathered around; the Gardaí are having an emergency press conference. They want to apologise; they've made a mistake. It was the wrong site. The wrong men. The wrong family and the wrong Travellers.

In recent times the HiAce van has been replaced by MPVs. An early memory was sitting in that particular van with my father and mother, who were driving from Sligo back to Dublin. September; school holidays were over. Many times in the classroom my community was referred to. Poets, writers. Listening to the description, knowing instinctively that they're talking about us. It was too dangerous to ask the question, yet there was a knowing. An adrenaline rush of pride, secretly and shyly imbuing the knowledge that Yeats's *Tinker* painting captured the faces of Traveller women like my grandmother and her mother. There's no acknowledgement from me or the teacher of what's happening while she turns the pages of the art-history book.

As an adult, my curiosity and taste is cultivated, defined where we are located in the archives of our museums. The bourgeois teachings and assimilation practice have ensnared me. Echoed by my forced inculcation of the elitism that's embedded in academia. Somewhere in my journey that social contract of respectability was signed. Despite all efforts of resistance, my persona has been moulded by the characteristics of the middle class, cultivated typically with reference to perceived materialistic values or conventional attitudes. Elevating myself out of poverty came at a price. They tell me my place is in a gallery. Where freedom is limited. Agency is lost. Subjectivity is made subservient to that ever-present settled critique. They look, they judge, they write. They speculate, anticipate. Yet in this exhibition my self is stolen.

There is little or no room for dialogue. They own the space and very soon they will own me.

On being brought to the National Gallery by an art historian to see portraits of my own people painted by another settled man, my companion suggested the third floor, the Yeats room. For a moment there was an uncomfortable hesitance. We made our way towards the lift. On several occasions my visits to this room invoked a sense of unease. With great enthusiasm my companion produced a library book about these particular paintings. The tinge of blue echoed through. My own viewing of these paintings was of wild coastal scenes, horse races, farmers, card players and local shops. The colloquialisms felt familiar. Yeats is believed to have said that the deep, intense blue was 'a colour that always affected him'.

A rage came upon me, feeling that spaces like this had always been closed off to people like me. Nonetheless, here we were on the walls, made sterile, immobile and objectified. Yet somehow the colours, the vibrant rawness of the paintings resonated, and my rage was overwhelmed by nostalgia for my own childhood. Irony is not lost on this presentation of us, of Travellers, as having an integral relationship with Irish identity. Us, with our aggravated history of misunderstanding and hostility, always the objects of the settled gaze. The paintings reminded me of places where often strangers would stop their cars to photograph us.

It's estimated that Yeats had twenty-four pieces that depicted Traveller imagery. He wasn't the only one. Nano Reid, Louis le

Brocquy and Mick O'Dea. Unlike other painters who made portraits of Travellers, Yeats pushed himself beyond the encampment and propelled his portfolio to include the female and male Traveller form. Slowly moving through Yeats's family room, more paintings of diverse figures. The clown, the person of small stature and the tinsmith. Sitting in silence, the chemistry between my companion and the electricity between my body and the paintings creates a complex pressure. Yeats does not romanticise Travellers; he paints faces that are lived-in; even the oil paint itself has a rich texture that feels authentic to our ethnicity. The tension of the legacy of misappropriation. The canon of artists and writers making their careers from art depicting a culture not their own, so that we Travellers become artefacts of Irish heritage devoid of any tangible recognition of our own agency. Tilting my head, my response is coded. The backdrop of my own narrative also curates the tension between the outside gaze and the inside landscape.

The question of ownership is rhetorical. These artefacts are housed in buildings where our living presence causes distress and subversion. This lies between the artist's settled identity and the Traveller of the painting's subject. Studying the painting, cautiously glancing, enquiring. The close proximity of my companion is telling. The conversation about the paintings is full of contradiction. Reticence engulfs me. The composure of my poise becomes unsettled. Turning, moving, attempting to create some distance. The interruption to our familiarity disorientates him. The sudden chasm creates confusion. It makes a new silence. My attention is ignited by the painting's brashness. Yeats's women are assertive, in content and form. His intentions come with a discerning invitation.

Boldness dares me. Whispering with absolute certainty: 'Travellers, Travellers, Travellers.' The word reverberates around the room.

Our conversation about the paintings was full of contradiction. Reticence engulfed me, and in the silence, the brashness and boldness of Yeats's women dared me. We both were drawn to the painting entitled *Singing 'Oh Had I the Wings of a Swallow'*, which illustrates a young woman singing for her supper, on a train in 1920s Ireland. Rapidly glancing at the painting, then turning towards me. His words: *gens du voyage*, the French word for Traveller people. A slow smile gathers momentum. We move closer to Yeats' painting. The passion of the Tinker woman. In this particular moment, the sense of being watched, being under surveillance, is overwhelming. The fear of punishment, of being found out, hangs heavy in the air between us.

The memory conjures up the songs that we sang as children, also the song of struggle and survival. My brothers and sisters would be in the back. Singing, laughing and fighting over lemonade and biscuits. Mam would have a quiet sadness. Soon the journey would be over. Tears, hugs and goodbyes were being prepared. The separation had no elegance. Tears from adult and child. My father looking into the distance, awkward with the power and status of nuns. My brothers and sisters looking out the back window of the HiAce van. The sterile smell of the institution, a combination of polish, boiled cabbage and pee all suppressed. My mother is stopped at the entrance.

The big house. The residential institution for children who became repositories of violence from the state. No state exams. No expectations. No value. No love. No individuality. Broken bones to match the many broken or suppressed identities. That place held the smell of stigma. All kinds of children were put into these places. Poverty flourishes in the midst of silent, unnoticed histories. It's where Traveller and settled met and formed an act of resilience against power and coercion. It was where the dirt of society gathered and flourished. The handover is swift. Nuns distract my mother by focusing on her pregnant belly. My body is pulled, my arms loosened from her neck. Her smell is vanishing rapidly. Within seconds firmness and hostility awakens. Clothes are stripped from my body. My head and hair are searched for lice. Different clothes with labels, numbers are put on me. There are no bright colours. The fabric is hard from too many washes. Automatically a young woman in a uniform, neither a nun nor a nurse, warns me to speak properly. Diction, the settled way of saying things.

At the Ballinasloe Horse Fair, a place where commercial and cultural material was bought, bartered and borrowed. Settled people wanted our ponies, our horses. Not always our presence. Our trip to Ballinasloe, like many other families, was a way of meeting our own. Families from various different camps around the country. A marking of the dead. A possible opportunity of marriage. An exchange of a song. Mostly, a territory that was ours. Where others sought permission to enter.

At the fair one year, when my father and mother were chatting with other adults, my sister and I spotted a small Shetland pony. Jumping out of the van without paying attention to how small we were, both of us hit the ground with a thump. Our motivation was to pet and ask could we feed the horse. After the fall, the crowds gathered. The owners of the Shetland allowed me to sit on the horse all that day, so I didn't have to walk. My sister was raging.

On the roads there would be families and trailers in every county. Familiarity and comfort in that insular recognition that was only known among us. Traveller iconography was the tall, round churn cans. With lids that were like soldiers' helmets standing outside gleaming chrome trailers. Every family had one or two to store water. My sisters and I would have spent many a long hour shining up the churn cans, which would gleam in the sun. The women would have washed clothes and blankets and then hung them on a bank behind the trailer. Getting water from a local pump, trying to boil it on an open fire. There was always a hidden compromise whether the precious water would be used to clean, cook or wash with.

Dad would always salute the men on the road. He knew their family names and where their people were from. Invariably the conversation with them would focus on finding a safe and clean place to camp for a couple of weeks. As these conversations were happening, there was a sense of urgency. My mother would start folding and putting items of crockery, jewellery and blankets away. Nothing was expressed verbally but it was the way my father was standing with the other men who were camped on the road. My mother, her business, gave us the signal to be ready. The eviction, the sense of fear and terror still puts a wrench on my spine. The bulldozers, the men in balaclavas – hired security by the state, the local politician and the priest fighting with each other. The priest defending a humanitarian cause. The politician amplifying the sentiments of those who did not want their town and village 'spoiled' by the Traveller aesthetic.

The beoirs and the children ignoring the politics of justice. Their attention was focused on keeping the children safe and knowing that there was no other planned place to move to. The aim was to pack as fast as possible. Some women and their husbands took an admirable stance. They weren't moving. The aggression. The men in their balaclavas sounded local. Maybe they served us in a shop, taught us in the school or even shook our hands in Mass. We were in the van; the trailer was locked and hooked onto the towbar. The negotiations were in full swing. Territory of land and road ownership was being argued. Occasionally there might have been a silent look between my mother and some of the neighbours camped alongside our trailer, who had circled the politician. That look carried an unspoken judgement. In response, my mother, with an infant in her arms, would make the baby wave back at the woman's stare. The wave of the baby is my mother letting them know that she understands why some Traveller women felt it was safer for their children to move before the confrontation with the men in balaclavas became too dangerous. My mother, like most women, recognises and understands in a non-verbal way how women of all generations are caught in a compromise.

Each name, symbol, ritual triggers. Ubiquitous with clarity even in the echelon of a settled environment. It's there. It's always there. Fragments of our identity wanting to be restored and acknowledged. The silent nod, the wink. The clearing of the throat. We know. Yet another town, another location and another sense of loss. Mam and Dad would remind us that their generation lived and moved in a barrel-top wagon. For so long the iconography of Traveller identity was so scarce and so hidden. The image of the barrel-top wagon resonated in a hazy way. That haze was made fuzzy by a juxtaposed set of emotions. We didn't see ourselves in the landscape or the cultural fabric in the way maybe settled artists did.

The barrel-top wagon seemed more pleasurable to settled people. Romantic. As if it was made for the television. Similar to the open-fire singalong. The wagon and the singalong became remote versions of who and what our culture represented. They told us a story about ourselves via a dominant settled gaze and narration. 'Knacker drinking'* became part of the settled youth vocabulary. The phrase was never subtle. There was no reflective or illuminative way to demonstrate that the refusal to let us in – access to pubs and other amenities – was a form of double pejorative positioning. It was almost part of a rebranding of some public-relations campaign where we sold ourselves to ourselves or maybe to a younger generation, while settled people looked on.

My father could not read. His generation seemed to have a built-in satnav. Occasionally, if we were in a town or a county that he didn't know that well, he'd whisper to one of us children to read the sign on the road. Only once did we tell him the wrong directions and add a good forty miles on to our journey.

Modernity generates new ways of expressing our ethnicity. Fluidity of culture brings expression that leaves no room for any

---

\* The phrase 'knacker drinking' is used in the vernacular to describe drinking in the outdoors or in a field. Travellers have been denied access into pubs or recreational facilities. In contemporary contexts the phrase is deemed racist and offensive, and will soon be part of hate crime legislation.

generation to become stagnant. Innovation brings a vocabulary that takes cognisance of our forebears' algorithms. An inbuilt curator narrates our undocumented history. Artefacts such as folklore and music create the conditions for a Traveller renaissance.

Houses, apartments and overcrowded, unserviced sites is where we find ourselves. Our young are isolated, disorientated and often dislocated from our spirit. The pull of progress. A code of hiding, pretending and shaming. The racism, be it minute or flagrant. It's ever-present and there is an intuitive practice of preparing. Fragments of our identity get lost in the debris of what is known as growth. Families are dispersed, stolen and broken. We became lost to a myth. Romanticised and sanitised.

The politics of survival. Activism, meetings, demonstrations, policies: they steal our dignity. The burden of representation, the knowing that this journey of repetitive struggles of survival will continue into several generations. There will be martyrs and icons. They will be honoured and adored in our history, music and art. They will be referred to as the heroes, the strong ones. Then there's the casualties. The ones that frequently find themselves asking: heritage, identity, ethnicity, what does it mean? The ones who vehemently deny. Every generation: it is their duty to criticise, question and respond to a sense of ignominy towards their identity being prescribed in the form of tradition. The kickback is communicated with fragility that reverberates a set of emotions to deflect the outside ridicule of racism. The ones who struggle with the fact that their children or grandchildren step out of an heirloom, a closet that has kept Traveller ethnicity in a tight knot. The ones that look away in despair when their children dance and celebrate a resurgence about who and what they want to be. There are no answers to the questions about ancestors' addresses or what town they came from.

Nostalgia relies on an unsafe memory. Complexity brings tension. Reinventing, reminiscing, emotional memories, feelings rise and fall. Similar to native indigenous people, the Māori, the Australian Aboriginal people, we reinvent the essence of our ethnicity. Be it urban or rural, a tear will always fall driving past sites. The vibrancy and tenacity of our ethnicity is not dependent on any particular setting. Traditions are being pulled and stretched in all directions. Our Pavee radar ensures we'll always recognise each other, embracing a new reality. Traveller iconography has become more subtle and sophisticated. The Traveller aesthetic will always have a delicate ease and elegance.

The rain has stopped. Pulling the key out of the ignition. Home is an apartment. The concrete environment allows for very little air and open spaces. Family, community connection; it's not here nor behind a high wall. There's a woman three doors down. Her surname... but I can't be sure. We look at each other. Suspicious. Hoping neither of us will give each other away. In the lift, the tight space, searching for a marker, an earring, an accent, reducing our ethnicity to something tangible. The niceties of casual encounters are passed between us. The onlooker, the third person, has no idea of the dynamics that are being played out. Instead he insists on referring to us as ladies. Our eyes meet at this moment. We catch, we both know, this time we got away with it. We fooled the settled man.

# The Speedway

## *Stephen O'Reilly*

My favourite time was around twenty past eleven at night when
the fairground jenny spun down and hundreds of coloured lights
slowly dimmed to darkness before me and I would stand there
with a styrofoam cup of coffee in one hand and a congealing
hamburger in the other, feeling like the Emperor of the Universe,
the master of all I dimly surveyed. Listening to the chink of keys
and money in the distance as somebody locked up, the laughter of
lovers outside the grounds as they went down to the beach or back
to their caravans. The smells of wax and diesel fumes, chips and
candyfloss. The smell of the sea and the peppery electric smell of
the dodgems.

I stood on the steps of the Speedway, its heavy carved
motorbikes and animals quiet now, their evening spent undulating
over wooden hills and valleys at breakneck speeds beneath the
glow of myriad coloured bulbs, winking in time to the tick of
the rider's terror. The long wail of a siren at that moment when

the lights went off, when the whole thing felt ready to fly apart in the darkness and scatter riders, motorbikes and animals across the grounds. The slow, giddy return to normal, shakily stepping off, legs stiff and surprised, a knowing smile at those waiting their turn. Those poor hoors who didn't know what they were letting themselves in for. The Northern boys standing aloofly by to collect the money from them as they clambered aboard, everyone wanting a motorbike rather than the bears or horses or dragons, which were seen to be somehow soft.

The Northern boys had motorbikes. Shiny Japanese yokes they rode into town at the start of the summer, staying in tents and caravans while they worked their way through the warm weeks, spraying scorn over those poor unfortunate idjits who could only dimly glimpse the scalding joys of speed and motion through a fifty-pence fairground ride. They stood up on the barriers around the edge of the Speedway's rippling platform, crudely tattooed arms folded, bodies leaning impassively inward against the spin of the machine. Cool incarnate while the punters squealed incoherently.

The girls loved them.

There was always one or two of them waiting patiently on the steps of the Speedway each night. All brown skin and denim, sometimes wearing the boys' heavy leather jackets given to them the evening before as some sort of contract. Down on their annual holiday to be replaced the following week again by someone new and just as pretty, smelling of salt and sweat and their mother's perfume. To disappear arm in arm, laughing and giggling up the town for chicken and chips or down towards the beach where the mysteries lay.

My first pay packet. My first real fight. My first kiss and the clumsy fumbling of youth all happened against the gaudy backdrop of those summers at the fairground. The slow passage of each day measured by the albums of Dr Hook, Hot Chocolate, Smokie and Sister Sledge blasting out of the fairground's tired eight-track.

I'd been at the graveyard that week. Some kid, a couple of years behind me at school, who had gone to bed and not woken up, and Hot Chocolate echoing out over the town from the giant single speaker mounted on the roof of the Speedway. The heavy bass of 'You Sexy Thing' reverberating from the walls of arcades and crooked rows of guest houses. One of the men behind me, conscious of the occasion, said in a low voice, 'I'd effing give him a sexy thing if I was standing next to him.' Rain dripped off the bearers as they lowered the small coffin into the ground, the crowd wincing at each hollow bump. The priest spoke out of a small black book, while an old man held an umbrella over his head with one hand, and one for himself with the other. His magnified eyes darted around the mourners behind thick black frames, looking for all the world like a man who had decided to give himself up and was uncertain of the treatment he might receive at his captors' hands.

The rain fell faster and harder. Some of the mourners began to lose their footing on the muddy inclines covered in marram grass from where they had chosen to view the proceedings. Slipping slightly and resuming their prayers with sheepish 'look what nearly happened to me' expressions.

Then it was over. They began to drift away from the small grave in huddled groups of twos and threes.

'Is there room in the car for PJ?'

'Could you drop us off at the corner?'

Most had walked the short distance out of the town behind the coffin and didn't fancy the walk back now that it was lashing down. There was a loud thud and they turned as one, back towards the grave, where two men with shovels were beginning to fill in the earth, anxious themselves not to get too wet. The heavy clods of mud and stones tumbling down onto the pine lid of the coffin. Inside the small box the noise must have been deafening and I couldn't see how anything alive or dead could have slept through it. I turned and left, eager to get to work. To get back to the music and the living and away from that miserable hole in the ground that had something to do with betrayal.

I worked for Mr Charles Fry on the darts stall.

Mr Fry was a very English gentleman who had been a Shakespearean actor decades before and was the owner of the most wonderfully subversive shirt I had ever seen. I'd been standing next to him one day, leaning out over the carpet-covered counter of the stall, chatting, and suddenly noticed something that made me laugh. The cream shirt had a pattern of fine purple lines, an intertwined mass of nude male and female bodies, coupled, exchanging joy.

Mr Fry usually wore that shirt once or twice a week and I had never noticed the detail before in the two years that I'd worked for him. From the distance it seemed to be no more than a relic of sixties psychedelia. Now, for some reason, I found my eyes continually drawn to it. I wondered where I could get something like that. I'd love to wear it to Mass, maybe. To sit there damned, a writhing mass of sin as the others traipsed up the aisle to communion to stick out their pink, wet tongues for the bland taste of salvation.

'Where did you get it?' I asked him eventually.

'I really don't know. My wife must have bought it for me.'

I could not imagine that. The not knowing where you got something. It spoke of a wealth of experience and the slow rub of time that was still alien to me.

Neither did I know Mr Fry's wife. She had died years before and I thought that she must have been an extraordinary woman but said nothing more about it, embarrassed by my fascination. Staring at the patterns of the shirt whenever its owner's back was turned. Wondering what it would be like to have someone, to hold someone like that. To have someone wait for me on the steps of the Speedway, wearing my leather jacket, which was grey, because Mr Fry had forbidden the wearing of black leather jackets behind the counter, not wanting his staff to look like hards.

She stood watching me and I could see the shape of her legs backlit inside her summer dress. Something glittered on her ankle while she projected an inner calm and certainty that I knew, even at fourteen, would never be entirely mine.

'Do you wanna go, wee girl?'

My best Northern accent. Broadening the vowels, drawling it out to her as a lure.

'That's awful. What do I have to do?'

'Sorry. Are you down for the week, then?'

'Aye. From Belfast.'

She looked older than I did. Long-limbed, shoulders beginning to redden slightly outside her dress. Face freckled and wary of me. I took that to be a good sign, desperately wanting to look slightly dangerous. Pleased with myself that I seemed to be holding her attention.

I handed her the darts, telling her to score under twenty with three darts, all darts must score, and that the attendant's decision was final. Like all good fairground games, it was deceptively simple.

'Go on, have a go.'

Two of the darts stuck but the third ricocheted off the wire of the dartboard and embedded itself in the heel of my runner. I presented her with one of the prizes off the shelf. A fluffy pink and purple monkey that had a toilet-roll body and fur that could have been made of asbestos for all I knew, or cared at that moment.

'Listen, why don't you come back later on tonight. I get off at ten.'

She looked directly at me, more amused than I would have liked, toying with the monkey's fur, which was coming away in little clumps that drifted off in the breeze from the beach.

'Sure. OK.'

'Really?'

'Why not?'

She looked up at the Speedway, where a shirtless Northern boy holding two styrofoam cups of coffee in one hand deftly grabbed hold of the spinning rail with the other to haul himself aboard against the centrifugal force of the ride.

'Do you know those lads?'

'Oh aye. Taught them all they know. Don't let the old guy see that monkey or he'll do the Hulk on it.'

And I laughed at that. The image of the elderly, refined Charles Fry turning into the Hulk, green biceps rippling and tearing through his softly pornographic shirt, trousers shrunk up around his calves with anger.

*

She came back for me that night with two of her friends and we went for a walk along the seafront, the others trailing behind. We talked about our towns, what we liked and what we hated, and just when I'd worked up enough courage to kiss her, she kissed me instead, and I felt the warmth of her body radiate through her thin dress into the cool night air and wondered why she tasted of salad cream. And did all girls taste of salad cream? Was that the natural female taste? Were there different flavours? What did I taste like? And then later when it was over, we walked back towards the fairground hand in hand.

I lost her on the Speedway.

I went to get them ice creams and when I came back the three of them were up on the ride with two of the Northern boys hanging out over them and I felt my stomach do a long, lazy flip, one of the ice creams sliding off its cone and onto my runner with a soft plop as I stood there like an idiot, knowing how this scene almost always ended, having seen variations of it enacted twice a day.

Binning the cones, I tore up the steps, watching the motorbikes and animals blur past, hesitating for a second while the Speedway built up even more speed, and as I finally leapt, the lights went out and the siren wailed and somehow I had a purchase on the platform, one hand desperately hanging onto the rail, relentless centrifugal force pushing me down into a crouch as I whirled around on the outer edge of the machine. Glancing up, I saw her look curiously over the side of the railing at me, perhaps suspecting some joke.

I let go and caromed backwards across the wooden slats on my behind, watching her recede, fetching up with a solid thunk against a pillar, the Northern boys hooting their derision as they surfed past.

'Are you all right?'

'Ah yeah. I'm grand.'

'We're going for something to eat,' she said. 'Are you coming?'

'I think I'll sit here a wee while. You go on. I'll see you later.'

I was afraid to move. The pain was enormous. It was all that mattered. I'd always assumed that 'breaking your hole' had just been a figure of speech.

She nodded.

'See you later.'

Only I didn't, but that didn't matter too much. Another door to childhood had closed behind me and there were still six weeks of the summer left.

The next time I'd have a better grip.

# Revelations

### Dave Lordan

The most shocking of the emerging stories held that one of these suddenly arrived, dreadlocked, Doc Marten-ed, combat-trousered wild ones had flashed his long, thick, swingable cock at a neighbour, from some clearing in the midst of their bizarre and (to all our eyes, my own included) alien encampment. There was nothing besides the encampment talked about by anyone on Bog Road that morning. Gossip, local-radio-inspired misinformation, and witnessed fact mingled and contended for dominance in every conversation that was had. So, by 10 a.m. the Mickey Swinger had achieved his local fame – so much of it that he has not been forgotten on Bog Road, even to this day.

It was a mobile commune of fire-jugglers and saw-players and acid-house ravers, of sixties free-lovers and eighties Crass acolytes, of hunt saboteurs and Bakuninist Wiccans, a menagerie of dropouts and irregulars aboded in the strangest of convoys – repurposed horseboxes, minibuses, ambulances, double-decker buses, HiAce vans, even army transport trucks. The commune had bloomed overnight in our Fairfield while we were sleeping. It could all have escaped from somebody's deeply feverish DT withdrawal dream or be something the Fairfield itself had dreamed into being – a Boschian collage formed from the time-freed fragments of thousands of fairs and circuses it had hosted through so many centuries past and gone, and dead to all but imagination – the great resurrector!

They were all real, though; they were all flesh and blood and full of piss just like us. They had convoyed here from the UK, ostensibly to enjoy and participate in our brand new Clonakilty Busking Festival, August 1988. This festival was the project of a committee of local businesspeople and live-arts lovers who wanted to find some way of livening the town up and making a few bob for the townspeople after a long and deeply demoralising recession. They hoped to attract a portion of respectable bohemia, polite balladeers to entertain at every street corner. In turn, the sound plan went, these world-class buskers would attract 10,000 middle-aged Dylan fans who would fill the B & Bs, hotels, pubs and restaurants – a kind of Christmas in August for Clon.

It was good plan, no doubt. *But*, says my old neighbour Muck to me one day below in no. 4, as he was stirring his White Lightning Stew (cider, mutton, carrots and spuds, salt and pepper to taste), *how do you make God laugh? Dunno,* says I. *Tell him your plans,* came the reply. And that was the way with the Busking Festival. Sure, folkies and respectable bohemians arrived in dribs from East Village, Brittany, the Isle of Skye... in enormous mobiles and quaintly hippified Volkswagen vans. But they were more than overwhelmed by far greater numbers of these ragged-trousered anarchists and barefoot council-estate refugees in lurid vehicles, luridly graffitied with Situationist slogans (*Beneath the pavement, the beach; Be realistic – demand the impossible; I take my desires for reality because I believe in the reality of my desires*), which the entire town was now attempting to decipher, some fearing they were cryptic verses from Satan's Bible announcing the end times.

The festival committee were horrified by this turn of events, and they were also afraid – was this going to cost more money than it raised? Was it going to ruin the town's touristic reputation, rather than make it? Sure, couldn't this mob of Gomorrans overrun the town, rob every premises in it, burn it to the ground, if they got going atall? Fear of a Hunnish sacking now gripped the imagination of shopkeepers and alcohol merchants, who, alongside the clergy, the Shickaloney and school principals, formed the ruling order in Clonakilty. Instead of throwing open the doors for the entire weekend, some were now contemplating putting up the shutters, just as they would for an Irish Traveller funeral or wedding. The pubs were hiring extra security, the supermarkets expected a tsunami of shoplifters. Something would have to be done about it, and done quick. It is said by certain sources – and I can't confirm or deny it – that an emergency, expanded, un-minuted committee meeting was held in a hurry. It is very probable, whisper certain sources, that the Gardaí were pressed upon to take immediate and forceful action to save the weekend from the barbarian hordes.

*He was going for a slash, brazen as you like and right out in the open, and when he saw her looking down at him from her upstairs window, he pushed it out so she would get a good look at it, and he grinning and guffawing at her the whole time, the filthy get.*

This is how my mom's friend relayed it, and she had heard it from another friend. Not only flashed then, but swung his mickey at her, it being the size of an elephant's trunk. Some believed the rumour and thought it a great disgrace, but others were sceptical: *Wouldn't she have needed binoculars to see even a prize-winning mickey from that distance – there were two or three furlongs in it, surely?* Others thought it was wish-fulfilment, her being a single lady in her early forties aboded with her elderly parents and rumoured never to have ventured far beyond Clonakilty.

*'Tis like the time they put something from Glastonbury in the soup below in Fiddlers Green and when I was walking home after I saw a naked Lady Godiva fly over on a jennet,* said Muck. And after another sup from his mug of Devil's Bit Broth (cider, turnips, onions, peas, salt and pepper to taste): *Do you know what, though? It mightn't have been her who started the rumour atall, but someone else just having the craic at her expense, aisy pickings that she is, the poor oul cratur.*

Nevertheless, she was not the only one on the terrace to be greatly perturbed by the arrival of a large band of unfamiliars, unannounced and uninvited, into our Fairfield. In centuries past, it was a literal Fair-field, and now served us as a playground, a sports pitch, and grazing for the few among us who still kept and traded horses and donkeys. By custom, it was considered to belong to the residents of Bog Road in common. This was not a legal truth – the deeds were held by the county council, but it was a moral truth established by long-held practice. For sure, we all saw it as our field and our field alone, and had even concocted a tale whereby the field had been left to us by some feudal gentleman long ago, but that his will had been nefariously destroyed by the county council to hide this fact. Anyway, our whole childhood and much of our adolescence took place in the Fairfield, which was big enough for all of us to do as we pleased – shifting, boozing, donkey-riding, rounders, soccer. We were also accustomed to the field playing annual host to a succession of circuses and funfairs. The older boys earned money helping to erect and dismantle the tents and rides. Smaller kids got free rides and tickets for being locals, and we befriended the children of the carnival workers too, for the while they were around. We were always down in the dumps when the colour and excitement left the field after the last circus truck pulled out. We all dreamed of running away with the circus but none of us ever had the guts in the end. *Round here,* said Muck, in between sucking on one of the cloves that provided his non-cider-based nourishment, *it's the circus runs away from us.*

These New Age Travellers were like the circus, but they were not the circus. They confused us and made us anxious. *Who in sweet Jesus's name were they atall atall? ... What's that bad, strong smell coming off them? Incense for devil-worshippers is it! ... That music, well, I wouldn't call it music, but whatever it is they're playing would go in and out through your head!*

Some were afraid they would be robbed or attacked, others of 'drugs' and what berserker things might occur under their influence; more were irritated by their disregard for conventional dress and grooming, or by their massed Englishness – the brutality of the Crown forces towards locals was within living memory still – many had the same accents and the same faces as the lumpen scum who had filled the ranks of the Black and Tans and raped and marauded their way through West Cork.

Really though, they were nothing like the proto-Brownshirts

that Lloyd George had sent over to massacre our grandparents. They were anarchists, punks, free-festivallers, ravers, a mobile rebellion, each one a modern Diogenes giving two fingers to the indignity of late-capitalist life. An older core had been on the road since the anti-nuclear campaigns of the 1950s, and the convoys had slowly grown as part of the beatnik and free-festival movements of the following decades. They weren't lazy. Anyone who lives a conventional nine-to-five life has little right to accuse those who pursue a difficult life of principled non-conformity of laziness. Besides, many worked as seasonal farm labourers and as the heavy lifters at summer festivals – work that would have killed those who accused them of being scroungers. Recently their numbers had swelled exponentially due to the political influence of hard-left punk culture, of the Thatcherite decay of UK civilisation, and the rise of underground rave, for which rapturous eruption their convoys were the vector. But no one on Bog Road knew any of that or had only a vague and warped sense of New Age Travellers picked up from hostile UK tabloids. Of course, they knew as little, or as wrong, about us as we knew about them, for neither of our kinds of people took up much space in papers or TV shows or novels, and when we did, the depiction was just as biased and inaccurate in either of our cases. The perverse and lying influences of mainstream media meant that when we stared at each other from the terrace and field and back again, it was inevitable that what we thought was distorted and unflattering. The scene was set for a confrontation.

By high noon the festival committee had – it is rumoured – un-minutedly EGM'd, conferred, concluded, and sure enough, at about three in the afternoon, a phalanx of squad cars arrived to the Fairfield gates and squads of baton-happy Shickaloney hopped out. The whole barracks must have been called up for this display. A dozen privates formed into a menacing baton-wielding line facing the Fairfield encampment. Among them were some of the most incompetent of the remarkably incompetent local force – full-time drunks who were finding it difficult to stand straight and were more likely to break their own heads with the batons than anyone else's. Some of my neighbours were already leaning out towards the Fairfield along the railings that ran the length of our raised terrace. Within a few minutes they were joined by most others – a row of congregated heads about a hundred strong, men and women, young and old.

The Shickaloney had also been spotted straight away by the New Age Travellers, who were undoubtedly expecting some such visitation – life on the road bringing with it constant tension with the Settler State. A delegation approached the Fairfield gate, men and women, one or two with small children in tow, or a breastfeeding infant. They were led by the long blond dreadlocked and plait-bearded one, who may or may not have flashed at our neighbour. I confess that my first priority was to see if the contours of his elephant cock could be made out through his combats and I doubt I was the only one to make this their principal investigation. Unfortunately, it was not spy-able – more of a periwinkle than an elephant's trunk, so, just like our own ones.

Attention quickly shifted to what the Shickaloney might be up to. By and large my neighbours did not like the Gardaí, thugs in uniform who were perfectly understood from long experience to have little to do with solving or preventing crimes, and much to do with prejudicial harassment of local workers and our own

Travellers – many of whom, members of families that had been violently forced off the road by the state, were our neighbours and friends and relations, and were there leaning and watching and considering alongside us now.

Fresh in many of our minds was the recent barbaric treatment of Jasper O'Driscoll, a homeless alcoholic who lived on waste ground beside the Fairfield. The weekend before, he'd been roughly arrested in front of us all and marched in handcuffs a mile through the town in the middle of the day in a sadistic Calvary of humiliation. When he left the station a few hours later he was covered in bruises, having had the shite beaten out of him in the cell. This was no unusual occurrence – there were more than a few on Bog Road who had experienced similar at some stage of their lives. Our Traveller friends had of course experienced much, much worse, including some having been kidnapped as children by the Guards and given over into the custody of sadists and child-rape rings in industrial 'schools'.

The Mickey Swinger stood forward and, going completely over the heads of the scowling Shickaloney in-between, appealed directly to the Bog Road Forum. The gist of it was: *We intend no harm, we're only ordinary people like yereselves trying to live as best we can, we'll cause no trouble, we won't stay long, and we will tidy up after ourselves*. My neighbours said nothing for or against; they were considering. They talked in hushed tones in groups of two or three and then passed their opinions up and down the railings either side of them – in such a way that a general agreement could be arrived at.

Next to speechify was the notorious fat-arse Sergeant Boyle, a low-IQ bully universally detested on Bog Road. Cunningly, he decided to play to the idea that we were the rightful owners of the Fairfield and therefore the arbiters of justice in this case. This meant if heads were broken and toddlers were batoned, as they inevitably would be were the state to carry out an armed assault on the commune, RTÉ and the other tabloid media could report it as having been done at our behest and with our enthusiastic support. Says the sergeant, *I can only remove them if ye make a complaint against them – I can't do anything if ye don't.* We all knew he was only dying to remove them. He was only dying to get the excuse to call in reinforcements from the bigger barracks in Bandon and Cork and ride on in like Custer at the Washita River. And the supplicants knew exactly what that would be like, having survived several years of the kind of UK state criminality usually reserved for the residents of the Falls Road or the Creggan, including the notorious state crime known as the Battle of the Beanfield in 1985, when not only toddlers but babes in arms were pepper sprayed and had their skulls cracked open. But we of Bog Road, helplessly relying on the mass media for information about far-away events, didn't know anything about that.

My neighbours continued consulting along the railings. The New Age Traveller delegation, fronted by Elephant-Cock, stood opposite in the ancient silence of pleading supplicants, awaiting judgement. It came soon enough. Our own next-door neighbour Tracy was first to declare, *We've no objection as long as there is no trouble.* And heads nodded all along the railings in agreement – including that of the woman who had supposedly seen the Vision of Cock. *No objection as long as there is no trouble,* a few more repeated. Elephant-Cock dropped to his knees, prayerfully lifted his hands, and praised us to the high heavens. Smiles and chuckles broke out among all the New Age Traveller delegation, and then leapt over the line of Shickaloney and spread to all of us along the terrace in no time, smiles and chuckles all round. Only the Shickaloney were left unable to smile. And that was that. The cops, disarmed, went on their way and, better still, a rapport had been established between the two tribes, who were now grinningly looking at each other from field to terrace and back again, a kind of astrological mirroring in which could be told each other's pasts, each other's futures.

That night an 'illegal' rave took place in the Fairfield in a circus tent; it may well have been the first such rave in Ireland. Even at a distance of 500 metres, in bed in the back room at no. 9 Fairfield Terrace, Bog Road, I could feelhear the bass vibrating through the floor and the wall and the mattress and into my blood and bones, *oomph-oomph-oomph-oomph-oomph-oomph*. Beating through me like a second, greater heart, like a heart that belonged to all in its radius and would raise us all up together to dance until dawn. It was a kind of music that I hadn't heard for at least 10,000 years: pre-historic, pre-urban, pre-class, and pre-cop, involuntarily animating, ritualistic, self-transcending, trance-inducing. I had just turned thirteen and I could not resist it. I dressed as quietly as I could, careful not to wake my two brothers, with whom I shared a bedroom, climbed out the back window onto the kitchen roof, leapt down into the back garden, scrambled over our back fence, turned left and then right down the back boreen and crossed the road into the field, making my way in a midnight daze, past campfires and jugglers and fire-breathers and acoustic strummers and didgeridooers and solo dancers and spinning trippers and passed-out revellers, to the rave. There amidst the 120 bpm music and the hummingbird-speed of the strobe and the circulation of chimney-sized joints of weed, hundreds of New Age Travellers blended with hundreds of locals who had trickled, streamed and then flowed here after the pubs closed, drawn as I now was by the irresistible bass beat, which had chimed with something age-old in their very organs too.

Immediately upon entering I started to dance, awkwardly, experimentally, judderingly, like St Vitus himself. A short, barefooted man with a long, plaited beard and tattooed all over – a forehead like Newgrange – approached me smilingly and passed me a half-full flagon. But half full of what? Perhaps it was the strobe lights, but it didn't look like cider. *What's in it?* I shouted at him at the top of my voice. *The good stuff*, he roared back. So I took a good slug out of it and it didn't taste any worse than Muck's White Lightning Stew, so I took another good slug, and another, and what a night I had after that, such a night that, more than thirty years later, I sometimes think I might still be at it and that half-flagon I supped on was the juice of ascension, the moly that uplifted me and rescued me from the nightmare of the contemporary, or at least showed me what escape from this grotesque and terrible nightmare we are all still stuck in might feel like.

# All the World's Ends

*Abby Oliveira*

April 2020 and the gods are taking the utter piss. This has to be the finest April weather I can ever remember, yet there's very little to be done about it, seeing as the world is ending. Again.

I'm already the colour of the Blackbird bar's flat white coffees that I've been daydreaming about so much. My thirty-three-weeks-gone belly is bare to the sun; a few of the younger women on the street can't hide how distasteful they find this, but needs must. To me, it has always felt right to go belly bare to the sun. I take a selfie and send it to my ma, then wish I hadn't because she might call me back. Today is a day when to even think of my family is to burst into tears. I'm terrified. But if I dwell on the fear then the wee yin within me might absorb it, mistaking it for something nutritious. Instead, I turn my attention to the oblivious old cat as he scratches his back on the concrete driveway, delighted to have my company for once. I'm envious of his cluelessness; bliss. I should be working, but I can't think. I'm terrible at resting. Even sitting here at my sun-trap of a front door isn't rest, but survival: I'm building up the vitamin D stocks after reading about studies carried out at Trinity College. I have so much video editing to do because I work self-employed in the arts and they (alongside everything and everyone else) live exclusively on digital video now, in binary code, on the internet, that place where we all spend most of our lives but that is as unfathomable as the heavens. Thank Christ for it.

1999 and a group of final-year girls are crammed around one computer in the library of Coleraine Girls' Secondary School. Line by line of text appears on the monitor at such a tedious pace that, by the time the page loads, most attention spans have karked it.

'What happens now?' I ask our lab tech, excited. I have notions of virtual reality, artificial intelligence, *Star Trek: The Next Generation*-level stuff.

'This!' He gestures at the screen as if to say, 'How could you possibly want more!'

The internet, the greatest revelation, the world's most mind-blowing technological achievement to date, was an astronomical disappointment. A heap of books on computers instead of paper as far as I could see. Maybe the *Star Trek* stuff was for the grammar-school ones, I thought.

Yet this internet was so advanced that it apparently couldn't cope with three zeros in a row and was going to kill us all come New Year's Day. The movie in my head of the first day of AD 2000 was a mash-up of computers randomly short-circuiting; sparks of electricity diving into the waters of a great flood where saucer-eyed people were drowning; fire; clouds parting like theatre curtains;

Jesus emerging with a face on him like a catwalk model; Ian Paisley live-commentating it all.

When my world did end – later in 1999, much sooner than expected – it looked nothing like that. It looked like my beloved granny Mina in Scotland being killed by the cancer nobody knew she had. It looked like the vast expanse of the Irish Sea as I stood on the ferry deck feeling every inch of the growing distance between me and the north coast of Ireland like stretched and ripped stitches. Mum couldn't afford the return ticket for us all after the funeral, being a single parent of five, so we were on a one-way ticket to live in Scotland. And all this in the middle of GCSE time, so I for one welcomed the triple-zero apocalypse; my future was fucked anyway.

Of course, when the first day of AD 2000 actually arrived, all that was different from all the other New Years I remembered was a monumental hangover. And the bodies of a whole new group of friends surrounding me in someone's stale-smoke-filled bedroom. New friends who embraced everything about me, who helped me rediscover reasons to start loving life again.

Tuesday afternoon and the neighbours are gardening, or hanging out whatever they've convinced themselves needed washing, or are heading out for their once-a-day wearing the gym gear they didn't use in January when the gym was still a chore. Turns out normality was far from normal, just familiar, but sure, we knew that. The Virus is the only topic of conversation: hopefully it'll be over come the start of May, says everyone. The jovial undertones to the neighbourly chats are vanishing. A month ago was a different story: a few surprise weeks off work, some shameless weekday seshing, it was all for the taking. Now the nervous laughter; paranoia on narrow pavements; everyone now a potential infection; everyone ready to scream. I can't let fear leak in. The new life inside me is recording everything. I might as well be sitting under a cloche in a fish tank as I watch and listen. I have that strange but familiar feeling of being half in and half out of my body, of being envious of inanimate objects and their inability to feel. There is nowhere to run away and hide from this, no part of the planet that isn't touched. The only way around is through. The most terrifying truth on Earth.

11 September 2001 and life is about to begin. Although I moved out of the family home and have been working full time at the bingo for a year, this is the day I regard as my first day of proper adulthood. Today I return to Portstewart to start a theatre studies course at the University of Ulster. I'm going to live in a different country from my family for the first time. If anything goes wrong, no one can take a short drive to save me. I'm not worried. I was the eldest child of a single-parent household for long enough; I know what survival is and I can do what I need to.

I don't remember exactly when it dawns on me that something earth-shattering has happened. I remember the bright, crisp day and the dark café. I remember all the other customers, every single one, being up from their tables talking to each other, hands over gaping mouths and ghost faces. Everclear's *Sparkle and Fade* album on full blast in my earphones: I don't take them out to hear what's being said. One of the waitresses brings a portable TV out to the counter, and everyone congregates around it. I can't see the screen; I can only see shoulders knotting and heads shaking over and over and over. I stare at the bubbles in my mug, feeling like my astral soul is leaving my body. Then I'm at the bus stop, no idea if I finished my coffee or not. Of course, by the time I get to Portstewart it's clear that whatever has happened won't be ignored. People are staring at TV screens in every window of every business I look in along the way. I have never seen anything like it. Later that night (or week, or month) I am glued to the news: the male reporter says, 'Everywhere, there is a real sense that things will never be the same again.'

May 2020 and lockdown has officially been extended by three weeks. There is a dearth of people willing to pick crops as the pay and conditions are so exploitative; this matters now, because the work can't be done by migrant workers. Nibiru was supposed to appear in our skies twice already this month, with a full-on collision predicted for a few days from now that won't happen. That hasn't ever happened, not since I first heard of the mysterious rogue planet when it was due to destroy us back in 2003. Instead, it chose to continue its interstellar dithering. It dithered even as our government helped slaughter Iraqi civilians in their hundreds of thousands; as millions of us took to the streets and couldn't stop them; as the Celtic Tiger got spectacularly high, overdosed, then died just as spectacularly. We drowned out its death grunts by watching *Zeitgeist*, the documentary of the late 2000s, recommended by a colleague who had an unshakeable faith in the conventions of living a good, conservative life. *Zeitgeist* ended up putting that particular colleague's head away, razed his certainties about the world to the ground. It did the same to many people, I hear.

Boris Johnson continues to haver shite: *Stay Alert* is the new buzz slogan (as if the Virus prowls the shadows of the streets like some phantom knickers-thief). The health secretary wouldn't advise hugging anyone until maybe probably likely a vaccine is conceivably ready for perhaps autumn, weather permitting. There are more fights on my social-media feeds. I could cheerfully choke at least ten of the bastards on there.

I'm still going belly bare to the sun whenever I can, remembering to keep rubbing my huge bump so that (according to the hypno-birthing and Ina May Gaskin books and the health visitor's leaflets sent out in lieu of a home visit) this baby feels that the world is a welcoming, safe, and loving place. And because *we are so blessed, so very lucky* compared to so very many. I repeat that mantra over and over in my mind, as if the wee yin is telepathic, as if it cancels out the negative vibes of my more frustrated thoughts. *We are blessed, so very lucky.* But sometimes, no matter how many times I repeat it, it isn't strong enough to fight back thoughts of the empty wakes and funerals, the fear for people who can't get life-saving surgeries or decent PPE or time off work, for those with literally not a penny, not a drop of fucking soap. Sometimes I cry as if I've any right or cause to, and the crying just goes on and on and on.

2010 and the Hermetic Order of the Golden Dawn – W. B. Yeats's old crew – say the world will end this year. There's definitely something in the air, I can feel it, but can't find the words. My lefty socialist pals reckon I'm just feeling the effects of the recession, of Ireland being sold out to save the bankers. One night we're partying in Victoria the jazz singer's flat, when she and Connor the pianist poet lean towards me, their eyes sparkling. 'Abby, can you feel the revolution coming?' asks Victoria. My stomach jumps with excitement. 'Yes!' That was it. A name for what I'd been feeling. Or so I thought.

Yet, inexplicably, I can't stop crying. Nobody knows; it embarrasses me to talk about it because life is great: I'm in a solid relationship, I'm respected in my career field, I have good relationships with family and a tight-knit friendship group. I have no reason to be randomly bursting into tears. My pals from the reiki and bio-energy healing group talk about the upcoming end of the Mayan calendar. They say the world is not going to end like the religiously obsessed are saying, it's just that we're approaching the end of the beginning of a new age. I love to discuss the idea, like I love discussing the idea of God or capitalism or black holes in space, but I have no faith in it.

Come late spring of 2011, I'm planning for the upcoming summer, a bright future, and I'm so excited. For a while I even think I'm fine again. But little do I know this is only the beginning of a depression that will last for five years. Come the winter solstice of 2012, I will have abandoned the career I love, abandoned my healing and meditation practices; my tight-knit friendship group will have unravelled beyond recognition. Yet the world will remain. Unrecognisable but intact.


'Remember Brexit?' I ask Martin. 'I miss Brexit. Such simple days.'

We laugh. We've done a lot of laughing over the past eight weeks, not least of all because we're going a bit stir-crazy. My belly has started to shake like Santa's whenever I laugh. It has been uncomfortable to laugh for the past few days, or cough, sneeze, sleep. I can feel my pelvic bones preparing for the next shock. It's time. A couple of days at most. *I am blessed, so very lucky*, and my body knows exactly what it needs to do.

I was born in 1982, among the first of the millennials. The me, me, me burnouts; the entitled, mollycoddled Peter Pans; the original snowflakes; and other arbitrary names invented to suggest that we're just too spoiled and coddled for this fair world (even more so than your average Westerner from a wealthy country). We were planted in constantly shifting sands. That invisible yet so influential guidebook that outlines the attitudes, motivations and rules of life, and the right way to live, was well decayed by the time we staggered into maturity. I can't remember a time in my entire adulthood when I felt certain about who the goodies and baddies were. Every generation before us might have felt the same, but it was never sold to us like that.

Yet we do have an unshakeable knowing of our own: a knowing that everything will be the opposite of grand. That everything is highly likely to fall to shit and nothing, not even the most seemingly solid of relationships, beliefs or laws, can or should be relied on as given, that the concept of 'security' in any aspect of life is a dangling carrot. We know that the centre won't hold, and the falconer is winging it like everyone else; it is what it is. Our entire adulthoods have been spent bracing for the end of the world in one form or another. Yet here we are, alive in the future we were repeatedly told we didn't have.

Now, we stare blankly at the latest world's end, the greatest threat yet, some say. Greater apparently than the Spanish flu, smallpox, polio, bird flu, SARS, swine flu, mad cow disease, the Taliban, ISIS, Nibiru, cancer, terrorism, Brexit, the Tories and

Trump all rolled into one. I don't know how I know, but I just know; we will know exactly what we need to do to survive. Just as we have done at all the world's ends before this.

The End.

# The Welding Rod's Contribution to World Literature

*Dermot Bolger*

My travels have led me across frozen lakes in remote Canadian forests and Arctic Scandinavian landscapes, but if asked for my coldest memory, only one place comes to mind. I leave my childhood home in the working-class Dublin suburb of Finglas before dawn on 27 December 1978. The sky is ink black, the sparkling frost turning pavements into treacherous skating rinks. I was a nineteen-year-old factory hand, keeping my balance by gripping walls. A car slides down McKee Road, the driver's face peering from a circle in the windscreen hacked clear of ice. On Jamestown Road I join a procession of other factory workers, walking in silence because it was too cold to shout greetings as we entered the Unidare industrial complex, returning to work after St Stephen's Day.

At 7.28 a.m. I punch in my card at the Oerlikon welding-rod

factory, where I will operate a compressing machine for the next eight hours. Back then this factory ran round the clock in three different shifts. Normally there were clamouring voices and a residue of warmth as the night-shift crew let the morning shift take over. But we were the first workers back after Christmas. An eerie silence haunted the factory. It was colder inside than out on the streets. I remember nothing about that shift when the racket of machinery resumed: men swapping jokes while deftly lifting trays of welding rods from a conveyor belt. I just recall the Siberian chill cutting into our bones as we awaited the hooter.

I was the youngest worker among men twice and three times my age, who looked out for me but took no prisoners and suffered no fools. A work-to-rule protest was led by a shop steward who seemed determined to foment unrest. Endless union meetings happened in the canteen. I spent my shifts singing to my compressor while using heavy levers to compress into solid 'slugs' a mixture of loose chemicals raining down from a conveyer belt onto the steel tray before me. These 'slugs' were pushed into the barrel of a machine into which steel rods were fired.

The rods emerged covered in a hardened coating formed by the chemicals. But if even one thumbtack mysteriously found its way into the chemicals, the machine shuddered to a halt and needed to be meticulously cleaned. When this happened, chargehands glared at me with justifiable suspicion because I was constantly approached by older workmates handing me metal slivers to discreetly drop into the chemicals I was compressing and therefore sabotage production.

Years later this gave me the opening line of my first novel, *Night Shift* – the welding rod's sole contribution to world literature: *He watched the superior smirk of the chargehand's arse vanish down the concrete path between the screeching machines and waited for Frankie's nod.* At nineteen, while scared of being caught, I regarded my workmates' requests that I commit sabotage as their way of letting me know that they trusted me enough to see me as belonging among them. I was exploited by the firm, which paid me a reduced wage because of my age. But looking back with a writer's detachment, I also suspect an exploitation of my naivety by some workmates. If caught, it was my word against theirs as to where those pieces of metal came from. In a tinderbox of industrial unrest, where the lay-off rule was 'last in, first out', management could make an example of me without the all-out strike provoked by sacking an older factory hand. However, industrial peace broke out and my crew started working against the clock for bonus payments at a pace that left me shattered.

When I finished school in 1977, determined to somehow one day earn a living as a writer, the railings of the Unidare complex were familiar to me. My brother worked for Tinsley Wire in there. Indeed *Night Shift* was written on an old typewriter 'liberated' from the Tinsley offices on my sixteenth birthday. Its disappearance was never solved, but for anyone wishing to conduct forensic analysis, the typewriter is on display in the Little Museum of Dublin. On teenage walks at night, beating out the rhythms of poems, I often heard the hooter announce the night shift at half eleven. With the introduction of free second-level education, I was the second family member to complete secondary education, although my big sister, who left school much younger and started writing much later, now outsells me many times over as a novelist.

If money had been found, I might have become the first Bolger to attend university, but while many classmates not going straight into jobs gained qualifications from technical colleges, I rarely remember university being discussed. But leaving aside financial considerations, I sensed that entering a middle-class environment like Trinity College would separate me from the world I wanted to write about, skewering my relationship with people to whom I felt an affinity and whose lives weren't captured in Irish literature at that point.

Perhaps my hesitancy had more to do with a tentative uncertainty about the type of writer I wanted to become, rather than from any antagonism towards such institutions. I had been befriended by the brilliant poet and social commentator Anthony Cronin, whose *Irish Times* 'Viewpoint' column was a radical beacon for young writers. From it I grasped the notion that (insofar as schools of poets exist) there seemed the possibility of a more interesting loose gathering of new poets emerging outside the walls of academia. Tony also talked about how, if serious about devoting yourself to writing, there was a lot to be said for burning as many bridges as possible before they diverted you into safer pastures. My refusal to apply for promotion in any job stemmed from this desire to sever all wiser financial options for my life.

I'm not recommending this to the new writers joyously welcomed into print in this anthology. It is the least practical career advice since John Butler Yeats told his sons, Willie and Jack, that a steady job had proved the ruin of many a good person. But in my particular circumstances it seemed right to leave myself unqualified to do anything except write, and the great, liberating joy of writing is that you need no qualification except talent; no one's permission or approval. Indeed, if wise, you blithely ignore not just the old-fashioned censorship that my generation sometimes needed to fight against, but ignore also the ever-changing list of rules that commentators try to impose on the types of imaginative characters who suddenly emerge from your subconscious. I hope every new writer in this book will enjoy great success, but if they do, they will have made too many sacrifices in achieving it to surrender their intellectual curiosity and play by other people's rules.

Before starting work in Oerlikon, I started a community arts group in Finglas called Raven Arts. We staged arts festivals usually attended by four people and a dog. My mother died when I was ten, my seafaring father was generally away on voyages, and during his absence his house became a makeshift arts centre, brimming with musicians and poets plotting to use any local space we could find. Such events were not without pitfalls. When we negotiated the use of a small corridor up a long flight of stairs above some shops, our guitar workshop was interrupted by two skinheads who suspended one participant above the top step and threatened to let him fall until a collection was taken up. While we imagined there was no money in art, it transpired there were considerable amounts to be made when you held the artist suspended above a steep staircase.

When tired of selling broadsheets by local poets in pubs, we branched into pamphlets. I remember my factory workmates each buying a copy of my first poetry pamphlet in the canteen during break on one night shift. I doubt if many read the poems, and I got slagged by each man before they shook my hand and wished me luck, because, whatever the hell I was at, they weren't going to be found wanting in supporting me. When we decided to publish actual books, we determined to not only publish local writers. Because we felt like marginalised outsiders, we welcomed any voice that seemed marginalised and outside the mainstream of what constituted Irish literature. I use this term in the sense of what it meant before books like Roddy Doyle's mould-breaking, self-published debut, *The Commitments*, blew apart the definition of Irish literature.

It may seem strange that European writers like Pier Paolo Pasolini and Paul Celan were published by us in Finglas, in addition to debut volumes by people like Patrick McCabe, Eoin McNamee, Sara Berkeley, Fintan O'Toole, Rosita Boland, Colm Tóibín and Katie Donovan. But part of finding your own voice means refusing to be pigeonholed. Raven Arts Press sprang from the punk explosion of 1977. If young people could start punk bands in sheds without knowing how to play their instruments, it seemed natural for us – with no money or knowledge of publishing, and indeed no actual shed – to start a publishing house as a platform for anyone who felt marginalised. Raven sprang from the needs of its particular time, just like this anthology launching sixteen unpublished writers stems from today's need for new voices to be heard. We just did it with more crooked pages and misprints.

The poet Paul Durcan (three of whose early books were published by us) described the Raven poets as having 'nothing in common except originality and dissidence'. Being outsiders, we sought outsiders. We found our first two poets in Sydney Bernard Smith, writing scurrilous experimental poetry on Inishbofin, and in the Birmingham-based poet Jule Wieland, whose poems captured the realities of visiting her then boyfriend in prison.

When laying out our first book by hand in a cottage in Dolphin's Barn, we needed to barricade the front door because local thugs tried to kick it down, convinced we were drug dealers, although our strongest substance was cow gum to crookedly glue the typeset poems onto pages. We had our first launch in the old Protestant church in Finglas. It seemed a good way to bring art to local people and we didn't want to go cap in hand to the literary establishment: we wanted to make them come to us – which is why Raven books had 'published in Finglas' on the back cover.

But was Finglas ready for poetry and were the Dublin literati ready for Finglas? Happily, a large number of locals turned up from curiosity, listened appreciatively and went home quietly. Our problem was the arrival of denizens from Dublin's literary pubs, eager to support Sydney Bernard Smith. Finglas seemed like 'Injun' country for them. One very famous painter sought directions from a well-dressed local youth before handing him a pound, telling the passengers in his car: 'The poor chap probably hasn't a bed for the night.'

We got to know this drunken painter well from repeatedly needing to carry him from the church by his arms and legs. He apparently found it blasphemous that Anthony Cronin was reading, and regularly interjected in a posh accent: 'Balls! Balls! A communist reading in a Protestant church!' The painter snuck back in every time we needed to eject another literary type, tanked up to brave the wilds of Finglas, while the vicar held his head in his hands and locals watched in bafflement. If we thought that bringing art to the masses was difficult, we discovered how exhausting it was to keep the masses safe from the artists. Finglas has produced great poets like Paula Meehan, Michael O'Loughlin (Raven's co-founder) and Rachel Hegarty, and great musicians like Christy Dignam. But it never produced a literary event as strange as when the literati arrived on safari, finding safety in numbers and fire water. Several were last seen engaged in an experimental dance workshop or a running battle near the taxi rank on the main street.

Flushed with modest success in selling our early volumes around pubs or in small bookshops, in my first interview I grandiosely mentioned an ambition to publish a first selected poems by, as I phrased it, 'the communist poet Charlie Donnelly' who died, aged twenty-two, in the Spanish Civil War. I received an angry communiqué from the poet Ewart Milne – a friend and contemporary of Donnelly's who shared his left-wing 1930s activism. I need to paraphrase this lost communiqué, but in essence Milne said: 'How dare you describe my friend Charlie as "a communist poet". We were both poets and, back then, both communists, but Donnelly was not "a communist poet": he was a poet first and foremost, who happened to be a communist.'

It wised me up to the dangers of neat classifications. The whole point of being a writer is to allow yourself complete independence of thought. If you get lucky, your work will surprise you, forcing you to delve deeper into your psyche and bedrock of innermost emotions than you perhaps wished to go. During such moments when you immerse yourself in imaginative voyages into your subconscious, you cease to belong to any class, creed or race other than your inner self and, if lucky, you may find that you actually become a stranger to yourself. I don't mean that you cease to belong to any class, creed or race in your perspective or attitude of everyday life. I just mean that all writers possess split personalities: the everyday part, which is fixed, and the imaginative part, which is beyond all definition.

I've never written any book not informed by my experience of growing up in a working-class suburb, by my experiences of how some people's perspectives of me changed when they discovered this and by my occasionally jaundiced scrutiny of the foibles and lives of such people. But, remembering Milne's retort, I reminded myself that I am not 'a working-class poet' but a poet shaped by my working-class background.

Writers are told to write about what we know, but, if we have truly lived, then we know about far more than just our own lives. My early experiences gave me sufficient insight to write a trilogy of novels set in Finglas – *Night Shift,* based on my factory days, *The Woman's Daughter* and *The Journey Home,* which explored the alienation of my generation growing up in 1980s Ireland in an era of high unemployment, with legislators afraid to legislate for the reality around them. But my sense of being an outsider, of not fitting into a certain perceived notion of 'Irishness', means that I also felt perfectly placed to write two very different novels – *The Family on Paradise Pier* and *An Ark of Light* – about a real-life upper-middle-class Protestant family, the Goold-Verschoyles. This family had looked forward to playing a role in the Ireland whose independence struggle they supported, but found that this Ireland afforded them no role.

Therefore, although from the opposite end of the social spectrum to me, my characters shared my early sense of feeling marginalised. The Goold-Verschoyle brothers immersed themselves in communism; the youngest son was taken prisoner by the Soviets for dissent during the Spanish Civil War and died in a Gulag – unbeknown to his family. The imaginative landscapes I traversed to retrace their footsteps were far removed from Finglas – places like Moscow and Barcelona in the 1930s, London during the 1926 General Strike or a remote Pyrenean village where one sister lived in poverty, trying to become a writer. But I felt no sense of appropriating classes or cultures, although I tried to listen in my heart to the judgement of the real-life people each character was based on. The only rule I could follow was the credo I've followed for decades. It is the sole advice I'd give any writer making their debut in this anthology, if they bother with advice. To write each first draft with passion in your heart and edit every subsequent draft with ice in your veins; to ensure you can morally justify to yourself anything you write; to imaginatively frequent places beyond your comfort zone and conform to no notion of what you are meant to write about; to never imagine you have the right to speak for anyone other than yourself or let others hijack your work in any simplistic fashion; to never set out to be a provocateur but not to be afraid to offend, if that is where your imagination leads.

To put it with more eloquence, let me root through a box under my bed. It contains one copy of each of the 127 books published by the press I started as a factory hand (which later became New Island Books). Among them is a collection of essays written by the poet, novelist and filmmaker Pier Paolo Pasolini shortly before his murder in 1975. I liked his advice to young writers so much that I printed it on the plain white cover of our edition of his essays. It reads: *Against all this you need only, I believe, do nothing other than continue simply to be yourselves; which means to be constantly unrecognisable. To forget at once the great successes and to continue, unafraid, obstinate, eternally contrary; to demand, to will, to identify yourselves with all that is different – to scandalise and to blaspheme...*

One morning in 1979 I received a job offer as a library assistant. It meant I would leave behind those factory gates. I told my workmates as we gathered in a local pub to give a send-off to a factory hand leaving for England. It was a wild, hilarious night: the first time I felt fully accepted among them. Every man wished me well. All agreed that we should meet again in that same pub on the following Saturday to give me my proper send-off. On the chosen night I arrived early. Two hours passed before I realised nobody was coming. I was just a kid who'd never truly earned my spurs. Those grown men meant no unkindness, but had already forgotten about me. It was a last valuable lesson I learned in the only university I ever attended before commencing my journey as a writer. I wish every new writer here success on the journeys they are embarking on.

# Working-Class Writing in Ireland Today: *The 32* and Beyond

## Dr Michael Pierse

*I am grateful to Dave O'Brien for his advice on some of the issues raised in this chapter, and to Fergal Finnegan for his counsel and commentary on earlier drafts. All omissions or errors, however, are entirely my own.*

When I first began writing *about* Irish working-class writing, the connections between the authors I studied seemed obvious to me. From Robert Tressell's *The Ragged-Trousered Philanthropists*, through Seán O'Casey's prolific work in drama and autobiography, to Brendan Behan's raucous and biting satire, to Paula Meehan's impassioned poetry and Christina Reid's provocative plays, class was so identifiably and indisputably central to these writers' experiences and their works. All had faced poverty in some form. All had used their craft to comment powerfully on class inequalities in the society around them. And their class perspective was undoubtedly part of why their works often shocked (or aimed to shock) readers and audiences – to jolt them into action. Irish working-class writers have diverse and sometimes conflicting interests and writing styles, but there is so much they share in common too. When I embarked on this research path in the early 2000s, however, it was surprising that these writers had hardly been linked together in Irish literary studies *as* 'working-class writers'. This seemed odd to a working-class student profoundly impacted by this literature.

So often we write about what we know or feel strongly about – not only creative writers (who know too well the dictum 'write what you know') but academics too, who frequently choose, as I did, to pursue scholarly interests that resonate personally, whatever the presumptions about dispassionate analysis that accompany academic practice. It is most often academic 'amphibians'* – people from working-class backgrounds who have entered the very middle-class world of academia – who are responsible for the growth in recent decades of global working-class studies. But if working-class commonality is something that socialists have always insisted transcends national boundaries, being working class also has very particular textures in different historical and geographical contexts. For one, the relative neglect of Irish working-class writing as a category contrasts with the relative (though still not nearly enough) attention that working-class writing has received in British

---

\* Michelle M. Tokarczyk (ed.), *Critical Approaches to American Working-Class Literature*, Routledge, New York, 2014.

life, not least because the history of class relations in Ireland has been so different from that in Britain.

Class in Ireland can only be comprehended in terms of the particularities of a very complex history of industrialisation, colonisation, emigration and partition. Grafting on the nearest available (British) model simply won't do. However, as recent research has shown,[*] the British-Irish context is vital in understanding the complexities of Irish class relations, given Ireland's historical role in providing labour to the British economy, for example. This short concluding chapter on class, writing, publishing and arts practice in Ireland attempts to mirror, from an Irish perspective, some of the analysis in Dave O'Brien's piece for this book's sister publication, *Common People*.

### Class in Ireland

Sometimes class can be difficult to navigate in an Irish context; for one, the language of class – terms like 'working class' and 'middle class' – doesn't have the same purchase in everyday Irish conversations as it does in England. 'Working class' is used quite a lot in Ireland, but there are many local variations in the language used to indicate class. Interviews conducted in the early 1980s, in Thomastown, Co. Kilkenny, during field research for Marilyn Silverman's book, *An Irish Working Class: Explorations in political economy and hegemony 1800–1950*, illustrate the everyday injuries of class in an Irish town: claims by one respondent that his millworker uncle was thrown off the county hurling team to make

---

[*] See David Convery, 'Writing and Theorising the Irish Working Class', in Michael Pierse (ed.), *A History of Irish Working-Class Writing*, Cambridge University Press, Cambridge, 2017.

way for a lesser player but farmer's son – and that this practice of elevating the sons of the better-off, regardless of ability, was common in the GAA; recollections of labourers being excluded from social gatherings reserved for the well-to-do; working-class people knowing where not to sit at Mass, where shopkeepers and 'strong farmers' always occupied special seats. All of this was part of working-class experience, but as Silverman acknowledges in her book, the language of class was a more localised matter, terms like 'landlords', 'shopkeepers', 'tradesmen' and 'labourers' fitting everyone into 'an all-pervasive socio-cultural map'. Similar situations are cited in other scholarship, where terms like 'grandees', 'money people' or 'poshies' indicate social structures that are roughly equivalent to one another but are named differently.

Classifying Irish people according to social class brings other challenges in terms of both perceptions and concrete economic differentials. Where people do self-designate as 'working class' and 'middle class', the designation can be misleading, though it nonetheless indicates levels of awareness of class divisions. Amárach Research, an Irish market-research and data specialist, conducted surveys in 2005 and 2011 in which, respectively, 35 per cent or 41 per cent of respondents in the Republic designated themselves working class – the 6-per-cent jump perhaps unsurprising given the aftermath of the 2007 economic crash. In terms of more large-scale quantitative analysis, research on class in the Republic of Ireland (ROI) most often utilises categories developed by the Central Statistics Office (CSO) in its classification of socio-economic groups (SEGs) such as Employers and Managers, Higher Professionals, Farmers, and Skilled Manual Workers. The working class is 'typically understood as the four "lowest" socio-economic groups

– that is to say manual workers and routine non-manual workers'.[*] While SEGs such as 'Skilled Manual' and 'Semi-Skilled' rarely make it into everyday conversation, clustering them according to what in everyday conversation people understand as 'working class' and 'middle class' can provide a useful starting point for considering what class is. On 2016 CSO figures, this would suggest a working class of around 46 per cent of the state's population, though as sociologist Kieran Allen has suggested, such methods of understanding class can be questionable for various reasons.[**]

## Class, publishing and the arts

Whatever metrics ones uses, however, unlike in Britain, there is no solid research in Ireland, north or south, on the class origins of Irish writers, journalists, translators, editors or publishers. In his chapter for *Common People*, O'Brien discusses official British statistics on the class origins of professionals in these areas. The Irish CSO holds no such data. The British data is relevant to the Irish context, nonetheless: Irish authors will often aim to get published by the big British publishing houses, and aspiring Irish publishing professionals will frequently aim to work in them; furthermore, the many social parallels between British and Irish life suggest that there will be similar patterns in the class barriers faced by working-class writers on this side of the Irish Sea.

A 2017 report on social mobility and the 'class pay gap' shows

[*]   Fergal Finnegan, 'Working Class Access to Higher Education: Structures, Experiences and Categories', in Ted Fleming, Andrew Loxley and Fergal Finnegan (eds.), *Access and Participation in Irish Higher Education*, Palgrave, London, 2017.
[**]  Kieran Allen, 'Ireland: Middle Class Nation?', *Études irlandaises*, 32:2, 2007. See statbank.cso.ie/multiquicktables/quicktables.aspx?id=cna07

that only 12 per cent of those who enter the creative industries in the UK are from working-class backgrounds.* O'Brien also cites UK Office for National Statistics research from 2014 that reveals 'almost half (47 per cent) of all authors, writers and translators in the British workforce were from the most privileged starting points (NS-SEC I), contrasting with only 10 per cent of those with parents from working-class origins (NS-SEC VI–VIII)'. In a recent British survey almost 80 per cent of those people in the publishing industry who identified themselves as working class felt that their background had adversely affected their career. This environment in Britain has consequences for Irish publishing, when, as Katy Shaw points out in her report on the *Common People* project, our nearest neighbour, Britain, is the largest exporter of books in the world, despite having only 1 per cent of the world's population, and when literary and publishing industries are the least socially diverse of all Britain's creative industries.**

Due to issues with sample sizes and the lack of specific data on Northern Ireland (NI), these British-based statistics cannot be confidently applied there. But the NI context is very much tied to broader UK policy trends on inclusion, with some specific local twists. Stormont ministers at the Department of Culture, Arts and Leisure (DCAL) have been keen, over the past several decades, to push inclusion in the arts, culminating, in policy terms, in the 2016 NI Assembly Committee for Culture, Arts and Leisure report,

* Sam Friedman, Daniel Laurison and Lindsey Macmillan, *Social Mobility, the Class Pay Gap and Intergenerational Worklessness: New Insights from The Labour Force Survey*, Social Mobility Commission, London, 2017.
** Katy Shaw, 'Common people: Breaking the class ceiling in UK publishing', *Creative Industries Journal*, 2010, DOI: 10.1080/17510694.2019.1707521

*Inclusion in the Arts of Working-Class Communities*, which aimed 'to pinpoint and understand barriers to inclusion in the arts faced by members of working-class communities'.

These barriers – economic, geographical, educational, cultural and psychological – will be familiar to working-class writers, practitioners and activists in the cultural sphere. Lack of time, transport and information, educational and financial barriers, and fish-out-of-water discomforts are all identified as hampering working-class engagement. There is, however, a further informational gap, which the report acknowledges. While it cites unsurprising indicative figures on socio-economic inequalities in attendance at arts events, its data is restricted to ticketed events – leaving out the many cultural activities in working-class areas that happen without tickets. Such data gaps are part of the problem for this relatively small, divided statelet, which is often left out of considerations in the UK (and in the Republic) and has inadequate data-gathering activity in terms of socio-economic inequalities in the arts locally. There are, however, NI-specific features that suggest the urgency of locally based research. For example, as the Arts Council of Northern Ireland (ACNI) noted in its submission to the report:

> Evidence suggests that Northern Ireland has levels of social exclusion that are well above other regions of the United Kingdom, living standards that have persistently lagged behind GB (with the main factors being lower levels of employment and productivity, as exemplified in our highest inactivity rate in the UK of 27 per cent).

The report recommends 'better data gathering around participation in arts and cultural activities', though it is unclear how this will be achieved. An additional issue of relevance to the current book is that, when working-class engagement as makers of art is considered, writing as a specific activity doesn't much feature. Writing projects that engage with working-class people, like Fighting Words* or *The 32*, are scarcely analysed in studies of class and participation in the arts.

In terms of publishing and class in the Republic, indicators suggest similar issues to those in evidence in Britain, and that greater attention to class origins by the CSO would yield important data for the analysis of working-class mobility. Education is a key factor in becoming a writer or publisher, and Ireland suffers from serious, long-term issues in terms of class inequality in the education system. The OECD's report on social mobility, *A Family Affair? Intergenerational Social Mobility Across OECD Countries* (2010), illustrates how having well-educated parents has a significant impact on social mobility across OECD countries and that Ireland has less educational mobility than the OECD average. A 2009 OECD report concluded that, if, as the analysis shows, coming from an educated family significantly increases the likelihood of gaining a tertiary education, then 'the penalty of coming from a low-educated family is particularly high in Ireland and Greece'. In its discussion of relative social mobility – what it terms 'sticky floors and sticky ceilings' – a more recent OECD report suggests that some occupations require job-specific human capital that parents transmit to their children.

---

\*   Fighting Words is an organisation that provides 'free tutoring and mentoring in creative writing and related arts to as many children, young adults and adults with special needs as we can reach', through cultural centres across Ireland, including in disadvantaged areas of Dublin and Belfast. See www.fightingwords.ie

These occupations included not only entrepreneurs and the self-employed, but also certain liberal professions, where skills and knowledge are transmitted that help lower the barriers to entry.

In *Common People*, O'Brien notes the importance of obtaining data, which isn't currently available in Britain, on the class origins of people in positions of power in publishing – on those who commission publications, for example. The relative lack of social mobility in Irish professional life suggests that further research on the backgrounds of arts and publishing decision-makers here would likely reveal important findings on the barriers facing Irish working-class artists. In areas such as publishing, where networking, residing in expensive cities and having family financial support to supplement poorly paid internships or entry positions are key, it is obvious that professional advancement is significantly impacted by background. Crime-fiction author and working-class north Dubliner Jo Spain has recently noted that 'if you're from a working-class background, you don't have a friend who's an agent or a relative in the publishing industry'. While this is true for most middle-class people too, the point stands: access to professional networks is no doubt a factor in the exclusion of working-class people from the publishing industry, as either writers or decision-makers. This does not in any way discount the importance of smaller Irish publishers that have acted as conduits to success, or routes to bigger publishers, for working-class writers. Culture Matters (which published the recent *The Children of the Nation: An Anthology of Working People's Poetry from Contemporary Ireland*), New Binary Press, New Island Books, Salmon Poetry, Liberties Press, Dedalus Books and *The Stinging Fly* are among the presses that contribute to a lively publishing scene in Ireland and provide important platforms for writers from working-class backgrounds.

## Community arts

Research on community arts in Ireland is also helpful in considering these issues. There is a misleading tendency to assume that working-class writing and community arts are more or less synonymous; working-class writers can be just as covetous of their isolation from the community – as committed to the individuality of their artistic pursuits – as writers from other social backgrounds. That said, community arts have been integral to the energy behind working-class writing in Ireland over the past four decades, as illustrated, for example, in the experiences recounted in Sandy Fitzgerald's *An Outburst of Frankness: Community Arts in Ireland – A Reader* (2004), or in recent research on Irish working-class feminist writers in Emma Penney's PhD thesis *Class Acts: Working-Class Feminism and the Women's Movement in Ireland* (2020).

Inner-city Dubliner and dramatist Peter Sheridan, who had in the 1970s been a practitioner of 'left-wing agitational drama', recalls a period of 'transition' in his own thinking around this time: 'When you realised that the next stage is that of bringing theatre to a community and making it happen in a community context, of making the audience the performers.'* As Penney's work shows, in the 1980s women like Cathleen O'Neill in north Dublin were coming to similar conclusions regarding poetry and prose, setting up their own writing projects, which in turn became building blocks for the feminist movement in Ireland. Finglas writer Dermot Bolger's activism in publishing around this time, setting up the independent publisher Raven Arts Press (1977–92),

---

* Quoted in Sandy Fitzgerald, *An Outburst of Frankness*, New Island Books, Dublin, 2004.

later co-founding New Island (1992–present), was part of this phase of challenging practices in publishing and the arts. Raven Arts operated along collaborative lines, 'dictated by the group of writers for the group of writers [...] maintaining a horizontal, collectivist perspective'.* This movement was part of a broader global phenomenon, of course – influenced by working-class writers' organisations, notably the Federation of Worker Writers and Community Publishers in Britain, whose work is explored in *The Republic of Letters: Working-class writing and local publishing* (ed. by David Morley et al., 2009). Celebrated working-class writers have often been exceptional, self-taught intellectuals who stood out from their communities while representing them. The most famous of these in Ireland, Seán O'Casey and Brendan Behan, gained fame on the international stage, but their audiences and their actors were mostly drawn from the middle classes. This new generation marked a sea change in this regard.

But the impact of this changing environment was far from instant in Ireland, where the Arts Council, established by the 1951 Arts Act, focused on 'excellence' and 'high' arts, narrowly defined, with all the elitism that such concepts often entail. The Irish Arts Council was described in the late 1960s/early 1970s by an anonymous senior civil servant as having 'little respect' in the Irish Department of Finance, due to the perception that its management had 'established a coterie or clique around themselves', as part

---

* Erica Meyers, 'Characters of Class: Poverty and Historical Alienation in Dermot Bolger's Fiction' (unpublished doctoral thesis), University of Edinburgh, 2015.

of an Irish arts world that was 'too in-grown and in-bred'.* In the early 1970s, artists associated with the Project Arts Gallery accused this closed arts world of 'symptoms of class bigotry'.

There were other barriers in the Republic too: O'Casey, Behan, Paul Smith and Lee Dunne, for example, had all encountered difficulties in terms of push-back from conservative powers when trying to represent the grittier aspects of working-class life; the latter two suffered significantly from official censorship (in place for books since 1929, but eased somewhat from 1967), during the era of celebrated 'slice of life' and 'angry' working-class writing in Britain. North of the border, a notorious example of the pressures facing working-class writers there is Sam Thompson's public spat with the Ulster Group Theatre board over the staging of his play of the shipyards, *Over the Bridge* (1960). The 1973 ROI Arts Act was partly a response to criticisms of the ROI's stifling climate of cliquishness and censorship – of who-you-know and what-you-shouldn't-know.

The new movements, operating in a more conducive climate, sought not only to portray working-class life, but to do so in ways that further democratised the arts – bringing in working-class audiences and, in the more radical practices, seeking to enable working-class people to write themselves. Here, various agendas met – cultural democracy, leftist agitation, the policy imperatives of organisations like Combat Poverty and the more humdrum agendas of governmental schemes to target unemployment. North of the border, the imperatives of peace-building would also bolster

---

\*     Brian P. Kennedy, *Dreams and Responsibilities: The State and Arts in Independent Ireland*, The Arts Council, Dublin, 1990.

community arts. When practitioners like Fitzgerald, Sheridan, O'Neill, Annie Kilmartin, Mowbray Bates, Martin Lynch and Des Wilson started out in the 1970s and 1980s on either side of the border, their varied forms of grassroots cultural activities – writing projects, workshopped plays, combinations of amateur and professional actors, and a focus on community venues – were, however, viewed by some as outlier activities, and for the arts establishment, the stuff of community development rather than Culture with a big 'C'. Plays and writing about poverty, the shaming practices of the social welfare system, militarisation and state violence, women's intersectional oppression, the injustices of the legal system and various other issues core to working-class experience began to emerge. The shoestring-budget projects behind these plays were unsurprisingly short-term, sporadic and unsustainable. Equally, they suffered from their inevitable subject matter; as Sue Richardson, who worked with the Women's Community Press that produced bottom-up writing on the heroin problem and working-class life in the early 1980s, recalls: 'It was very radical.'* Fitzgerald recalls a seminal meeting of community arts groups in the North Star Hotel, Dublin, in 1983, which was attended by 'no more than fifteen organisations', then 'the majority of community arts groups working in the thirty-two counties'. This group evolved into the CAFE collective, which drew on parallel initiatives across other cities on the island and put new impetus behind lobbying for progressive change. While the cross-border partnership fell away, on both sides of the border community arts began to blossom.

*   Quoted in Fitzgerald, *An Outburst of Frankness*.

In the Republic, European structural funds and government 'back to work' grants supported community arts growth in the 1980s. In 1985 the Arts Council set up an Arts Community Education Committee, which supported now more long-term development of community arts organisations, though employment-related funding was, for a time, far greater than Arts Council support. One of the issues with this, as Fitzgerald identifies, was the impetus towards employability in schemes that catered for the arts in working-class life; art for art's sake, or for the sake of personal intellectual development or expression, was arguably an afterthought, at least for those with the purse strings. Continued lobbying by organisations like CAFE was key in prising open a closed understanding of the state's role in cultural democracy, and increased funding for arts in working-class communities ensued in the 1990s, when the 'Arts Plans', which continue to be produced to the present, brought recognition that the state's arts infrastructure was heavily skewed towards the middle classes. While there have been significant changes in approach in working-class inclusion in the arts over the past four decades, problems remain. A more recent report (2014) highlighted evidence that people from disadvantaged backgrounds were equally interested in the arts but were 'many times less likely' than their better-off counterparts to participate in cultural events.

In the North, a range of organisations, mainly working in theatre from the 1970s on, also pushed the agenda. The Fellowship Community Theatre, the activities in arts and activism centred around Des Wilson's People's Theatre in Springhill House, Belfast Community Theatre Group, Charabanc, Tongue in Cheek, Ballybeen Community Theatre, Dock Ward Community Theatre, Frontline Community Drama and eventually the North's own

Community Arts Forum (CAF) – which would lobby an ACNI reluctant to accord funding to less 'mainstream' activities – all grew apace. Community drama thrived in Belfast and Derry, Derry Frontline and JustUs theatre groups being among them, drawing on the experiences of working-class communities, situating performances in those communities, and in some cases fostering organic working-class writing. Charabanc, for example, interviewed mill workers for its play *Lay Up Your Ends* (1983), and brought these 'millies' in to see the resultant play. JustUs workshopped plays from the spoken and written experiences of West Belfast locals, producing, also, new working-class dramatists like Brenda Murphy and Christine Poland. All of this creativity was impelled by the need of people experiencing intense violence and oppression to find a voice, which was much of the impetus behind the largest community festival in Ireland, Belfast's Féile an Phobail, itself a major sponsor of working-class talent.

A changing funding environment encouraged the rising tide. Significant support came from government regeneration initiatives, and later from EU peace funding and the UK Lottery. As the cultural historian Robert Hewison (2014) has shown, from the instalment of the New Labour government in 1997, arts funding was ramped up across the UK, with a new focus on its role in combating social exclusion.* This new government's direction of travel also steered ACNI towards greater community engagement. ACNI's attitude to community arts changed dramatically in the 1990s – a transformation described with wonderful hyperbole by

---

* Robert Hewison, *Cultural Capital: The Rise and Fall of Creative Britain*, Verso, London, 2014.

one community arts practitioner, Gerri Moriarty. The changed relationship between community artists and ACNI in the 2010s would, from a pre-2000s perspective, 'have been regarded as a notion as difficult to comprehend and as unlikely to become a reality as the eradication of smallpox would have been to individuals living in the nineteenth century'.

This changed environment has been underlined by progressive policies from Stormont, which has repeatedly emphasised the targeting of social need in culture and arts funding. ACNI's funding for community arts rose from the mid-1990s, and along with the expansion of other forms of funding, confidence and ambition in the sector grew. A wide range of working-class writers are active north of the border, particularly in theatre groups like Etcetera (which supports Loyalist working-class writers), Green Shoot and Kabosh, at least in part due to ACNI and governmental funding targeted at areas of social need.

## The situation now

The ROI Arts Council's 2006 report, *The Public and the Arts*, identified social differences in terms of arts audiences: skilled working-class people were half as likely as middle-class people to have attended a concert hall or opera house, semi-skilled/unskilled working-class people less than half as likely as middle-class people to have attended the theatre. Working-class people were also far less likely to have purchased creative writing of any kind. It is no surprise that a 2016 report reveals that working-class, non-employed, lower-income and lone-parent households will typically have fewer books than wealthier cohorts, but other findings also stand out: the extent of a child's reading is 'strongly associated with mother's education, with the children of graduate mothers 2.6 times more likely to read every day than those whose mothers have lower secondary (Junior Certificate) education or less'. Boys are particularly impacted in this regard: 'A very significant proportion of boys from working-class or non-employed backgrounds (33–36 per cent) report that they do not read for pleasure at all.' Whatever the advances in policy, and the upheavals just outlined in community arts, working-class children are still the least likely to develop the skills required to become writers and public intellectuals.

Part of the fascination with the working-class writer, or artist, is with people who are assumed to be fit only for the less cerebral forms of labour having the gumption and audacity to enter the domain of those society has often designated as the possessors of that mystical artistic gift – 'genius'. As Mowbray Bates put it, 'a large part of the impetus for this kind of work is very deeply personal. It's a rebellion against conditions and circumstances, of your upbringing, of your experience, of what you see around you. It's rebelling against "them".'* Such sentiments need to be historicised and contextualised, of course; as we have seen in this chapter, the relationship between the working class and creative writing in Ireland has changed over time. However, as is also apparent, there is much about these perceptions that resonates in Ireland today: for working-class people to get their fair share of the creative pie, a lot more will have to change – the rebellion against 'them' must continue, across policy agendas, community activism, on university campuses, in arts projects and through more initiatives like this, *The 32*.

---

\*    Quoted in Fitzgerald, *An Outburst of Frankness*.

# The Contributors

Claire Allan is an international bestselling author from Derry in Northern Ireland. A former journalist, she published eight contemporary women's fiction titles before turning to crime, or more specifically domestic noir, in 2018. Her debut thriller *Her Name Was Rose* has sold more than a quarter of a million copies. When not writing thrillers, she can be found penning romantic comedies under her alias of Freya Kennedy.

Kevin Barry is the author of three novels and three story collections, most recently *That Old Country Music*. His awards include the IMPAC Award, the Goldsmiths Prize, the *Sunday Times* EFG Short Story Award and the European Union Prize for Literature. His stories and essays have appeared in the *New Yorker*, *Granta*, *Harpers* and elsewhere. He also writes plays and screenplays. He lives in County Sligo.

Dermot Bolger's fourteen novels include *The Journey Home* and *An Ark of Light*. His debut play, *The Lament for Arthur Cleary*, received the Samuel Beckett Award. Other plays include *The*

*Ballymun Trilogy* (charting forty years of a working-class suburb) and an adaptation of *Ulysses*. His selected poems, *That Which Is Suddenly Precious*, appeared in 2015. Bolger championed new writers, firstly through Raven Arts Press, which he founded as a teenage factory hand, and later through co-founding New Island Books.

Kate Burns was born in Belfast in 1956 and grew up in Andersonstown. She attended St Genevieve's Secondary School and St Dominic's High School. In 1978 she graduated with a B.Ed. in English with Dramatic Art. In 2015, following the death of her husband, she retired from teaching and returned to creative writing, undertaking courses through the Queen's University Belfast Open Learning programme. She is currently studying at Queen's for an MA in Creative Writing.

June Caldwell's short story collection *Room Little Darker* was published in 2017 by New Island Books in Ireland and in 2018 by Head of Zeus, UK. Her debut novel *Little Town Moone* is forthcoming with John Murray.

Martin Doyle is Books Editor of the *Irish Times*, which he joined in 2007. He previously worked for *The Times* and is a former Editor of the *Irish Post*. He edited *A History of The Irish Post* (2000) to mark its thirtieth anniversary. He was an extra in the last ever *Father Ted* and is still dining out on it.

Roddy Doyle has written twelve novels, including *The Commitments* (1987), *Paddy Clarke Ha Ha Ha*, for which he won the Booker Prize in 1993, *The Woman Who Walked into Doors* (1996), *Smile* (2017) and, most recently, *Love* (2020). He has also written several collections of stories, a memoir of his parents, *Rory and Ita* (2002), and eight books for children, including *The Giggler Treatment* (2000) and *Greyhound of a Girl* (2012). He lives and works in Dublin.

Paul Dunne is a young writer from Tallaght, Dublin. He graduated from Trinity College Dublin with a B.A. in English Literature and Film Studies, and an M.Phil. in Creative Writing. Paul's writing seeks to ambitiously explore, reflect and capture contemporary Ireland with an emphasis on working-class stories, characters and their distinct voices as expressed through demotic dialogue. He is working on his first novel and a collection of short stories centred in Tallaght.

Trudie Gorman is an award-winning writer and poet based in Dublin whose work explores the personal and political interplay between class, gender and the body. Trudie has performed her poetry across Ireland and the UK and has published pieces in *Poetry NI*, *I believe Her* and *Two Metre Review*, and has been broadcast on BBC Radio London. Trudie was selected for Poetry Ireland Versify Series in 2019. Her performance poem 'The Opposite of Survival' was shortlisted for the Creative Future Writer's Award 2019. Trudie is currently working on her first collection of poetry in partnership with Poetry Ireland.

Marc Gregg is a queer writer and classical vocalist raised in Lisburn, Northern Ireland. He studied Music at Goldsmiths, University of

London, which is where his love of the strange first took off. Since then, he has co-produced and written the show *Soap Opera* for BBC Radio Ulster as well as review pieces for the *Journal of Music*. Currently, he is experimenting with whatever writing will have him, mainly poetry and short stories. @FightingMarc

Angela Higgins is the mum of two young men, partner to one, yogini, creative and sea woman working in an education authority. She has taught in schools, prisons, universities and community settings. She is a lifelong student and in 2018 her suppressed interest in creative writing was unleashed at a Creativity and Change course at Cork Institute of Technology. Angela lives in Wicklow, and is a school starter, instigator, swimmer, sailor, kayaker and very amateur gardener.

Dublin-born Jason Hynes grew up on the Northside of the city, where he still lives. He writes for a range of media including radio and TV and has been IFTA-nominated for his short film 'Two Fat Ladies'. In 2013 he received a scholarship to study a Master's in TV Fiction at Glasgow Caledonian University. When not being interrupted by cats, he continues to work on a series of Dublin-based stories.

Riley Johnston is an English teacher from Belfast. 'Improper' is her first piece of published work and she is currently working on a novel. Riley is a member of Belfast Jazz Orchestra where she plays trumpet. She is also a socialist activist and member of political party People Before Profit.

Erin Lindsay is a writer and editor from Tallaght in Dublin. She completed her degree in Journalism with Gaeilge in 2017 and has been working with words ever since. As a journalist and broadcaster, she's worked with some incredible people on stories around culture, the arts, women's health and lifestyle. She now spends her time searching for grammatical errors in work documents, and voraciously reading fashion magazines.

Dave Lordan is a writer and community educator from Bog Road, Clonakilty, West Cork, with an interest in multimedia and collaborative creativity. He is the author of five books of poetry, prose and essays, as well as sole creator or collaborator on numerous multimedia projects ranging from soundscaped audio books to podcasts to radio drama to a suite of highly regarded poetry videos. Find his work at www.davelordan.com, www.lordanslit.com and www.facebook.com/davelordancreativity

Originally from Blanchardstown, Dublin, Alison Martin is a playwright, writer and editor. As well as writing extensively for print, Alison recently contributed to the Super Paua theatre company's audio drama series and RTÉ's *Keywords* podcast. Alison has a particular interest in the Irish language, theatre for young audiences and television drama. Currently an Associate Artist with Axis as Gaeilge, Ballymun, Alison lives in Wexford with her three children, Beck, Ríonadh and Ferdia.

Rosaleen McDonagh was appointed to the Irish Human Rights and Equality Commission in May 2020. She is also a member of Aosdána. Presently Rosaleen's piece *Walls & Windows* is being commissioned for a production in the Abbey Theatre. *Contentious Spaces* has also been commissioned by the Project Arts Centre for production in 2021. Rosaleen's collection of essays will be published in September 2021 by Skein Press.

Linda McGrory grew up in the seaside town of Buncrana, Co Donegal, and has worked as a journalist for more than twenty years. A former staff reporter with the *Irish Examiner* and *Derry Journal*, she has freelanced extensively and has edited magazines on adult literacy. She is a graduate of English and Philosophy from NUI Galway and holds a post-graduate diploma in Applied Communications. She lives with her husband in Greencastle, Co Donegal.

Lisa McInerney's work has featured in *Winter Papers*, *The Stinging Fly*, *Granta*, the *Guardian*, *Le Monde*, the *Irish Times*, various anthologies and on BBC Radio 4. Her debut novel *The Glorious Heresies* won the 2016 Women's Prize for Fiction and the 2016 Desmond Elliott Prize. Her second novel, *The Blood Miracles*, won the 2018 RSL Encore Award. Her third, *The Rules of Revelation*, is due May 2021.

Lyra McKee was born in 1990 in Belfast. She was an award-winning investigative journalist; she was featured as one of *Forbes*' '30 Under 30' and named as a rising literary star by the *Irish Times*. McKee was fatally shot during rioting in Derry in 2019. At the time of her death, she was working on a piece of investigative journalism entitled *The Lost Boys*, which remains under review with Faber & Faber and those closest to her.

Danielle McLaughlin's short story collection *Dinosaurs on Other Planets* was published in 2015 by The Stinging Fly Press. In 2019, she was a Windham-Campbell Prize recipient, and won the *Sunday Times* Audible Short Story Award. Her first novel, *The Art of Falling*, was published in 2021 by John Murray.

Eoin McNamee was born in Kilkeel, Co Down. He has written seventeen novels including *Resurrection Man*, *The Ultras*, the *Blue* trilogy and *The Vogue*. He also writes for cinema and television. He is Director of the Oscar Wilde Centre in Trinity College Dublin.

Paul McVeigh's debut novel, *The Good Son*, won the Polari First Novel Prize and the McCrea Literary Award and was shortlisted for many others including the Prix du Roman Cezam. Paul was a playwright in Belfast before moving to London to write comedy with shows touring the UK and Ireland including the Edinburgh Festival and London's West End. His short stories have appeared in the *Irish Times*, *Stinging Fly*, *London Magazine* and anthologies such as *Being Various*, *Common People* and *The Art of the Glimpse*. They have also been read on BBC Radio 3, 4 and 5 and Sky Arts. He was editor of the *Belfast Stories* and *Queer Love* anthologies and *Southword Journal*. He is associate director of Word Factory, the UK's national organisation for excellence in the short story, and co-founder of the London Short Story Festival. Paul interviews authors and reviews for the *Irish Times*, and his work has been translated into seven languages.

Maurice Neill was born in Belfast in 1959 and educated at Belfast High School, Queen's University and University of Ulster. He was a journalist at Ireland's first Sunday newspaper *Sunday News*, the *Belfast Telegraph* and *Reuters*. In 1999 he received a commendation in the Northern Ireland Press and Broadcast Awards and in 1997 a special commendation in the Irish section of the European Journalism Awards. He is a life member of the National Union of Journalists.

Michael Nolan is from Belfast. His work has appeared in *The Stinging Fly, Fallow Media, Lifeboat* and *Winter Papers*. He is the fiction editor of *The Tangerine* and is currently studying for a PhD in Creative Writing at Queen's University Belfast.

Abby Oliveira is a writer, performer, lyricist and theatre-maker based in Derry. She has been an eminent member of the Irish spoken-word scene for over a decade. She performs regularly at events and festivals throughout the UK, Ireland and abroad, and has toured work in Australia, New Zealand (via support from Arts Council NI) and Singapore. She has had work commissioned by BBC Radio 4 and Foyle, RTÉ Radio and more.

Stephen O'Reilly took up part-time employment in order to spend more time writing and shortly afterwards won the 2019 RTÉ Short Story Competition with his tale of apathetic androids in 'Honey Days'. He is the recipient of a Molly Keane Memorial Award and has been shortlisted for a Seán Ó Faoláin Prize. His work has appeared in *Neonlit: The Time Out Book of New Writing*, *Southword*, *The Galway Review* and various other anthologies.

Rick O'Shea is a broadcaster with RTÉ – weekdays on RTÉ Gold and presenting *The Book Show* on RTÉ Radio 1. He has been a judge for the Costa Book Awards and IWC Novel Fair, Dalkey Literary Awards judging chair, and literary curator for the UCD Festival and Waterford Writers Weekend. He runs the 35,000-member Rick O'Shea Book Club, chooses the quarterly 'Must Reads' lists for Eason and recommends books on RTÉ Radio 1's *Today Show*.

Dr Michael Pierse is Senior Lecturer in Irish Literature at Queen's University Belfast. His research mainly explores the cultural production of Irish working-class life. He is author of *Writing Ireland's Working-Class: Dublin After O'Casey* (2011) and editor of the recent collections *A History of Irish Working-Class Writing* (2017) and *Rethinking the Irish Diaspora: After the Gathering* (co-edited with Dr Johanne Devlin Trew).

Senator Lynn Ruane is an independent member of Seanad Éireann, representing Trinity College graduates in the Oireachtas since 2016 and serving as the deputy leader of the Seanad Civil Engagement group during that time. She was elected to the Senate while President of Trinity College Dublin's Students' Union, where she gained entry as a mature student through the Trinity Access Programme. Her legislative priorities in office have focused on equality of access in education, gender equality and reproductive rights, tackling socio-economic inequality and advocating for progressive reforms of drug, migration and social welfare policies. Prior to her entry to politics, she developed addiction programmes for fifteen years as a community worker in west Dublin. She is the author of the award-winning memoir *People Like Me*.

Theresa Ryder was assistant to the late author J. P. Donleavy for many years before graduating with an MA in Classics and a teaching degree from Maynooth University. Her first short story submission won the Molly Keane Creative Writing Award. She is a regular contributor to the award-winning #WomenXBorders project in the Irish Writers Centre. She has completed her first novel and is currently working on a memoir of the Donleavy years, a new novel and a short-fiction collection.

Jim Ward is from Salthill, Galway. From a working-class background, he went to university on a scholarship and studied engineering purely to land a job. He has, nevertheless, experienced employment and unemployment. Now a tour guide, he is published for poetry and stories in Irish and English. He is the author of two plays – the award-winning *Just Guff* and *Three Quarks*. He is seeking a publisher for his first novel, *Rednecks in Suburbia*, and is a published cartoonist.

Elaine Cawley Weintraub is an educator, a cultural historian and a writer finding her voice as a passionate advocate for all those whose voices are not heard. Her own experiences as a woman and a member of the working class, along with her Irish identity, have shaped her world view and taught her to value all cultures and experiences.

Unbound is the world's first crowdfunding publisher, established in 2011.

We believe that wonderful things can happen when you clear a path for people who share a passion. That's why we've built a platform that brings together readers and authors to crowdfund books they believe in – and give fresh ideas that don't fit the traditional mould the chance they deserve.

This book is in your hands because readers made it possible. Everyone who pledged their support is listed below. Join them by visiting unbound.com and supporting a book today.

Michael Creamer
Riah Creighton
Teresa Crew
Liz Cronin
Maggie Cronin
Conor Crummey
Helen Cullen
Michelle Culligan
Liz Cullinane
Emma Cummins
Paul Curley
Siobhan Curley
Kevin Curran
Matthew Curran
Peter Curran
Lee Currid
Shane Curtin
Gráinne Daly
Justin David
Sarah Davis-Goff
Sharon Dempsey
Eoin Devereux
Samuel Dodson
Louise Doherty
Miche Doherty
Mark Donoghue
Sarah Bobby O Donovan
Shona Donovan-Thoma
Maura Dooley
Louise Doughty
James Downey
Rory Downey
Sarah Downey
Emma Downey Burns
Niamh Downey Kelpie
Kevin Doyle
Daniel Duffy
Eva Duffy
Michelle Duffy
Chloe Dunne
Emer Dunne
Ken Dunne
Ken Dunne
Paula Dunne
Elizabeth Durkin
Eugene Egan

Jessica Egan
Ken Elkes
Ann Elliott
Avril Erskine
Wendy Erskine
Virginia Evans
Marc Fairclough
Fiorenzo Fantaccini
Finbarr Farragher
Caroline Farrell
maria farrell
Melissa Fegan
Anthony Ferner
Sergio Ferreira
Shirley Finlay
Doreen Finn
Arlene Finnigan
Garrie Fletcher
Maggie Fogarty
Sarah Franklin
Chris Frawley
Elizabeth Fredericks
Melissa Fu
Maria Fusco
Jacqueline Gaile
Bríd Gallagher
Eithne Gallagher
Mary Gallagher
Cathy Galvin
Frances Gapper
Heidi Gardner
Polly Geoghegan
Barbara Giglione
Guin Glasfurd
Sinéad Gleeson
Claire Goff
James Gracey
Anne Grant
Peter Grant
Joanne Greenway
Julie Gregg
Anne Griffin
Anne Griffin
Yvonne Griffiths
Damian Grudzien
Bridget Hamilton

Dr Michael A. Hann
Claire Hanna
Carmela Hannon
Sharon Hardwick
Robin Hargreaves
Sean Harkin
Shaun Harkin
Ruth Harrison
Nicola Heaney
Neil Hegarty
Mark Hennebry
Adeline Henry
Conal Henry
Fi Henry
Eve Hickey
Vincent Higgins
Esther Hoad
Caelainn Hogan
Cat Hughes
Joanne Hunter
Charlotte Hutchinson
Damien Hyland
Irish Cultural Centre
    Hammersmith Ltd
Jean
Mandy Jenkinson
Colleen Jones
Carrie Kania
Neil Kaplan-Kelly
Amanda Kavanagh
Geoffrey Keating
Andrew Kelly
Maureen R Kelly
Robert Kelly
Viv Kemp
Fionnuala Kennedy
Marnie Kennedy
Shirley Kennedy
Alice Kennelly
Orla Kennelly
Eilish Kenny
Laura Kenwright
Andrew Keogh
Dan Kieran
campbell killick
Carrie King

Georgia Kirrin
Catherine Kirwan
Jenny Knight
Simon Kövesi
Sven Kretzschmar
Miriam Laird
Kathleen Langstroth
Fion J. Lau
Adam Laverty
Angus Laverty
Alexandra Law
Mavis Le Page Leathley
Caroline Lea
Evalyn Lee
Katie Lindsay
Liz Lyons
Brendan Mac Evilly
Ann MacLaughlin-Berres
Margaret Madden
Caroline Magennis
Shauneen Magorrian
Bernard & Kathleen
  Maguire
Sabrina Mahfouz
Jimmy Marsden
Róisín (Hann) Mason
Matthew
David Maxwell
Anne Mc Kiernan
Carmel Mc Mahon
Frances McAleese
Ciara Mcallister
JL McCavana
Alan McCormick
Ruth McCracken
Alison McCrudden
Paula McDonald
Angus McDonogh
Emma McEvoy
Tara McEvoy
Brid McGinley
Rebecca McGlynn
Mary McGrath
Shane McGuinness
Henrietta McKervey
Ryan McKinney

Ciaran McLarnon
Stuart McLaughlin
Paul McMichael
Aidan McQuade
Jane McVeigh
Kevin McVeigh
Helen Megan
Sinead Mercier
Anne Michail
Niamh Michail
Katie Millard
John Mitchinson
Ger Moane
Damhnait Monaghan
Caroline Moore
Anne Moreau
Kevin Morrison
Steven Moss
Molly Moylan Brown
Anne Mulkeen Murray
Judith Mulkerin
Declan Mulligan
The Munster Literature
  Centre
Anna Marie Murray
Carlo Navato
Louise Neill
Mary-Clare Newsham
Deirdre Ní Fhloinn
Sinéad Ní Scollaígh
Liz Nugent
Máirtín Ó Catháin
Pádraig Ó Tuama
Gráinne O' Toole
Kerth O'Brien
Sorcha O'Brien
Clare O'Dea
Denise O'Donoghue
Patrick O'Donoghue
Áine O'Gorman
Caoimhe O'Gorman
Jenny O'Gorman
Eimear O'Herlihy
James O'Meara
Cathleen O'Neill
Fiona O'Neill

John O'Neill
Mark O'Neill
Sheila O'Reilly
Rick O'Shea
Karen O'Sullivan
Sara O'Sullivan
Tina O'Toole
Katie O'Toole Byrne
Richard O'Beirne
Lara O'Brien
John O'Donnell
Maeve O'Higgins
Trisha Oakley Kessler
Jennifer Orr
Jeremy Osborne
Jacinta Owens
Ian Peddie
Ellen Pentony
Ann Perrin
Shirley Perrott Mound
peterfromderry
Michael Pierse
Stef Pixner
Justin Pollard
Katie Pollard
Jonathan Pool
Thomas Pool
Alison Collison Powell
Gill Powell
Eve Power
Peter Power-Hynes
Tricia Purcell
Cora Quigley
Gràinne Quinn
Lucy Quinn
Liz Raleigh
Claire Redmond
Trish Reilly
Jane Roberts
Frances Robinson
Brenda Roche
Margaret Rochford
Sarah Ronan
Max Roveri
Lynn Ruane
Jennifer Rudden

Lisa Rull
Deborrah Russell
Eoin Ryan
Michelle Ryan
Robert Ryan
Christina Schönberger-
  Stepien
Rose Servitova
Breda Shannon
Liz Sheppard
Julie Sheridan
Dr Michael Short
Karell Sime
Wendy Sinnamon
Lorna Sixsmith
Marianne Skelcher
Amy Slack
Hanna Slattne
Fiona Smith
Olivia Smith
Scott Smith
Malcolm Spatz
Caroline Sproule
Janice Staines
Colin Stakem
Katherine Stanton
Henriette B. Stavis

Siân Steans
Markus Steck
Cathryn Steele
Gabriela Steinke
Luke Stobie
Jo Stones
Deirdre Sullivan
Swiss Centre of Irish
  Studies
Daniel Syrovy
Sue Targett
Carrie Thompson
Ali Thurm
Christina Timmins
Gráinne Tobin
Colm Toibin
Maile Topliff
Jo Tracy
Jess Traynor
Bridget Tucker
Ann Tudor
Emma Tyrrell
Jo Unwin
Seamus Vanecko
Eva Verde
Sally Vince
Paul Vincent

Michael Vincent Brennan
Peter Viner-Brown
Debbi Voisey
Dave Wakely
Sarah Walsh
Denise Walters
Emma Warnock
Paul Waters
Tracey Weller
Brian Wharton
Lorraine Whiteway
Anne Whittock
Andrea Wilkinson
Eva Wilkinson
Venetia Wilks
Catherine Williamson
Sarah Wilson
Sasha Wilson
Shaun Wilson
Andrew Winder
Gretchen Woelfle
Ann Wright
Shannon Yee
Martina Zandonella
Zurich James Joyce
  Foundation